AMERICAN FILMS OF THE 70S

Conflicting Visions

Peter Lev

AMERICAN FILMS 70s
OF THE
Conflicting Visions

UNIVERSITY OF TEXAS PRESS  AUSTIN

An earlier version of Chapter 10, "Whose Future? Star Wars, Alien, *and* Blade Runner,*"*
appeared in Literature/Film Quarterly *vol. 26, no. 1 (1998). Reprinted by permission.*

Requests for permission to reproduce material from this work should be sent to
PERMISSIONS, UNIVERSITY OF TEXAS PRESS, P.O. BOX 7819, AUSTIN, TX 78713-7819.

∞ The paper used in this book meets the minimum requirements of ANSI/NISO Z39.48-1992
(R1997) (Permanence of Paper).

LIBRARY OF CONGRESS CATALOGING-IN-PUBLICATION DATA

Lev, Peter, 1948–
   American films of the 70s : conflicting visions / by Peter Lev—1st ed.
      p.   cm.
   Includes bibliographical references and index.
   ISBN 0-292-74715-2 (cl. : alk. paper)—ISBN 0-292-74716-0 (pbk. : alk. paper)
   1. Motion pictures—United States—History. I. Title: American films of the seventies.
II. Title.
PN1993.5.U6 L44 2000
791.43'75'097309047—dc21   99-053348

FOR SARA

Contents

Preface xi

Introduction: "NOBODY KNOWS ANYTHING" xv

Part 1

CHAPTER 1: HIPPIE GENERATION 3
Easy Rider
Alice's Restaurant
Five Easy Pieces

CHAPTER 2: VIGILANTES AND COPS 22
Joe
The French Connection
Dirty Harry
Death Wish

CHAPTER 3: DISASTER AND CONSPIRACY 40
Airport
The Poseidon Adventure
Jaws
The Parallax View
Chinatown

CHAPTER 4: THE END OF THE SIXTIES 60
Nashville
Shampoo
Between the Lines
The Return of the Secaucus Seven
The Big Chill

Part 2

CHAPTER 5: *LAST TANGO IN PARIS:* OR ART, SEX, AND HOLLYWOOD 77

CHAPTER 6: TEEN FILMS 90
American Graffiti
Cooley High
Animal House
Diner
Fast Times at Ridgemont High

CHAPTER 7: GENERAL PATTON AND COLONEL KURTZ 107
Patton
Apocalypse Now

CHAPTER 8: FROM BLAXPLOITATION TO AFRICAN AMERICAN FILM 127
Shaft
Superfly
Claudine
Leadbelly
Killer of Sheep

CHAPTER 9: FEMINISMS 142
Hester Street
An Unmarried Woman
Girlfriends
Starting Over
Head over Heels/Chilly Scenes of Winter
Coming Home
The China Syndrome

CHAPTER 10: WHOSE FUTURE? 165
Star Wars
Alien
Blade Runner

Conclusion 181

APPENDIX 1: TIME LINE, 1968–1983: AMERICAN HISTORY,
AMERICAN FILM 187

APPENDIX 2: FILMOGRAPHY 199

Notes 205

Bibliography 221

Index 229

Preface

This book is an interpretive history of American films of the 1970s. It argues that the films of the period constitute a dialogue or debate about the nature and the prospects of American society. The dialogue passes through both aesthetics and ideology; these two concepts ultimately merge in what I call, for lack of a better term, an artistic "vision." In Part One of the book, I present films which express conflicting positions on the question of social change. Should American society move toward openness, diversity, and egalitarianism, welcoming such new developments as the counterculture and the anti–Vietnam War movement? Or should America change by refusing to change, by stressing paternalistic authority and traditional morality? I follow this debate through a dozen years and several genres or cycles. Part Two of the book broadens the dualistic argument of Part One by examining some of the specific issues explored by the films of the 1970s: the Vietnam War, the sexual revolution, the status of teenagers, African American culture, the women's movement. The dialogue here emphasizes pluralism; it becomes more a clamor of competing voices than a dialectical exchange.

Further, within specific constituencies there is a range of positions and a range of accommodations to Hollywood convention. The final chapter of this section restores a dialogue between liberal (or progressive) and conservative; it synthesizes issues of sex, race, and gender with an ideological interpretation of three science fiction films.

My book has been loosely influenced by the Russian literary critic/historian Mikhail Bakhtin, from whom I borrow both the concept of dialogism and a skeptical attitude toward literary canons. Dialogism, for Bakhtin, is the idea that the novel as literary genre is a complex amalgam of overlapping and competing languages (historical, class-based, group-based, specifically artistic). The heterogeneity of the novel is such that authorship becomes almost irrelevant—except that the author blends the different languages.[1] I present a dialogue of competing styles and meanings between films, between film and literary source, and within films (using, at times, production history to explain a divergence between collaborators). As to the canon, Bakhtin wrote literary histories far more wide ranging than the standard texts and anthologies. For example, he traced the origins of the novel back thousands of years, to Greek and especially Roman texts.[2] I have more modestly added exploitation films (*Joe, Superfly*), rarely discussed works (*Shampoo, Starting Over*), a Euro-American hybrid (*Last Tango in Paris*), and low-budget independent films (*Killer of Sheep, Hester Street*) to the emerging list of "essential" 1970s films (e.g., *Chinatown, Jaws, Nashville, Star Wars*).

American Films of the 70s: Conflicting Visions is clearly not a comprehensive history of film in the 1970s. It discusses in detail about forty films, which were chosen primarily to illustrate and support the book's argument. Diversity, quality, personal taste, and limits of access were secondary criteria. I regret the omission of many fine films, especially *The Godfather* and *Taxi Driver*. They were left out because they added relatively little to the discussion in Part One. In general, I believe that no film history can be either comprehensive or objective. There are occasions which call for a survey approach (many films, a few sentences on each), but the more in-depth approach essayed here is a better way to get at the multiple branchings and connections of film history.

I have taken some liberties with the concept of "decade." The book starts in 1969, with *Easy Rider*, because this is the year when the social movements of the late 1960s most strongly impacted Hollywood. Many of the films of the early 1970s, and even the later 1970s, can be seen as responses to this moment of radical challenge. The book also extends into the early 1980s, with *The Big Chill* (1983), *Blade Runner* (1982), and *Fast Times at Ridgemont High* (1982), because artistic movements and styles do not abruptly end at the turn of the calendar. My subject is still, roughly, the films of the 1970s.

As an aid to those readers with only a hazy awareness of the social and political events of the period, I have included a brief time line of American history for the years 1968–1983. This time line may be found at the back of the book, between the conclusion and the filmography.

Writing a book is a long journey. I would like to thank the following individuals and institutions who helped me along the way. Your expertise, enthusiasm, and good counsel are very much appreciated:

In California: Mark and Patricia Treadwell, Don and Sue Silver, Stephen Mamber, and the libraries of UCLA, USC, and the Academy of Motion Picture Arts and Sciences.

In Illinois: Jeffrey Chown.

In Maryland: Yvonne Lev, Sara Lev, Jim Welsh, Greg Faller, Barry Moore, Steve Weiss, Ron Matlon, George Vázquez, David Harley, Martin H. McKibbin, Roland Chambers, Dean Esslinger, John Haeger, Video Center, and the libraries of Towson University, the University of Maryland College Park, and the University of Maryland Baltimore County as well as the Enoch Pratt Free Library. Special thanks to the Faculty Research and Faculty Development Committees of Towson University for their financial support of my research.

In Montana: Paul Monaco.

In New York: The Museum of Modern Art Film/Stills Archive, Jerry Ohlinger Archives.

In Pennsylvania: Rebecca Pauly and the library of Franklin and Marshall College.

In Texas: Jim Burr and the entire staff of the University of Texas Press.

In Washington, D.C.: The Library of Congress.

"NOBODY

KNOWS

ANYTHING"

Introduction

Screenwriter and novelist William Goldman, writing in 1982, suggests that the first rule of Hollywood is "Nobody Knows Anything."[1] Goldman explains that film industry producers and executives do not know in advance which film will be a box office success and which film will be a failure. Blockbuster movies such as *The Godfather* were written off as inevitable failures during production, and *Raiders of the Lost Ark* was turned down by all the Hollywood studios except Paramount. Any number of big-budget productions have done no business, whereas low-budget sleepers such as *Easy Rider*, *American Graffiti*, *Rocky*, and *Porky's* have done phenomenally well. Nobody knows anything.

Goldman's formula can be historicized by dividing Hollywood sound film into three periods. In the first period, from the late 1920s to the mid-1950s, Hollywood executives did in fact know a few things. The film audience was more or less stable (especially in the first part of this period), and a well-developed system of stars and genres was in place. Further, the Hollywood major studios owned chains of first-run theaters, so every film from the

Hollywood majors could expect a carefully planned release. Executives and producers could be confident that a well-made film following established conventions would find at least a moderate audience. It is also worth mentioning that studio executives at this time were experienced showmen with an intuitive understanding of what would play for an audience. This intuitive sense can be represented by a story about Harry Cohn, the legendarily crude head of Columbia Pictures. Cohn supposedly said one day, "I know it's a bad film if my ass itches. If my ass doesn't itch, the film is OK."[2]

Cohn's seat-of-the-pants approach does suggest that he knew at least a little bit about which films would work. But in the 1960s and 1970s, the film audience shrank and fragmented, and the verities of the old studio system fell apart. Stars and genres were no longer enough to sell a picture. *The Sound of Music* (1965) was an enormous box office success, but its follow-up, *Star!* (1968; same genre, same star), was a resounding failure. Established writers, directors, and producers, many with track records stretching back for decades, were suddenly out of favor with a film audience now consisting primarily of young people. In desperation, major companies bypassed established talent to take a chance on younger producers, directors, and actors. Several important films were produced in this way: *Bonnie and Clyde* (1967), *The Graduate* (1968), *Easy Rider* (1969), *Midnight Cowboy* (1969), *M.A.S.H.* (1970), *The Last Picture Show* (1971). But the second wave of youth films, descendants of *Easy Rider* such as *Getting Straight* (1970), *The Strawberry Statement* (1970), *Zabriskie Point* (1970), and *The Last Movie* (1971), were colossal failures. The 1970s were the true era of "Nobody knows anything," a period of uncertainty and disarray in the Hollywood film industry.

By the time William Goldman was writing his book *Adventures in the Screen Trade* in 1982, a new set of rules and regularities was being established in American films. Stars were once again important, with the new actors introduced in the 1970s—Nicholson, De Niro, Pacino, Hoffman, Streisand, Streep—becoming the established talents of the 1980s. Businessmen, not showmen, were running the Hollywood companies, so emphasis was put on the assembling of "packages" (marketable stars and directors) plus such presold properties as sequels, comic books, and best-selling novels. The younger audience had stabilized and become at least reasonably predictable. Beginning with *Jaws* (1975) and *Star Wars* (1977), Steven Spielberg and George Lucas had pioneered a return to simple, optimistic genre films. Finally, the film industry was beginning to stress advertising and market research as key elements in film planning. To summarize, in the 1980s film executives once again thought they knew a few things.

Those who value creativity and risk taking in the arts are strongly attracted to the "Nobody knows anything" period of the 1970s. The average quality of films may have been better at the height of the studio period (for example, in 1939); but for sheer diversity of aesthetic and ideological approaches, no period of American cinema surpasses the films of the 1970s. The example I gave above of films like *Easy Rider* and *Midnight Cowboy* leading to "second-generation" youth films such as *Getting Straight* and *Cisco Pike* is itself somewhat misleading, because it ignores all the other things that were going on in the period. The 1970s in film were not only the era of youth culture but also a period of antiwar satire, of right-wing vigilantism, of blaxploitation, of women's liberation, of blatant sexism, of family values, of new family units. If nobody knows anything, then everything is permitted.

Creative moments in film history often take place in periods of social and political conflict. This generalization applies to German silent film during the Weimar Republic, to Italian neorealism after World War II, and arguably to the French New Wave of the late 1950s (the period of the Algerian War, and also of a controversial youth culture exemplified by the novels of Françoise Sagan). Creative periods in film also seem to coincide with film industry instability, as in Italian neorealism, the French New Wave, and possibly the German silent film (here the government-sponsored UFA studio did provide a few years of stability). Both sociopolitical controversy and a film industry in rapid flux were characteristic of American film in the 1970s.

The sociopolitical context of the late 1960s and early 1970s can be summarized as political and generational strife. Many movements of social change were underway: the civil rights movement, feminism, gay liberation, the environmental movement, the hippie generation. And the various attempts to block these movements, to "turn back the clock," strongly influenced millions of Americans. The Vietnam War polarized the generations, especially since the young were subject to a military draft. In addition to the war, Americans suffered a series of shocks: the assassinations of Robert Kennedy and Martin Luther King Jr. (both in 1968), the oil price shock and resulting inflation, the Watergate scandal.

Meanwhile, the film industry was enduring shock and controversy of its own. The end of the Production Code meant a new license for Hollywood films, resulting in *Midnight Cowboy*, an X-rated film, winning the Academy Award for Best Picture in 1969. Young talents got the chance to direct feature films, while established veterans such as Vincente Minnelli and Billy Wilder struggled in the new, anything-goes environment. The box office dropped off sharply in 1968–1969, leading to talk of a "film recession." David Bordwell and Kristin Thompson report that the major studios lost $500 million between 1969 and 1972.[3] In response, movies became more violent (*The Wild Bunch, A Clockwork Orange*) as well as more sexual (*Last Tango in Paris*). Despite these rapid changes, no producer could predict the film audience's mood. According to Robert Sklar, "of the scores of movies released every year, only a handful captured the attention of the public."[4] Nobody knows anything.

One could argue that the film audience of the 1970s, made up primarily of teenagers and young adults, pushed the American film industry to overemphasize the impact of the hippie generation and the antiwar movement. But even in these circumstances, the cinema of the counterculture was balanced by numerous action movies propounding conservative social values. If the early 1970s were the period of youth culture on film, they were also the period of right-wing cop films starring Clint Eastwood and Charles Bronson. These films feature a lot of action, a lot of anger, and a studied indifference to the rights of minority groups and other social outsiders. So, an overview of the early 1970s would have to see a split in the social and cultural values presented by American films, rather than focusing on an experimental and socially critical "New Hollywood." This split corresponds closely to the political divisions in the country around 1970: "Hawks" vs. "Doves," the "Generation Gap," and so on.[5]

However, no binary opposition completely describes the range of American films in the 1970s—or, for that matter, in any decade. Cinema creators and cinema audiences have a wide variety of interests, a point which often eludes systematizing critics. This point can be illustrated in a couple of different ways: first, by analyzing the range of American films made in one year; and second, by discussing a few specific films in some detail.

Consider the American feature films made in 1975. From one perspective, this was a year of transition between the rebellious films of the Hollywood Renaissance circa 1970 and the optimistic genre films to come. The more political and experimental films of 1975 are marked by a certain exhaustion (e.g., *Nashville, Shampoo,* and *Night Moves*), whereas the new trend is anticipated by the overwhelming success of *Jaws*. Indeed, *Jaws* is an excellent prototype of the late 1970s and early 1980s blockbuster—simple story, masterful technique. *Jaws* shies away from controversial issues to present an elemental, mythic story. One can add that Steven Spielberg was much younger than the directors of *Nashville, Shampoo,* and *Night Moves,* so that we might be describing a changing of the guard. The New Hollywood of 1970 was already struggling, already being replaced by the "Movie Brats" of 1975.

But what does this progression omit? What other American movies were appearing in 1975? Well, the old Hollywood of the 1940s and 1950s was still around, represented by such films as *The Hindenburg,* directed by Robert Wise, and *Rooster Cogburn,* directed by Stuart Millar and starring John Wayne and Katherine Hepburn.[6] Charles Bronson appeared in *Hard Times* and *Breakheart Pass;* Clint Eastwood starred in *The Eiger Sanction.* G-rated films such as *Benji* and *Adventures of the Wilderness Family* did well at the box office. Films on women's roles included *Alice Doesn't Live Here Anymore, Crazy Mama* (an interesting Roger Corman film), *Smile,* and *The Stepford Wives.* Neil Simon adapted two of his own plays for the screen, *The Prisoner of Second Avenue* and *The Sunshine Boys.* Star vehicles stretched from *Funny Lady* (Barbra Streisand) to three Burt Reynolds pictures. Afro-American films included the blaxploitation *Cleopatra Jones and the Temple of Gold* and the *American Graffiti*–influenced *Cooley High.* Independent features covered a tremendous range, including Joan Micklin Silver's *Hester Street,* James Ivory's *The Wild Party,* John Waters's *Female Trouble,* Russ Meyer's *Supervixens,* and also James Collier's *The Hiding Place,* a film financed by the Reverend Billy Graham's organization.

The Academy Award winner for the year, *One Flew over the Cuckoo's Nest,* deserves special attention. On the one hand, this can be seen as a

New Hollywood, socially critical film. Nurse Ratched represents the Establishment, the combination of Big Government and Big Business which supported the Vietnam War and steadfastly blocked social change. Jack Nicholson, who plays the rebellious McMurphy, is an icon of the new cinema of the 1970s. On the other hand, the film is quite conventional in technique and completely accessible on the literal level. It is absorbing as a simple story with no metaphoric or allegorical dimension. And if one wants an allegory, *Cuckoo's Nest* could be read as a broadly humanist fable attached to no specific period. It could even be called a simple (though not necessarily optimistic) genre film—with the genre being the fight against tyranny.

The *Cuckoo's Nest* example illustrates my second point: that beyond the complexity of interpreting a large group of films of a particular era, individual films can present a complex set of ideas. *Cuckoo's Nest* can be interpreted as a response to a specific political moment and a specific kind of oppression. It can also be enjoyed as a myth or fable about repression in general. I would suggest that the considerable popularity of *Cuckoo's Nest* resulted from its tendency to generalize, and thus to attract a broad spectrum of viewers.

To further examine the heterogeneity of the period and the complexity of meanings within individual films, let us consider *American Graffiti* and *Chinatown*. *American Graffiti*, a surprise hit in 1973, is a prime example of what Paul Monaco calls the movement toward nostalgia in American films of the 1970s. Nostalgia, per Monaco, is "memory without pain," and therefore a strategy for evading the tumultuous social conflicts of the early 1970s.[7] *American Graffiti*'s setting and approach certainly fit this formulation, as it takes place in a small, peaceful California town in 1962—before John Kennedy's assassination, before the Vietnam War, before the counterculture. And the film's multiple protagonists are very much concerned with their own problems, with private life, rather than with pressing social issues.

Despite this conservative, backward-looking agenda, *American Graffiti* can also be seen as part of the anarchic, wildly innovative American film renaissance of the 1970s. It seems to have created a new paradigm for the teenage comedy or "teenpic." Structural conceits of *American Graffiti*, including the ensemble cast, the compression of time, the rock music score, and the view of teenagers as an autonomous subculture, have been copied and refined by dozens of films. Further, this last point, the autonomy of teens, is at least potentially a basis for criticism of the adult world. The joy and the egalitarianism in George Lucas's teen world are sadly lacking in the world of adults. Of course, one could reply that the autonomy of teens is more a marketing strategy than a true freedom. But Lucas's creation on film of a teenaged culture separate from the adult world clearly has at least some of its roots in the antiestablishment youth culture of about 1970.

If nostalgia is memory without pain, then *Chinatown* (1974) is memory with the pain. In this film, Jack Nicholson wears a spiffy white suit, Faye Dunaway is a fashion plate, and Los Angeles in the 1930s looks sunny, clean, and stylish. But all of the film's secrets are terrifying, and they ultimately plunge the spectator into the abysmal depths of human nature. *Chinatown*'s trajectory is modeled by the scene in which director Roman Polanski, in a cameo role as a cheap hood, slashes Nicholson's nose and dirties the detective's calm, unlined face. In just such a way will *Chinatown* destroy the surface calm of Los Angeles. Following the conventions of the mystery genre, the character played by Nicholson uncovers evidence of man's baser nature. But reversing those same conventions, in *Chinatown* the John Huston character, the monster of capitalism gone wrong, definitively wins the day.

Chinatown is the best of the mid-1970s films mourning the death of the 1960s dream. All of the movements of social reform have amounted to very little; our lives are run in unseen ways by the barons of capitalism. Government is thoroughly corrupt; the water scandal in the film, based on historical events in Southern California, is a metaphor for such things as the OPEC oil cartel, the Agnew bribery case, and the Watergate break-in and cover-up. *Chinatown* goes so far as to preach the virtues of passivity, for by meddling in things he doesn't understand, the Nicholson character brings about the death of his beloved. The film's signature line echoes in our ears: "Forget it, Jake. It's Chinatown."

But let us return for a moment to the surface of the film. Consider those elegant costumes, and the Faye Dunaway character's gorgeous Colonial Revival mansion. Add to this the message of passivity, and there is something strangely comforting about Robert Towne and Polanski's re-creation of the Thirties. Nothing can be done, so why not enjoy the sensual memories of times past? There is a nostalgic and escapist element to *Chinatown* after all, and in this regard it is something like *American Graffiti*. This second level of criticism is not meant to nullify *Chinatown*'s status as a film of incisive social criticism. Instead, it points to contradictory levels of meaning in a very complex film.

I would argue that *Chinatown*-style complexity is characteristic of a number of American films of the 1970s, and of considerably fewer films in the 1980s and 1990s. The 1970s on film is marked by several distinct and sometimes contradictory currents, currents which can be analyzed both in overview and within individual films. This flow of conflicting ideas is what makes the seventies extraordinary. For me, the era of "Nobody knows anything" is the most exciting and most experimental period of the American feature film.

Whither goest thou, America,

in thy shiny car in the night?

—Jack Kerouac, *On the Road*

Part
1

Movies read or interpret the cultures in which they

exist, just a beat behind the present tense of events.

—Helene Keyssar, *Robert Altman's America*

Chapter 1

Easy Rider

Alice's Restaurant

Five Easy Pieces

Hippie Generation

The roots of *Easy Rider* lie primarily in the Hollywood B movie, also known in the 1960s as the "exploitation film." Producer/actor Peter Fonda, director/actor Dennis Hopper, actor Jack Nicholson, and cinematographer Laszlo Kovacs had all worked for Roger Corman's production unit at American International Pictures. The story idea of *Easy Rider*, credited to Peter Fonda, stems from exploitation movies Fonda had acted in for Corman, especially *The Wild Angels* (motorcycles) and *The Trip* (drugs). As Ethan Mordden points out, the exploitation movie was a way "to treat a theme of the day with some abandon."[1] Big-budget films from the Hollywood majors had standards of craftsmanship and taste which made for fairly conservative filmmaking. Exploitation films were supposed to be about sex and violence, rather than story, which means they could take liberties with the "well-made narrative." Films such as *Wild in the Streets* and *The Wild Angels* express something of the anarchic energy of 1960s youth culture. But the downside of the exploitation film (aside from sloppy technique) is that one never knows if the filmmakers are in any way committed to their material.

"Exploitation film" suggests not only a disinterest in film content but an actual bamboozling of the audience. It can be dispiriting to watch films where writing, acting, and technical crafts are so bad that the film doesn't seem to be trying. In *The Trip*, for example, the LSD trip itself has some interest, but for the rest of the film the actors are just going through the motions.

The innovation of *Easy Rider* was to apply the low-budget production methods of the B film to a deeply felt, contemporary subject. The screenplay, written by Fonda, Hopper, and Terry Southern,[2] traces the adventures of two long-haired motorcyclists, Billy (Dennis Hopper) and Wyatt, often called Captain America (Peter Fonda). They buy cocaine in Mexico, sell it in Los Angeles, and set off on their "bikes" for Mardi Gras in New Orleans. Along the way they have several encounters with characters and scenes emblematic of rural and small-town America: a farmer with a Mexican wife and a large family; a hippie commune in the desert; a parade where they are arrested for "parading without a permit"; a jailhouse encounter with George Hanson (Jack Nicholson), a lawyer with ACLU sympathies; a restaurant where the local sheriff and his cronies make threatening remarks while some giggling teenaged girls ask for a ride. The evening after the restaurant scene, as Wyatt, Billy, and George sleep in the open, they are attacked by vigilantes with clubs. George is killed, his head beaten in. Billy and Wyatt continue on to New Orleans, visiting a high-class bordello in George's honor. They stroll around Mardi Gras with two prostitutes, and all four take LSD in a cemetery. This leads to uncomfortable imagery and a certain amount of soul-searching. With a quick cut, the two motorcyclists are on the road again. A rural type in a pickup truck shoots at Billy, to scare him, and wounds him badly instead. The truck then circles back and the shooter kills Wyatt. The camera rises in the only helicopter shot of the film, revealing green pastures and a river as the "Ballad of Easy Rider" ends the film.

The production situation of *Easy Rider* throws some light on its unusual qualities. Originally, the film was planned as an American International release, with actors Fonda and Hopper taking over production duties as well. However, producer Fonda got a better deal from BBS Productions, an independent company affiliated with Columbia Pictures. BBS, a partnership between Bert Schneider, Bob Rafelson, and Steve Blauner, was sponsored at Columbia by Abe Schneider, Bert's father. BBS had made a lot of money on

"The Monkees" TV show, and was now willing to take a chance on a low-budget "youth movie." Novice filmmakers Fonda and Hopper were given a good deal of autonomy but were expected to stay within the $365,000 budget. Fonda and Hopper's inexperience led to some awkward moments but also to an opportunity to create a different kind of film.

Easy Rider is a modest film which gained tremendous "weight" because of its placement in cultural history and its overwhelming reception. It was a runaway hit in North America and Europe, eventually earning $60 million. *Easy Rider*'s success led to much discussion of the "new generation" of American youth and to new approaches to making films. The "hippie generation" or "counterculture" had by 1969 been established as a force in popular music, with San Francisco rock, British rock, and so on, but had made little impact on the film industry aside from the previously noted B pictures. Peter Fonda describes the cultural void filled by his film: "In 1968, we had our own music, art, language, and clothing, but we didn't have our own movie."[3] Suddenly, with *Easy Rider*, the culture of long hair, drugs, and rock and roll was prominently featured on the world's movie screens.

The impact of *Easy Rider*'s release can be gauged by looking at what else was playing in American movie theaters in July 1969 when the film came out. *Variety*'s July 23, 1969, edition reports that the three top-grossing films for the previous week are *The Love Bug* from Disney, *True Grit* from Paramount (starring John Wayne), and *April Fools* from National General. Other noteworthy films in the top ten are *Romeo and Juliet* (Zeffirelli version), *Where Eagles Dare*, *The Wild Bunch*, and *Oliver*. In places eleven through thirteen, *Chitty Chitty Bang Bang* and *Funny Girl* rank just ahead of *I Am Curious, Yellow*. Further down the list are Old Hollywood films such as *Sweet Charity*, *MacKenna's Gold*, and *If This Is Tuesday, It Must Be Belgium*; youth culture films such as *Midnight Cowboy*, *If*, *Che*, and *Putney Swope*; and the long-running, uncategorizable *2001: A Space Odyssey*.[4] Overall, the list shows tremendous diversity, but no particular pattern. It's a portrait of a film industry in disarray, where traditional blockbusters are no longer reliable, but nothing has taken their place.

Stephen Farber sums up the period in *Film Quarterly*'s Winter 1969–1970 edition, saying that "Summer 1969 may well turn out to be one of the crucial moments in American film history. . . . Almost all of the big, expensive, traditional-style commercial films . . . have failed miserably." Instead, "the changing movie audience . . . has finally registered its preferences" for youth films like *Easy Rider, Midnight Cowboy,* and *Alice's Restaurant.* Further, the studios are excited by the success of the new, "small" movies. "Right now they want every film to look like *Easy Rider.*"[5] In a very brief period, Hollywood had moved from investing in traditional, big-budget productions to an enthusiasm for new talents and experimental, low-budget films. The American film industry seemed to be undergoing a major shift, and *Easy Rider*'s success was the primary catalyst.

The narrative of *Easy Rider* is a journey consisting of several loosely linked adventures, plus footage of Wyatt and Billy on the road. The journey is not particularly suspenseful or melodramatic, but it does have mythic roots. It is first of all a celebration of the beauty, promise, and diversity of America, consciously connecting traditional elements (e.g., the small farmer, the magnificent desert landscapes) with new initiatives (e.g., the hippie commune). In discussing the scenes set in the desert Southwest, Dennis Hopper acknowledges the influence of "John Ford's America"; it was Ford's Westerns which established Monument Valley as emblematic of the power and majesty of America as both a social/political and a natural/geographical entity.[6] The names "Wyatt" and "Billy" also clearly descend from the Western genre. But *Easy Rider* is not really a Western, since the direction of travel is West to East and the heroes head not to an open frontier but to a closed land of bigotry. The desert spaces of the first half of the film are much more appealing than the lush, built-up spaces of the film's second half. As soon as the heroes enter into the organized life of the small-town parade, they are arrested. As George Hansen says in a campfire monologue, the Americans of 1969 give lip service to freedom but are terrified of the real thing.

This overarching symbolism gives substance to a story which is often slight. The opening scenes are hurried; we learn little about the backgrounds and motivations of Wyatt and Billy. Lee Hill notes that several expository scenes were cut, which puts the film's emphasis on action and visuals.[7] Later, the journey scenes focus on the people the heroes meet; therefore any changes in Wyatt and Billy happen unobtrusively. The actions of the Southern bigots are explained primarily by George Hanson's monologue. Another hint comes from the flirting of the teenaged girls with the three "hippie" visitors. Wyatt, Billy, and George threaten the patriarchal order of the town, and therefore (the film suggests) they are attacked. But aside from these hints, the violence of the film is underdetermined. In general, *Easy Rider* follows the B film in stressing theme and visuals and omitting the psychological depth of the well-made plot.

However, there is more to *Easy Rider* than a sketchy plot. The visuals are very important, and they communicate with a non-narrative directness unusual in Hollywood cinema. The several montages of Fonda and Hopper riding motorcycles are themselves images, or descriptions, or synecdoches of freedom. Out on the open road, no clocks, no limits, just man guiding machine. Laszlo Kovacs's photography glides lovingly over the customized Harleys, showing details of wheel and chrome as the bikes are in motion. In one scene, Dennis Hopper veers across the road, and the camera zooms out slightly to include him in an unobtrusive image of freedom. Another scene, this time more emphatic, compares riding motorcycles to flying, with the musical accompaniment "So You Want to Be a Bird." Some images are presented with a kind of reverence: the earth, water, and sky of the Southwest; the rancher's family at dinner and the commune members saying grace; the early morning scene with sky peeking through an abandoned shack; the pot-smoking scene in an Indian ruin. Other images are confining or ugly: the jailhouse scene and especially the acid trip in the cemetery. Here, 16 mm shooting on a rainy day creates an ugly, depressing, confining mood, as the actors (Fonda and Toni Basil in particular) play out psychodramas amidst the monuments and statues.

Easy Rider is an odd mixture of the obvious and the subtle and is therefore open to several different levels of interpretation. For some critics, the film is a kind of nouveau exploitation film, provocative but incoherent. The hip, contemporary nature of the subject does not make up for a thinness of both plot and character. Jeff Greenfield finds both the verbose Billy and the taciturn Wyatt/Captain America irritating in their shallowness.[8] Diana Trilling complains about the drug angle of the film, saying it never comes to grips with the moral implications of dealing cocaine.[9] Margie Burns is strongly critical of the film's violence, calling it a "trivializing echo of the fate of three Mississippi Freedom Riders." Overall, Burns sees *Easy Rider* as a demonization of the rural South and therefore a rationale for the rapid growth of suburbs.[10]

A second type or level of interpretation is provided by Stephen Farber, who finds *Easy Rider* interesting as a sociological rather than artistic text.

Easy Rider COLUMBIA PICTURES.
Billy (Dennis Hopper) and Wyatt (Peter Fonda) on the open road. Courtesy of Jerry Ohlinger Archives.

For Farber, the great achievement of Hopper, Fonda, and Southern is that they feel the pulse of young America. They are very good at reflecting the fantasies of alienated youth, less astute at shaping these fantasies into artistic form.[11] I would certainly agree that for many viewers, the tour of an alternative America was the key element of *Easy Rider*. The film encompasses the drug culture, bikers, hippies, the commune movement, a revived interest in the American Indian, and an excellent rock and roll soundtrack. In itself, the soundtrack suggests the vitality and diversity of American youth culture in 1969, via such performers as the Byrds, Bob Dylan, Steppenwolf, The Band, Jimi Hendrix, and so on.

A third interpretation of the film sees an overall coherence expressed by mise-en-scène and music as well as dialogue and plot. For Henry D. Herring, *Easy Rider* is "a song to the possibilities of the 1960s . . . a quest for genuine selfhood and personal freedom." [12] Images of alternative America and music about freedom (Steppenwolf, "Born to Be Wild") and nature's beauty (The Byrds, "I Wasn't Born to Follow") carry a sense of life's possibility. The musical score, chosen by Dennis Hopper, usually avoids the pleonasm of repeating exactly what the image says; it enhances, it counterpoints, it deepens the themes of the film. On the level of plot, Herring thinks that the film makes distinctions between Billy and Wyatt's quests for freedom. Billy "remains bound to strictures that parallel the bondage of the larger society: time, cashing in on the big money," a need for behavior that makes sense.[13] Wyatt is more relaxed, more of an individual. There is at least a chance that Wyatt can achieve "the complexity of a self both connected and free." [14]

Easy Rider supports all of the above interpretations, and more. Its great strengths, and great weaknesses, can perhaps be explained if we consider *Easy Rider* as an "amateur" film, in both senses of the term. As a first film by director Hopper and producer Fonda, *Easy Rider* is sometimes less than professional in construction. For example, the Mardi Gras scenes were shot in a great rush, by non-Hollywood camera operators (Laszlo Kovacs was hired afterward), because Peter Fonda was mixed up about the dates of Mardi Gras. One should not expect much coherence in those scenes. Also, I think the filmmakers do evade some of the hard questions implicit in the film: they do not take an attitude on the cocaine sale which finances the journey, nor do they convincingly motivate the violence that ends the film. However, *Easy Rider* is also a film made by people who love cinema— "lover" being the other meaning of amateur. They have crafted a beautiful and original film relying heavily on visuals and music. Also, by shooting quickly, on location, and with a mobile camera they have demonstrated the potential of low-budget production to create striking imagery of the open road.

A key to understanding *Easy Rider* is the Wyatt/Captain America character. Billy is a fairly obvious character, a loudmouth whose constant stream of chatter masks his insecurity. The quiet, observant Wyatt is more enigmatic. Is Wyatt a deeper, more thoughtful character than Billy, or is he just as superficial, just as unsatisfactory in suggesting a new direction for American youth? Herring suggests that Wyatt can be profound, but Jeff Greenfield finds him clichéd and irritating. My own reading of this character is that he is sweet, passive, and open to experience. Wyatt/Captain America is receptive to the various characters met on the road, and thus in a sense he generates the narrative. He is not at all a comic-book, action-oriented superhero (the nickname "Captain America" is interestingly ironic); instead, his dominant characteristic is sensitivity. But with thirty years of hindsight, Wyatt cannot be read as a guru or prophet. Some of his comments are pithy and sweet, as when he agrees to give two commune women a ride because "We're eating their food." Other comments are silly and clichéd, for example "I'm hip about time, but I just gotta go." And occasionally, Wyatt's instincts are just plain wrong. After observing the hippie commune's pitiful attempt at agriculture—no plows, no irrigation even though a river or canal runs through the land—Wyatt proclaims "No, they're going to make it."

Wyatt's most provocative comment comes late in the film, during the final campfire scene. Billy, shaking off recent events including George's death, exclaims, "We've done it. We're rich, Wyatt." Wyatt responds "You know, Billy, we blew it." This could be a statement on drugs, on the unpure origins of the journey. It could be about an ultimate failure to connect with the America outside the big cities. It could even be a metalinguistic comment on the impossibility of creating a new culture using the structures of the old, as David James suggests.[15] The emphasis on personal failure could lead the viewer back to interrogate the film. But ultimately this is a gnostic comment, a gesture at profundity that is not necessarily profound. The comment defines a fragile and contingent character who cannot easily summarize his experience.

To further consider the power and naïveté of *Easy Rider*, let us focus on two additional issues: the violence directed against the protagonists, and religious imagery in the film. The violent ending is a difficult compromise between a need for narrative closure and a desire not to trivialize a complex social situation. If *Easy Rider* is a genre film, in the motorcycle and/or Western genres, it needs to come to a strong and probably violent climax. If *Easy Rider* is a semi-exploitation movie, it can avoid thoroughly explaining the ending. But to stereotype and demonize the rural Southerners in the pickup truck would diminish a film which is surprisingly complex in its judgments.

So, the filmmakers treat the deaths at the end as, in a bizarre sense, accidental. The good old boys in the pickup truck want only to scare Billy with the shotgun. Though the shooter is trying to miss, he ineptly hits his target. The men in the truck then kill Wyatt in a gesture of self-protection. The ending becomes tragicomic (like the ending of Godard's *Pierrot le fou*), and its "message" is split: (1) America is a violent place, with near–civil war between classes, regions, and generations; (2) the deaths we see are nevertheless unusual, excessive, accidental. This compromise is a good try, but ultimately it is more about exaggerated, B movie violence than about social comment.

However, it is possible that the viewers of 1969 saw *Easy Rider*'s ending as, among other things, a response to the political rhetoric of the time. According to Jonathan Aitken, in George Wallace's third-party run for President in 1968 an oft-repeated line was "if one of them hippies lays down in front of mah car when Ah become President, that'll be the last car he lays down in front of." [16] The semi-accidental shooting of the hippies in *Easy Rider* may be a symbolic representation of this kind of extremist rhetoric. Patrick McGilligan, biographer of Jack Nicholson, makes the same point in a succinct phrase: "The killings were allegorical, of course." [17]

Easy Rider's religious dimension is subtler and more satisfying than its treatment of violence. The film has a diffuse spirituality, a nature-loving pantheism well-represented by the song "I Wasn't Born to Follow." There is also at least an attempt at Christian symbolism. According to Herring, Wyatt is at times presented as a Christ figure: "The whorehouse is an old church, he comes into the room on the word "Christe" in "Kyrie Eleison" and his prostitute is named Mary." [18] In another striking Christian connection, Wyatt, on LSD, sits in the lap of a statue of the Virgin Mary. Also, Wyatt's death at the end is never shown; it is simply indicated by a hurtling, burning motorcycle. Could this omission (probably the result of a low budget) also be creating the chance of a Resurrection? There are two possible explanations for the Christian symbolism. One is that Hopper and Fonda do want to suggest a connection between the murdered hippies and Christ—though Hopper, in an interview, chose to link them instead to the two thieves of the Crucifixion story.[19] Another explanation would be that the filmmakers ultimately reject the Christian references—the bordello as church is hardly a positive reference, and while on the Madonna's lap Wyatt says, "I hate you so much."

The last few moments of the film draw heavily on religious imagery without affirming or denying a link to Christianity. Wyatt dies (we think), and the camera ascends via helicopter to a point far above the ground. The details of bodies and burning motorcycles are lost in an image of green land and beautiful river. The helicopter shot could be an ascent to heaven, following Christian tradition, but it is more immediately an affirmation of the bond with nature. Wyatt and Billy's tragedy is only a tiny point in the continuity of nature, an idea brought home by Roger McGuinn's lyrics for "The Ballad of Easy Rider": "River flows, it flows to the sea, wherever it flows, that's where I want to be." This shot highlights the strengths of the film: original imagery, original thinking. *Easy Rider* is a film which broke the Hollywood mold.

Alice's Restaurant is based on a popular song, Arlo Guthrie's long (nineteen minutes) talking blues, first released in 1967. The song tells two autobiographical stories. First, it recounts how Arlo was arrested on Thanksgiving weekend in Stockbridge, Massachusetts—for littering! Second, it describes Arlo's induction physical at the Whitehall Street, New York City, office of the Selective Service. The link between the stories is that Arlo is turned down for the draft because of his criminal record. The song "Alice's Restaurant" is not really about Alice or her restaurant, which is part of its charm. The song is full of false leads, odd inclusions, and equally odd omissions. It does finally get to the point, Arlo's rejection by the draft, but much of the pleasure lies in the telling.

In adapting this narrative song for the screen, writer/director Arthur Penn and co-writer Venable Herndon faced a series of problems: (1) the song "Alice's Restaurant" was well-loved by a youth audience, and this created an expectation that the movie would closely follow the song; (2) the song offers little context and no character development; (3) the autobiographical song was closely identified with Arlo Guthrie, but Arlo had no acting experience; and (4) the song alternates between realist narrative and caricature. The filmmakers found ingenious responses to all of these challenges. They added new episodes and an emphasis on character to the story without contradicting the general outline of the song. They even added new passages of Arlo playing guitar and telling the story; one characteristic of a talking blues is that it is infinitely expandable. Arlo Guthrie does play himself in the film, which limits the protagonist's emotional range but also creates an interplay between documentary and fiction. Most of the other main parts are played by actors, but Officer Obie (William Obanheim) appears as himself. Stylistically, the film is primarily in a realist mode, but in the littering and draft physical episodes Arlo's sarcastic narration comes to the fore, accompanied at times by broadly farcical visuals. For example, as Arlo describes telling the army shrink he wants to "Kill! Kill! Kill!," we see Arlo and the shrink gleefully jumping up and down. The caricatural moments and the voice-over excerpts from Arlo's talking blues remind us that *Alice's Restaurant* is a construction, a fictional expansion of a real situation and a song.

The film's story begins with Arlo enrolling in a Montana college to escape the draft. But both Arlo and his friend Roger are beaten up and run out of town by unfriendly locals in cowboy garb. Arlo returns to the East and stays for a while with his friends Alice and Ray Brock, a couple who offer hospitality to a number of young hippies in a deconsecrated church in Stockbridge. Arlo also spends time in New York City, visiting his father Woody Guthrie, the legendary folk singer, and playing in small folk clubs. Woody is in bed, paralyzed, suffering from the nerve disease Huntington's chorea. The two main events of the song, littering and the draft physical, are presented at length in the film. Arlo and Roger are arrested by Officer Obie, the crime is thoroughly documented, and Arlo's sentence is a "twenty-five-dollar fine and pick up the garbage." At the induction center, the film (like the song) describes the dehumanizing process of an institutional physical in great detail.

The film's major addition to the song's plot lies in the characters of Alice, Ray, and a young heroin addict named Shelly. Alice and Ray, a couple perhaps in their thirties, establish a sort of extended family/youth hostel/ hippie commune where young people drop in, stay awhile, then drift away. Their ideal of a community based on voluntary association is presented as an alternative to the more conventional institutions of family, school, church, and government. What the young dropouts in this community find objectionable in mainstream society is not confronted head-on, but one powerfully suggestive scene provides some clues. Arlo, visiting Stockbridge, finds an old friend, a black man named Jake, at Alice and Ray's. Jake, a Vietnam veteran, now has a metal hook replacing one of his hands. The film emphasizes the hook via silent reaction shots of Arlo, Jake, and Shelly, but does not otherwise explain it. The spectator is supposed to make the link between a crippled young man and a faraway, unpopular war.

The film suggests some less-than-altruistic motives for Ray and Alice's generosity to the hippies and dropouts that surround them. For Ray, the commune is a way to stay young, to race motorcycles and deny responsibility. He is highly competitive with his younger friends, and is terribly disappointed when he finishes behind Shelly in a motorcycle race. He can also be violent; he hits Shelly and Alice in moments of rage. Robin Wood suggests that Ray has a latent homosexual attraction to Shelly, which would partially explain some rough horseplay between the two as well as Ray's odd use of the term "baby" in talking to Shelly.[20] Alice wants to mother everyone, and to offer her body to assuage all hurts, including her own. She sleeps with Shelly on one occasion, and she offers herself to Arlo as well. Alice founds the restaurant as a way to extend and commercialize her maternal instinct, but this venture struggles because no one but Alice will be responsible for it. The commune lifestyle has not magically transformed the imperatives of making a living, nor has it erased the distinctions between "men's work" and "women's work." Arthur Penn and his collaborators deserve credit for showing the unresolvable tensions of communal living—*Easy Rider* was not so candid in its commune scene.

Alice and Ray's commune experiment is ultimately not able to help Shelly. Shelly, a confused and unhappy young man who uses heroin to block out his troubles, is almost a son to the couple. However, Ray's competitiveness and Alice's compensatory sexual response make Shelly even more confused. After being off drugs for several weeks, Shelly reverts to heroin use. When confronted by Alice and Ray, he roars off on his motorcycle. Soon Shelly is dead of a heroin overdose. The film memorializes Shelly with a stylized scene of Joni Mitchell singing a requiem in a snowy graveyard. As Stephen Farber suggests, Shelly "is meant to stand for all the problems that are too intense for a loving family to solve, pain too twisted and unmanageable to be absorbed into Alice and Ray's pastoral ideal."[21]

Alice's Restaurant makes an interesting link between the hippies and the Old Left. Woody Guthrie is the bard of the union and political struggles of the 1930s and 1940s, and Arlo clearly idolizes his father. In a memorable scene, Pete Seeger (another figure linking Old Left politics and the popular culture of 1969) and Arlo play and sing "Pastures of Plenty" in Woody's room. "Pastures of Plenty" is a Woody Guthrie song about migrant farmworkers, cut off from the affluence they serve. This duet suggests that the hippies represented by long-haired Arlo have inherited some of the moral and political ideas of the Old Left. However, the film has previously under-cut this connection with a scene involving Arlo and Ruth, the middle-aged manager of a folk club in New York. Ruth gives money to pay Shelly's back rent and then starts reminiscing about the good old days of the Movement. Then she quickly makes a sexual advance to Arlo, which he rejects. Arlo leaves the club, his welcome at the folk club presumably ended. As with Alice and Ray, the good works of the club manager stem from a personal and limited agenda. She is not so much generous as wishing to recapture a romantic image of herself, and this puts a pall on the presentation of the Old Left generally.

The draft physical scenes in *Alice's Restaurant* are surprisingly apolitical. Yes, the song and the movie satirize the institutionalized process which turns young men into killers-in-training. No one in the induction machinery is interested in Arlo as an individual. He is poked and prodded and asked only one question: "Kid . . . have you ever been arrested?" He is eventually rejected by the draft because of his Stockbridge arrest, another encounter with an unthinking, unresponsive government agency. But *Alice's Restaurant* is not about draft resistance or opposition to the war in Vietnam; it is about one young man's lucky escape from the draft. There are a few lines about organized resistance in the recorded (1967) version of the song: Arlo suggests that young men tell the Army shrink "You can get anything you want at Alice's Restaurant," and then walk out. But these semi-serious lines are omitted from the film. Opposition to the war in Vietnam may be intuited from the overall wintry tone of *Alice's Restaurant,* and from the specific image of Jake with a hook replacing a hand. But although the film presents a general opposition to American "business as usual," it does not explicitly challenge United States policy in Vietnam.

Like *Easy Rider, Alice's Restaurant* has a religious aspect. The commune is in a deconsecrated church, with the pews torn out so that people can actually live in the building. On Thanksgiving Day, the ritual meal bringing people together at Alice and Ray's is visually paralleled with images of the other churches in town. We see a montage of exterior views of New England churches, with a congregation singing "Amazing Grace" on the soundtrack. Then we switch to an interior view of Alice and Ray's church, and discover that this "congregation" is doing the singing. The sense seems to be that the gathering at Alice and Ray's is creating a community and a spiritual bond similar to what is happening elsewhere. A further step in this direction is Alice and Ray's remarriage and homemade "reconsecration" of the church after Shelly's death. This is an attempt by Ray to reestablish the spirit of the commune with a brief, satirical ceremony and a big party. If a church is primarily a community, and good works, perhaps even a state of grace, then Alice and Ray's home is a church.

Despite Ray's frenzied attempt to throw a party, *Alice's Restaurant* ends on a somber note. Alice is shown in a long take at night on the steps of the church, alone in the cold. She is not ready to forget Shelly's death, or her husband's casual violence, or the "woman's work" which defines her role in the commune. A carefully designed camera shot, simultaneously zooming in and tracking back (with short lateral movements, as well) while the image remains about the same size, emphasizes the instability of this moment.[22] The wordless ending shot is a far more effective way to express the limitations of the new youth culture than Wyatt/Captain America's comment "We blew it." *Alice's Restaurant* is not primarily about Alice, but it ends with her pain.

The year 1969 was the high point of the youth culture's encounter with cinema, the moment at which enormous changes seemed to be possible. *If,* Lindsey Anderson's British film about student revolt, won the Grand Prize at Cannes, and *Easy Rider* won the prize for Best New Director. *Midnight Cowboy* won the Academy Award for Best Picture. *Easy Rider* was the blockbuster of the year, and *Putney Swope, Alice's Restaurant,* and *Medium Cool* received good reviews and fair-to-good audiences. Among the other New Hollywood films of the moment were *Bob & Carol & Ted & Alice, Downhill Racer, Goodbye Columbus, That Cold Day in the Park, They Shoot Horses, Don't They?, The Rain People,* and *Last Summer.* In 1969, film content, film style, and the film audience all appeared to be rapidly transforming.

Given this atmosphere of positive change, it is interesting to note how modest and muted *Easy Rider* and *Alice's Restaurant* now appear, especially in their relation to social change. Both films are about, and presumably addressed to, middle-class white youths. *Easy Rider* suggests a multicultural society in its scenes of the Southwest, and *Alice's Restaurant* includes an occasional black or Asian face, but neither film has much to say about race or class. Further, both films are surprisingly negative about the possibilities of the hippie lifestyle. The commune of *Easy Rider* is an excellent example of how *not* to do agriculture, and the deaths of George, Wyatt, and Billy are hardly a positive statement about freedom. *Alice's Restaurant* balances the good humor of Arlo Guthrie's song with a more melancholy view of Alice and Ray's extended family. The film shows deep flaws in the couple's reaching out to alienated young people. Vincent Canby's review cements this point by noting that in 1969 (two years after the events shown in the film) the real Alice and Ray are already divorced.[23] Perhaps the main virtue of *Easy Rider* and *Alice's Restaurant* is lucidity. They show how difficult it is to live even a little bit differently.

If 1969 was a banner year for new films and new talents in American cinema, 1970 was a year of retrenchment. Most of the films about youth culture and student revolutionaries produced by the Hollywood studios in the wake of *Easy Rider* were less than popular at the box office. Thomas Schatz describes a "deluge of youth-cult films" that were "obviously calculated in their appeal to America's disenfranchised (but ticket-purchasing) young." Specific films he mentions are *Getting Straight, The Strawberry Statement, Move!, Joe,* and *Little Fauss and Big Halsey.*[24] He could have added *RPM, The Revolutionary, Cisco Pike,* and perhaps even Michelangelo Antonioni's American-made *Zabriskie Point.* Some of these films were obviously derivative (which I think is Schatz's point), but it also seems likely that audiences in 1970 were no longer comfortable with confrontational youth films. Acceptance of drugs and drug pushers lasted only a few months, thus dooming *Cisco Pike,* and films about student revolutionaries faced opposition both from college-aged liberals seeking authenticity and from frightened people of all ages (a much larger group). The two biggest hits of 1970 were *Love Story* and *Airport,* genre films about simple, easy-to-grasp problems.

One exception to this trend was *Five Easy Pieces* (1970), the next important film from BBS Productions, the producers of *Easy Rider.* The film was directed by Bob Rafelson, a partner in BBS, and it confirmed the star status of Jack Nicholson. Rafelson had previously directed the Monkees in *Head* (coscripted by Nicholson), an exercise in neo-Beatles slapstick. *Five Easy Pieces* is a more substantial effort, which builds on the road movie element of *Easy Rider* as well as on Jack Nicholson's role of George Hanson in the earlier film. In *Easy Rider*, George was the prodigal son of a privileged Southern background, a liberal-leaning attorney whose father's influence kept him out of trouble. In *Five Easy Pieces*, the background of Bobby Dupea is still privileged, but now he is escaping his family of distinguished classical musicians by working as a rigger in the Southern California oil fields.[25] He lives with a waitress named Rayette (Karen Black) from the Deep South who listens to the music of Tammy Wynette.

One theme of *Easy Rider* was that the frontier was closed; there was nowhere for adventurous young people to go. This theme is seconded by *Five Easy Pieces*, where Bobby's geographical displacements do not bring him happiness, fulfillment, or peace. The closing of the frontier is announced metonymically within the film when Bobby picks up two female hitchhikers headed for Alaska. The unhappy, aggressive hitchhiker played by Helena Kallionotes complains incessantly about human filth and announces that "Alaska is cleaner." Though Bobby makes fun of this character ("That was before the big thaw"), his own quest is similarly irrational and impulsive. He journeys first to Puget Sound, where he finds only pretention and alienation on his family's island estate. Then he sets off (for Canada?) with Rayette but abandons her at a gas station and hitches a ride on a logging truck bound for . . . Alaska. Bobby may understand the futility of escape, but he cannot get beyond it.

Though *Five Easy Pieces* is not a hippie film, it does fit into the 1960s youth culture project of building a new life. In *Easy Rider* and *Alice's Restaurant* this project was expressed via new forms of communal living. *Five Easy Pieces* explores the alternate approach of changing one's social class. Bobby Dupea, concert pianist, becomes a blue-collar worker. Aside from working in the oil fields, he is shown drinking, bowling, playing cards, and having sex with a woman he meets in the bowling alley. Bobby's best friend is Elton, a hell-raiser with a wild laugh who is eventually arrested for jumping bail on a robbery charge. That Bobby is more attracted to partying than to the entire package of working-class values is shown in a conversation with Elton about kids. Elton married his wife when she became pregnant, and by now he enjoys having a kid. He expects Bobby to do the same thing with Rayette (though she never announces a pregnancy on-screen), but Bobby objects and stalks off. At this point Bobby quits the oil fields job and sets off for his family's island home—with Rayette.

The film's attitude toward its two featured social milieus seems to me uncertain. The interlude in the oil fields provides Bobby with friends, work, an opportunity to blow off steam. Yet he cannot entirely enter into a working-class identity. He objects to Elton's telling him what to do, and he never completely accepts Rayette as his lover and partner. Rayette's characterization throws some light not only on Bobby's hesitations, but also on the filmmakers' ambivalence about a working-class subculture. Rayette is simple, affectionate, dependable, genuinely in love with Bobby. She can be perceptive, but she sometimes seems dumb to the point of caricature. When she interacts with Bobby's family at dinner, her remarks seem both off-the-wall and clichéd. Rayette is also characterized by "her" music, the songs of Tammy Wynette. These simple, emotional tunes do provide a sense of cultural setting, but they lack the sophistication and depth of the classical music associated with Bobby's family.

If the working-class lifestyle is not entirely satisfying, the cultured intellectual milieu of Bobby's family is even less fulfilling. On the island, Bobby's brother, sister, and father live in an isolated, highly artificial way. All of them are, in one way or another, crippled: the brother wears a neck brace, the sister is emotionally starved, the father has had two strokes and cannot speak. The father of this film, present but yet absent, is uncannily like the Woody Guthrie (also a musician, also paralyzed) of *Alice's Restaurant*. The difference is that Arlo Guthrie loves and admires Woody, but Bobby has no particular love or respect for his father.

By far the most interesting resident of the Dupea estate is Catherine van Oost (Susan Anspach), who is studying piano with Bobby's brother Carl. Catherine seems content with the quiet island setting and the long hours of practice, but when pushed a bit she makes love passionately with Bobby, or Robert, as he is called on the island. Then she backs off, citing fairness to Carl but also doubts about Robert. In a memorable speech, Catherine says: "If a person has no love for himself, no respect for himself, no love of his friends, family, work, something, how can he ask for love in return? I mean, why should he ask for it?" Catherine is certainly a poised and articulate young woman, unlike Rayette. With no chance to continue a relationship with Catherine, Bobby/Robert leaves the island.

Gregg M. Campbell has proposed that Catherine, not Bobby, is at the center of *Five Easy Pieces*. For Campbell, the film is a feminist work by scriptwriter Adrien Joyce (a pseudonym for Carol Eastman). Catherine is the "true heroine," and even Rayette "is essentially more dignified and human than the male protagonist."[26] Campbell admits that Catherine's choice of a sheltered, limited existence may be a "cop out," but he then labels this choice "the profound flaw of accepting the tragic nature of life" (tragic because pain, conflict, limits are inescapable).[27] This is an interesting construction, but I do not think the film supports it. Clearly, Bobby is the main character of *Five Easy Pieces*; the narrative follows his adventures and his dilemmas. And though Catherine is capable of intelligence and dignity, the film connects her with the crippled lassitude of the island estate. She chooses the "rest home," as Bobby labels it, over the challenge of the unknown. Because she opts for the safe and easy approach, Catherine is a less memorable proto-feminist figure than the Alice of *Alice's Restaurant*.

We are left with the troubled Bobby as the thematic as well as narrative center of *Five Easy Pieces*. Bobby is at home nowhere. He has a tremendous energy to explore, to enjoy, to struggle, to "light out for the territory" like a modern Huckleberry Finn. He is a kind of hippie without the signature clothing or the naïve clichés. The film affirms Bobby's brief moments of spontaneous connection with the world: the camaraderie with Elton, playing piano on a moving flatbed truck, the famous restaurant scene (Bobby tries to get what he wants in a coffee shop which accepts no substitutions), the lovemaking with Catherine. But most of the time, Bobby is enfolded by absences and contradictions. Rayette is loving but stupid, Catherine smart but distant; neither is entirely "there" for him. His father is present yet absent. Elton is his friend but not his friend—when angered, Bobby calls Elton an "ignorant cracker." Even on a metaphysical level the film is beset by contradictions. Thus, one of Carl's intellectual friends proposes that rationality is a byproduct of human aggression, a hypothesis that denies its own basis in reason. More mundanely, Bobby's final abandonment of Rayette is shown in long take, prominently featuring a gas station sign: "Gulf."

Stephen Farber cautions that *Five Easy Pieces* is very much a film about an individual and that it resists social explication.[28] Nevertheless, I would point to two social themes in the film: first, a continuation of the restless exploration of *Easy Rider* and *Alice's Restaurant*, the search for a more authentic way to live; second, a misanthropic sense of the uselessness of such a search. In *Five Easy Pieces*, the audience can empathize with Bobby's

Five Easy Pieces COLUMBIA PICTURES.
Bobby Dupea (Jack Nicholson) playing piano on a moving truck. A moment of spontaneous connection with the world. Courtesy of Jerry Ohlinger Archives.

quest for fulfillment, happiness, connection to other human beings. But problems of identity are crushing, and little can be expected from this quest. Bobby may, in fact, be heading for death at the end of the film. The driver warns him, "Where we're going, it's colder than hell."

Bobby's difficulties may stand for the impasse of a generation, for whom traveling, intoxication, and sexual license do not solve underlying problems. As with *Easy Rider* and *Alice's Restaurant*, this film's primary virtue may be its lucidity.

Chapter 2

Joe

The French Connection   **Vigilantes and Cops**

Dirty Harry

Death Wish

Easy Rider, Alice's Restaurant, and *Five Easy Pieces* suggest that at least some of the youth culture films of 1969–1970 were modest and self-critical in their approach, and that they aimed at reaching a broad audience. *Alice's Restaurant* is the most specifically political of the three films, but it is very far from being militant. Nevertheless, it would be naïve to expect that "hippie" films represent any sort of consensus or even leading direction in the Hollywood output of the years around 1970. Among the very diverse works of this period, we can isolate a group of films that are conservative reactions to the same disruptions and social movements figured in the hippie generation films.

Joe is a version of the exploitation film, a film simultaneously excited and repulsed by the hippie lifestyle. This low-budget film was produced by the Cannon Group, a company which in 1970 was known for soft-core sex movies ("nudies," in the slang of the time). The key creative personnel for the film were unknown at this time, successful and famous later in the 1970s. The writer was Norman Wexler, later the writer of *Saturday Night Fever* and co-writer of *Staying Alive*. The director-cinematographer was John G. Avildsen, who was eventually to direct *Save the Tiger, Rocky*, and *Lean on Me*. As *Joe* and the later films demonstrate, both Wexler and Avildsen have a special affinity for urban working-class and middle-class settings.

The plot of *Joe* involves a young hippie girl, Melissa Compton (Susan Sarandon), who lives in the East Village with Frank, her drug dealer boyfriend. After an overdose of amphetamines, Melissa lands in the hospital. Her father, Bill Compton, confronts the boyfriend, a thoroughly nasty character, and in a moment of rage kills him. Then the father has a drink in a local bar and meets Joe Curran (Peter Boyle), a metalworker who mouths off about hating hippies, blacks, gays, and so on. Joe says he'd like to kill a drug dealer, and Compton lets slip that "I just did."

This seems to be an idle boast, but after news accounts of Frank's death, Joe takes it seriously. He tracks down Compton not for blackmail but to offer congratulations and friendship. In extensive scenes comparing the lives of a $160-a-week worker and a $60,000-a-year advertising executive, Joe and Compton meet, have a few drinks, get better acquainted. Eventually, Mr. and Mrs. Compton go to meet Joe and his wife, at Joe's apartment in Queens. Mary Lou Curran and Joan Compton chat in the kitchen, while Joe takes Bill Compton to the basement to show off his gun collection. The scene is a bit uncomfortable for all, especially when Joe pats a startled Joan Compton on the butt. However, the Comptons think they must stay on Joe's good side—he knows their secret.

When Melissa leaves the hospital and learns the truth about Frank's death, she runs away. Compton searches for her every night in Greenwich Village, and one night Joe offers to help. Their search takes these middle-aged men to a wish-fulfillment hippie orgy (Joe cannot pronounce the word "orgy"), where their wallets are stolen. With guns from Joe's collection in hand, they track the thieves to a commune in the countryside. They kill one of the commune members, and then, to protect themselves (the same rationalization as in *Easy Rider*), they shoot everyone present at the commune. Compton shoots a young woman in the back as she tries to escape. Then the camera angle shifts, and we see it is . . . his daughter.

Until the shock at the end, *Joe* seems to be supportive of the right-wing alliance of worker and manager. Joe is the most sympathetic character in the movie, a warm, gregarious, but very frustrated human being. He feels threatened at work, threatened in the street, threatened by his own children. A decorated war veteran, he talks about fighting for his idea of America at home (the main title for *Joe* uses lettering derived from the pattern of the American flag). Compton is a less impressive character (some reviewers commented on the flatness of Dennis Patrick's acting), but his killing of Frank seems in the film's terms to be more or less justified. Frank is a worm; critic David Denby (writing in 1970) describes him as "perhaps the vilest character in recent American films."[1] Frank has corrupted Melissa and has endangered her life. But what enrages Compton the most is Frank's talking about Melissa's sexuality, especially her Daddy hangup. Compton responds by pounding Frank's head against the wall, inadvertently killing him. The film then follows the logic "hippies are scum and therefore to be exploited" until it reaches its inevitable conclusion, the death of Melissa. But this is where the film's rationale explodes. If by one logic Melissa is hippie scum, by another she is Compton's daughter and therefore precious. The ending destroys the right-wing logic of what has gone before but provides no alternative view of the world, no approach to reconciling generations, races, or classes.

Joe is an interestingly incoherent film. It appeals to conservative spectators who fear the social difference of the hippies, the blacks, the drug dealers. It also appeals to more moderate spectators who object to disruption and lawlessness from any side. In a further twist, *Joe* suggests that the same spectators who fear the hippies are also excited and fascinated by the hippie lifestyle—specifically by recreational drugs and "free love." This aspect of the film, presented mainly via the orgy scene, has a dual meaning of its own. First, it shows the hypocrisy of men who value their own sexual freedom but are horrified by this same freedom extended to the young (and especially to women). Second, the orgy scene to a large extent leaves plot and character development behind to exploit and stereotype an idea of hippie sex. Among other things, *Joe* is a "nudie" which aims at shocking and thrilling its audience.

In an interview with the *New York Times* soon after the release of *Joe*, Peter Boyle expressed concern about the film's reception (even though this was the film which made him a recognizable movie star). Boyle felt that the film was supposed to be a critique of blue-collar conservatism and a call for an end to violence—both in Vietnam and at home. However, in the wake of the working-class demonstration on Wall Street in favor of the war in Vietnam, Boyle worried that *Joe* was being welcomed as a film expressing the divisive concerns of the "Silent Majority." Instead of critiqueing an irresponsible political position, the film was fueling that position.[2]

A film, or a novel, or a painting, is always more than the authors' intentions; a film involves an interaction between the images and sounds (the text), and the audience. In the case of *Joe*, this interaction is particularly fascinating. A text with several possible meanings is interpreted in one main direction because of current events. An incoherent text becomes a rightwing text. Peter Boyle is probably naïve in suggesting a liberal slant to the film (though this is one possible direction for interpretation) because its conservative appeals are so evident. The film is called *Joe*, not *The Death of an Innocent* or some such title, to highlight the most charismatic character. And Joe the character happens to be bigoted, violent, and *pleased* with his assault on anyone who is different. In a key moment of the film, he tells Compton that shooting the hippies can be fun. Turning *Joe* into a liberal social satire may have been possible, but it would have required the skills of a Stanley Kubrick. The young New York audiences who stood up and talked back to the screen ("Next time we're going to shoot back, Joe") did not miss the point;[3] they correctly interpreted *Joe* through the filter of current events.

Whereas *Easy Rider, Alice's Restaurant,* and *Five Easy Pieces* all made unconvincing gestures at expanding the horizons of "youth culture" to include other social classes or groups, *Joe* presents a rather convincing alliance between classes. The film figures not only the "Silent Majority," but also the Republican alliance that has dominated American politics since 1968. Joe and Compton are unlike in speech, dress, and income, but alike in conservatism, patriotism, and their definition of masculinity. Both fear social change and demonize the Other—in this case, the hippies and drug dealers. Both rely on subordinate, compliant women but allocate to themselves a realm of masculine freedom (drinks after work, sex with the hippie women). Both are willing to use violence to "protect" freedom—their own freedom, not necessarily the freedom of others. This agenda makes psychological sense for Joe, who is threatened on all sides. It makes a more calculating social sense for Compton, who is near the top of the heap and wants to stay there.

Although *Joe* is in some ways crude, it does a nice job of showing the contrasting settings of hippie-bohemian East Village, lower-middle Queens, and upper-middle Manhattan. Frank and Melissa's small apartment is grungy, messy, and inconvenient. The bathtub is right in the main room— probably so that we can watch Melissa take a bath. The literal filth of the apartment blends with a metaphorical filth of drugs, criminality, and hippie sex. This is presented visually in an early scene where Frank has dirt in-grained on the soles of his feet, even though he has just bathed. Melissa, though she lives in the same apartment and bathes in the same tub, seems to be clean and more-or-less wholesome. The Comptons live in a spacious apartment overlooking Central Park and are defined by expensive fabrics and clean, modern decor. The Currans live in more crowded surroundings with new but low-cost furniture and homemade curtains. However, both of the "adult" apartments are meticulously clean, which suggests a "Citizen / Other" division between the adult couples and the hippies.

Kristin Ross, in a recent study of French culture of the late 1950s and early 1960s, has discussed dirt and cleanliness as ideologically loaded terms. Her hypothesis is that "clean" was connected to "modern" and used as a xenophobic distinction between middle-class Frenchness and various Others, including peasants and especially non-Europeans (e.g., Algerians). Foreigners were often soiled by definition ("dirty Arab"), and this main-tained a distinction between France and the Third World at a moment when colonialism was ending.[4] In *Joe*, and American culture generally, dirt seems to be connected with sex (as in "filthy pictures") and criminality, rather than with explicit markings of social class. But the notion of "dirty" as an Us/Them distinction is as useful in 1970s America as in 1950s and 1960s France, and will be taken up again in this chapter.

Compton is an executive. He works in a large office characterized by shiny surfaces and a lack of clutter. Joe is a factory worker. His place of business is hot, noisy, and indifferent to fashion. In other respects, though, the two male characters are strongly linked. The names are almost equiva-lent: Joe Curran and Bill Compton. The cadence of syllables is identical, and both men are defined by strong, one-syllable masculine nicknames. Curran is clearly Irish, Compton not-so-clearly English in origin, but in melting-pot America these backgrounds are sufficiently close to suggest commonality of interest. Additionally, Joe and Compton have similar home lives: conventional, supportive spouses, and problems with teenage or young adult kids. On a personal level, Joe admires Compton's balls; Compton, after all, "did something" about the drug dealers. Compton, on the other hand, likes Joe's directness. Unlike the devious people in the advertising business, Joe tells you exactly what he thinks.

As an exploitation film, *Joe* is able to shuck the limitations of plausibility and get right at the fears of middle-class America. Almost all of the films of 1970–1971 are cautious and indirect about the profound stresses affecting the American community: the Vietnam War, riots in the black ghettoes, campus revolts, and so on. This is a period of great instability in which fighting in the streets is not only a possibility but occasionally a reality. Hollywood films typically avoid this kind of conflict; they try to attract an audience by being controversial but not confrontational. *Joe,* however, wades right in, imagining a peak of generational conflict: "Suppose I killed my daughter's hippie boyfriend?"

The French Connection (1971) is a well-made crime film about a successful, large-scale narcotics bust in New York City. It focuses on a conflict between tough, hard-nosed police detective Popeye Doyle (Gene Hackman) and elegant French heroin smuggler Alain Charnier (Fernando Rey). Doyle and his partner Russo (Roy Scheider), unwinding at a nightclub, notice a Brooklyn luncheonette owner with a suspicious wad of big bills. Following a hunch, they uncover contacts between Sal Boca (the luncheonette owner), drug financier Joel Weinstock, and Charnier. After long and fruitless surveillance, the operation against Charnier and Sal has been called off when Charnier's strongarm assistant Pierre Nicoli (Marcel Bozzuffi) tries to ambush Popeye. Popeye pursues Nicoli in a tremendously exciting car-versus-subway train chase scene and kills the would-be assassin. Then the police and federal agents combine to capture 120 pounds of heroin at the moment of transfer from Charnier to the American crooks. However, Charnier escapes from this confrontation, and several of the Americans receive little or no punishment for their parts in the narcotics scheme.

The French Connection is a very efficient, suspense-creating machine of a movie. It relies heavily on visuals to present the rhythm and feel of criminal activity and police investigation. At several points, fast-moving scenes are thrown at the spectator without exposition; acting more or less like detectives, we must somehow integrate them into the flow of narrative.

For example, no explanation is given of the killing of an undercover agent in Marseilles; because the killer is Nicoli, we eventually connect this with Charnier's operation. Also, a scene of a late-model Lincoln being loaded onto a boat in Marseilles is not explained; we later deduce that it must contain the shipment of heroin. In New York, Nicoli promises to take care of Popeye; but it is some minutes later, and without access to the sniper's point of view, that we discover someone is shooting at Popeye. By minimizing exposition and making the spectator work, *The French Connection* adds a modernist twist to a traditional genre.

Much of the film is taken up with "police procedural" sequences: how to tail a pedestrian with three men on the streets of New York; how to tail a suspect's car with two cars; how to arrange a wiretap; how to test heroin for purity (the crooks do that). Occasionally, the procedural details break into a full-blown chase, as in the famous sequence in which Popeye chases Nicoli. This is a remarkable scene for its gritty New York setting under the elevated train, and for the way a quotidian scene is transformed into breathtaking speed and danger. According to director Friedkin, the chase was filmed at real speed in the real location (a subway and several New York city blocks would be impossible to fake).[5] The car was in minor collisions three times, and in the scariest moment Popeye almost hits a woman pushing a baby carriage.

If *Joe* suggested a class alliance between blue collar and white collar, *The French Connection* is a populist film on the side of the working man. Doyle and Rizzo are lower-middle-class cops, living modestly and resenting the monied comfort of the criminals they hunt. One nicely observed scene shows Doyle outside a restaurant on a wintry day, eating pizza and drinking bad coffee, while Charnier and Nicoli dine elegantly within. There is a certain amount of class resentment in the scenes of the crooks staying in elegant hotels, driving fine cars, and so forth. The rich are shown as either having criminal secrets to hide (Charnier) or as spoiled, pampered, and naïve (the French TV star, played by Frederic De Pasquale, who imports the Lincoln as a paid favor to Charnier). Rich and poor meet in an interesting night club scene, where Sal and his organized crime cronies have all the money, but Popeye has power and status as a policeman. With the potential to physically attack, to arrest, to make trouble for the nightclub, a policeman has

The French Connection TWENTIETH CENTURY-FOX.
Gene Hackman plays Popeye Doyle, a hardworking, lower-middle-class narcotics cop. Courtesy of Museum of Modern Art/Film Stills Archive.

a certain amount of masculine force in night-time Manhattan, and shots of Popeye living it up at the nightclub show him reveling in this force.

The French Connection carefully avoids making a political statement in its primary conflict. Popeye's adversary is Charnier, a corrupt French businessman and therefore not included in the stresses and strains of American sociopolitical life. Charnier is bringing in heroin, which is assumed to be a bad thing. The days of "mellow" drug pushers (*Easy Rider*) are long since over. To a large extent, the film's morality recalls the most traditional of Westerns—we are for the white hats (the cops) and against the black hats (the crooks). The drama of *The French Connection* arises for the most part from *how* the white hats win out.

However, the film does get more complicated than this by suggesting that the cops have a subculture of their own. In rough, tough New York, they abide by their own rules, which are not exactly the same as the rule of law.

For example, Popeye and Russo terrorize an African American bar full of narcotics users not once but twice in the film. This has very little to do with plot or theme; it is primarily to set a violent tone. All they find out is that there are no hard drugs around, thus setting the scene for Charnier's shipment. But the casual violence of these scenes, which include a police beating outside the bar reminiscent of 1994's Rodney King incident, suggest that policemen follow the rules of their subculture, not of the law. Popeye insults blacks and hits blacks because he is "allowed" to do so. His job gives him little monetary award, but a fair amount of power. In *The French Connection*, society puts up with the police subculture in exchange for social order.

The film is generally in favor of giving police the broad powers they need to be efficient, and it at times ignores the abuses that result. Popeye Doyle, violent, impulsive, and dedicated, is regarded as a hero. According to William Friedkin, Popeye is the kind of tough cop that's needed in the very difficult, perhaps impossible, fight against narcotics.[6] However, at the end of the film, Doyle's behavior does come under scrutiny. In the showdown with the criminals, Doyle is intensely searching for Charnier in the many rooms of an abandoned industrial building. He almost shoots his own partner, Russo. Then he does shoot Mulderig, one of the federal agents on the case. Ironically, Mulderig had complained much earlier that the last time he and Doyle worked together, a good cop got killed. Russo is horrified by this turn of events, but Popeye, obsessed, hurtles off into the darkness in search of Charnier. The film ends on a freeze frame of the dark, wet interior of the building. Who knows who else Doyle may have shot, after the freeze frame? *The French Connection*, generally supportive of a macho police subculture, ends with a terrifying moment of doubt.

Dirty Harry (1971) is another powerful action movie about a morally questionable cop. It presents a film-long confrontation between San Francisco police detective Harry Callahan (Clint Eastwood) and deranged killer Scorpio (Andy Robinson). Scorpio begins by shooting, from long range, a young woman swimming in a rooftop pool. He also kills, in the course of the film, a ten-year-old black boy, a policeman, and a fourteen-year-old girl. In the film's concluding moments, he hijacks a school bus and threatens the lives of several young children. Callahan, known as Dirty Harry, makes apprehending Scorpio a personal priority. However, after he succeeds in trapping and wounding Scorpio in Kezar Stadium at night, the district attorney declines to prosecute because of lapses in legal procedure. Scorpio then evades Harry's unofficial surveillance by paying someone to beat him up and blaming Callahan. This sets up the final action scene on the school bus. Though ordered not to interfere with Scorpio's request for ransom money, Callahan saves the kids, kills Scorpio, and throws away his San Francisco police star in disgust.

Dirty Harry presents a San Francisco overrun by crime and sexuality, as represented by the red-light district, a woman known as "Hot Mary," a homosexual in the park, a sexual threesome involving two women and a man, a bank robbery which takes place as Harry eats his hotdog lunch, a frequently robbed liquor store, and of course Scorpio himself. Scorpio is a character without backstory, but his long hair and peace symbol belt buckle identify him with the hippies, the antiwar movement, and the social changes of the 1960s. In terms of local San Francisco history, he is also identified with the serial killer known as Zodiac, a notorious figure who wrote taunting letters to the newspapers and was never caught. Scorpio preys on the weak and kills for pleasure, which makes him unpredictable and hard to stop. Only Harry's fanaticism, equal to or greater than Scorpio's, is able to stop the killing.

Harry himself is out of control. He is called "Dirty Harry" because of his general misanthropy, because he takes all of the police department's dirty jobs, and because he does not stay within the limits of law and custom. A relevant usage of "dirty" circa 1970 would be "illegal, unethical, and violent," as in "dirty" espionage or a "dirty" war. Note that this is a quite different metaphoric use of "dirty" from the "dirty hippies" in *Joe*, or the "dirty foreigners" in Kristin Ross's *Fast Cars, Clean Bodies*. "Dirty" is a rich, multivalent term in modern Western societies. In *Dirty Harry*, the argument for illegal and unethical operations would be that society is breaking down, conventional lines of authority are ineffectual (neither the mayor nor the district attorney has a clue about how to fight crime), and only heroic action which goes beyond arbitrary rules can stem the tide.

The key point where individual heroism and law diverge in *Dirty Harry* happens after Harry has delivered ransom money for fourteen-year-old Ann Mary Deakin to Scorpio. Scorpio kicks Harry several times and decides to kill him. Chico (Harry's new partner) distracts Scorpio but is wounded himself. Harry knifes Scorpio in the leg, but Scorpio escapes. Later that night,

Dirty Harry WARNER BROTHERS.
Clint Eastwood as tough, cynical cop Harry Callahan. Courtesy of Museum of Modern Art/
Film Stills Archive.

Dirty Harry WARNER BROTHERS.
Harry Callahan (Eastwood) gets all the dirty jobs. Here he rescues a would-be jumper from a building ledge. Courtesy of Museum of Modern Art / Film Stills Archive.

Harry gets a tip that Scorpio lives as an illegal squatter in Kezar Stadium, and he enters the stadium without a warrant. He kicks open doors, scares Scorpio out onto the playing field, wounds him with a gunshot. Then Harry extracts the location where Ann Mary is being held by grinding his foot into the wound on Scorpio's leg. Unfortunately, Ann Mary is already dead. At this point, we cut to the district attorney's office, where the D.A. complains about Callahan's procedural lapses: no warrant, not reading the suspect his rights, extracting a confession via physical abuse or torture. Callahan is shocked (but not too shocked). What about the girl? What about her rights? At this point a Judge Bannerman, called in by the D.A. as a consultant, says that he understands Harry's point, but that under the law Scorpio cannot be charged.

This scene could have been played as a conflict between two valid points of view: the need for swift action versus the need for legal safeguards. The

D.A. could have subjected Harry to blistering criticism because he blew the case. Harry could have gotten a search warrant within minutes, I assume, for such an emergency situation. Because of his lone wolf approach, a killer will go free. Harry then could object, with vehemence, that a young girl's life was in danger. But the film does not play the scene this way. The D.A.'s criticism is fairly mild, and both he and the legal expert seem defeated in advance. The way is left clear for Harry's fanaticism.

Beyond this legal argument, Harry turns out to be a rather complex, and not always heroic, character. The film suggests that his tough, unyielding, unfeeling side stems from a personal tragedy. His wife was killed in a traffic accident, by a drunk. To compensate, or perhaps to hide from his grief, Harry has become a fanatical, at times sadistic, cop. He believes in nothing, certainly not in law or government; nothing except his own limited ability to right some wrongs. In a further twist, Harry is linked visually and thematically to Scorpio. Both are tall, both have long hair (Scorpio's longer than Harry's), both are good with weapons. Both peer out over the city from high perches; John Baxter proposes that Harry is San Francisco's "avenging angel," Scorpio his "satanic" challenger.[7] In one extraordinary moment, their subjectivities even seem to merge. At Kezar Stadium, the avenging Harry approaches the wounded Scorpio. Harry demands to know where the girl is. Scorpio protests that he has rights. Harry begins to step on Scorpio's wound. Threatening music (the "Scorpio motif") comes up, the focus becomes soft, and the camera floats up and away (helicopter shot). We therefore miss the exact method Harry uses to get information from Scorpio. A realistic shot seems to be transformed into someone's subjective perception, but whose? Both of these wounded adversaries could be experiencing an out-of-body experience created by pain, fatigue, and emotion.[8]

In its technique, *Dirty Harry* is a mixture of realism and what Jack Shadoian calls "symbolic fantasy."[9] The location shooting in San Francisco is meticulously realistic, especially in detailing the predicaments and tragedies of the victims: the naked, asphyxiated Ann Mary pulled from a hole in the ground, the young kids on the bus. The scenes involving police routines are good action fare, often understated but with riveting moments of tension. Except for Harry, none of the characters is well developed. The D.A., the mayor, even Chico and his wife are presented in an economical shorthand, and Scorpio derives some of his power from *not* being described or understood. Harry himself is an odd character, half embittered detective and half Superman. The mythic or Superhero aspects of his character derive in large part from the Sergio Leone Westerns, where Eastwood played the strong, silent Man with No Name, a Western good-bad guy with an amoral, nihilistic streak. Audiences identify with this character without necessarily expecting him to uphold the Good and the Just. The Superhero aspect of Harry resides with his powerful gun, the .44 Magnum, and the ritualized speech with which he baits criminals to try their luck. Other larger-than-life qualities of this character are his impressive, silent silhouette, his well-tailored clothes (though in a bow to realism, Harry worries in an early scene about damaging his $29.50 slacks), his ability to withstand pain, his appetite for the dirtiest, most demanding police work. Dirty Harry is even shown as a Christ figure; the scene where Harry is tormented by Scorpio takes place against the backdrop of an enormous cross on San Francisco's Mt. Davidson. Harry's individual, macho passion is presented as San Francisco's best hope against crime. In its emphasis on a larger-than-life hero *Dirty Harry* is almost *Batman*, except that this particular hero is physically and emotionally vulnerable, liable to break like a tightly wound spring. At the end of *Dirty Harry*, the prognosis does not look good for either Harry or the city of San Francisco.

Popular with audiences, *Dirty Harry* was harshly attacked by the leading American film critics. Pauline Kael called the film "fascist medievalism" as well as "right-wing fantasy." [10] Andrew Sarris described it as "one of the most disturbing manifestations of police paranoia I have seen on the screen in a long time." [11] Roger Ebert said, "The movie's moral position is fascist." [12] Although *Dirty Harry* affirms individual heroism, and not any sort of collective political movement, it does advocate a more-or-less autonomous police power. Harry Callahan has only contempt for his bureaucratic superiors and for the liberal court decisions protecting citizens' rights (e.g., the Miranda decision). The filmmakers have provided this character with a situation—the kidnapping of Ann Mary Deakin—in which the due process of search warrants and suspects' rights could do grievous harm. However, even Eastwood's sympathetic biographer Richard Schickel notes that the film overstates its case—in emergency situations like this, the suspect's right to remain silent (as guaranteed by the Fifth Amendment and the Miranda decision) might not apply. [13]

I would describe Harry not as a fascist but as a vigilante. His agenda is not racist or dictatorial; it is, in an American context, right-wing, conservative, law and order. In the second half of the film Harry disobeys a series of orders and solves the Scorpio threat using his own values and methods. He becomes a police vigilante. John Milius (an uncredited writer on *Dirty Harry*) describes Harry Callahan like this: "Dirty Harry is not really the police; he's kinda a fella that's acting on his own." Milius seems to approve of Harry's vigilante stance; he connects it to the Second Amendment's right to bear arms.[14] I disagree with Milius; whatever the motivation, police vigilantism is scary. Does the nightmare of Scorpio justify a cop unrestrained by law or government?

Director Don Siegel and star/producer Clint Eastwood[15] were surprised by the outpouring of criticism against Harry's social stance. They regarded *Dirty Harry* as a good action film, with an up-to-date and somewhat ambiguous hero. Siegel made the point that he did not necessarily agree with the hero;[16] Eastwood, more conservative politically than his director, defended the film's approach to law and order.[17] To some extent, *Dirty Harry* is a victim of its own economical and highly visual construction. In many scenes, a lack of verbal exposition and a heightened visual sense present Harry as a Superhero and San Francisco as a den of evil. Although other scenes combat this view, the film overall does have a comic-book quality which simplifies its sociopolitical perspective. *Dirty Harry* tries to address the tangle of competing rights (suspect's rights, victim's rights, society's rights) brought to the fore by liberal Supreme Court decisions of the 1960s, but it is too simple and too biased to be the definitive film on these issues.[18]

In his visual exposition of Scorpio, director Siegel seems to have outsmarted himself. Speaking to Stuart Kaminsky, Siegel describes creating visual cues to suggest that Scorpio is a mentally ill Vietnam vet. Siegel thinks that the peace symbol belt buckle is a symbol of self-delusion: "It seems to me that it may remind us that no matter how vicious a person is, when he looks at himself in the mirror, he's not capable of seeing the truth about himself . . ."; Scorpio "really feels that the world is wrong and he is right, that he really stands for and believes in peace."[19] This psychological construction is ingenious, but visual symbols tend to diverge from predefined, unitary meanings. Many commentaries on *Dirty Harry* see the peace symbol on the belt buckle as a simpler construct, an identification of Scorpio with the hippies and the antiwar movement. The attempt at psychological depth thus becomes an index of social conflict.

In general, *Dirty Harry* is clearly a film to the right of *The French Connection*. It supports not only the subculture of the police but also the extreme individualism of a hero with no use for established authority. The possible metaphoric extension of this vigilante cop to something like South American death squads (political assassination teams, often composed of soldiers or police officers) is indeed frightening. Perhaps as a "correction" to this reading, the next Dirty Harry film, *Magnum Force* (1973), shows Harry foiling the plans of a police death squad. In *Magnum Force*, Harry is clearly a man, not a Superman, and he chooses the current system of law enforcement, with all its flaws, over the predictable abuses of the secret death squad. The correction suggests that Eastwood, despite his continued defense of the original *Dirty Harry*, prefers Harry as an aggressive, unorthodox cop, and not as a social avenger.

In *Death Wish* (1975), the issue of fighting crime with extralegal means has lost most of its ambiguity. Charles Bronson plays Paul Kersey, a successful architect in New York City. One day a racially mixed group of young hoodlums follows his wife and daughter home from the supermarket. They kill the wife and rape the daughter, who ends up in a mental hospital. Kersey, though showing no outward emotion, begins to prowl the streets and subways of New York at night, inviting attack. When threatened by muggers, he becomes efficiently violent himself, killing and wounding a wide variety of punks.[20] Kersey is eventually caught by the police, but instead of holding him as a criminal and inviting extensive coverage from the press (which sympathizes with Kersey), they tell him to get out of town.

Kersey takes a train to Chicago. At the Chicago train station, he sees some young hoods terrorizing a victim. Kersey gives the hoods his best smile and mumbles "This is going to be fun." A concept which in *Joe* was thoroughly outrageous (hunting hippies with a rifle can be fun) has in *Death Wish* become formulaic, routine (hunting young criminals is both fun and socially beneficial).

Joe, The French Connection, and *Dirty Harry* examine ideas of vigilantism and/or excessive police violence in an original and sometimes ambiguous way. In all three, a right-wing perspective on the necessity of extralegal violence is balanced by a certain amount of doubt (less doubt in *Dirty Harry*

Death Wish PARAMOUNT PICTURES.
Paul Kersey (Charles Bronson) is a vigilante hunting young criminals. Courtesy of Museum of Modern Art/Film Stills Archive.

than in the other two films). In *Death Wish*, however, there is no ambiguity. The Bronson character has been injured, and he strikes out to respond. He is not hindered by the law or by organizational strictures; indeed, the police more or less approve of his actions, which is another reason why they choose not to arrest him. About the only complexity in *Death Wish* lies in the way Kersey stalks his prey. He appears to be a victim, ripe for plucking, but he is instead a ruthless predator. The title *Death Wish* seems to mean "a desire to kill" rather than "a desire to die"; although absolutely fearless, Kersey does not behave suicidally.

Harry Callahan in *Dirty Harry* presents an impassive, unfeeling, misanthropic face to the world. The film eventually gets around to explaining this public face and shows that Harry cares passionately about the death of the innocent and the pursuit of the guilty. Kersey in *Death Wish*, on the other hand, maintains an unfeeling impassivity from the death of his wife through the rest of the movie. He has a tiny range of emotion: bleak smile, uncaring stare. This impassivity, like Eastwood's cool nonchalance, may derive from the films of Sergio Leone; Bronson was one of the stars of *Once upon a Time in the West*. Bronson's stare suggests an anger that is beyond pathology, anger that is simply a given. This persona of stolid anger proved surprisingly popular with cinema audiences; Bronson became, in the mid-seventies, one of America's most popular movie stars.

The issue of urban crime was inflected, in the early 1970s, to cover attitudes toward social change, young people, and drugs. Movies such as *Joe*, *The French Connection*, and *Dirty Harry* use crime to attack social difference and mount conservative defenses of middle America. However, these films are surprisingly ambiguous in their populist sentiments, responding to the complexity and turmoil of the period. *Joe* is an antihippie movie, but it concludes by criticizing the older generation. *The French Connection* is a police-centered action film which includes a terrifying final scene of Popeye stalking anything that moves. *Dirty Harry* is another police-centered action film, but it focuses on fractures between the rank-and-file police, the city bureaucracy, and the law. Only in *Death Wish*, made a few years after the other films, does the cop/vigilante film become formulaic, with the character played by Charles Bronson methodically blasting away at urban gangs.

Chapter 3

Airport

Disaster and Conspiracy

The Poseidon Adventure

Jaws

The Parallax View

Chinatown

The period from 1970 to 1975 in the United States was a time of "malaise," to use a term later popularized by Jimmy Carter. The Vietnam War continued, even though official U.S. policy spoke of Vietnamization and peace. The booming economy of the 1960s staggered into a period of recession *and* inflation, impelled by the war but especially by the OPEC oil price shock. The price of gasoline quadrupled in a few months because of OPEC's rationing of supply. Americans queued up in their cars to buy the meager amounts of gas available. Politically, the United States was rocked by the Watergate scandal, a demonstration of widespread duplicity and illegal activity in the Nixon White House. In general, the early 1970s was a period of soul-searching in the United States, a period which demonstrated the limits of American power and security in the world.

The disaster movie is a staple motif of Hollywood cinema. A group of people saves itself from imminent disaster; the theme can be found in adventure, science fiction, horror, and other genres. The threat of disaster may stem from nature, or human folly, or alien invasion, or supernatural agency.

Whatever the cause, the dynamic of salvation is the same: the group uses the diverse talents of its members to survive the threat. This is the dynamic of *Metropolis* (1926), of *Hurricane* (1937), of *Independence Day* (1996).

However, the phrase "disaster movie" is specifically associated with a cycle of films in the 1970s, beginning with *Airport* (1970) and proceeding through *The Poseidon Adventure, Earthquake, Airport 1975, The Towering Inferno,* and so on. This set of big-budget, highly successful movies is characterized by two distinct appeals. First of all, it presents a fairly simple set of dangers and thrills. A physical, highly visual predicament threatens the group, which must respond in difficult and dangerous ways in order to survive. Second, disaster movies can be read as metaphors of the general malaise of American (or Western) society. The nature of the threat, the makeup of the social microcosm, and the specifics of the response all present an ideological view of the troubled America of the years 1970–1975.

In *Airport,* the operations of a major airport and the safety of a large airliner are threatened by a single, desperate man and by the conflicting needs of various constituencies (airport board of directors, airport manager, airline companies, neighborhoods adjoining the airport). An unemployed demolitions expert plans to blow up a Rome-bound airliner in order to collect on travel insurance and thus provide for his family. This individual killer is more pathetic than threatening; *Airport* does not provide a large-scale villain for our entertainment. The emphasis of the film is on the employees and resources of the air transportation industry, and on how they are mobilized to meet this threat. The threat itself seems to be unavoidable; a busy, complex, and highly technological institution such as an airport will always be somewhat endangered by what in military terms would be called sabotage.

Airport is an ensemble film which features a large cross-section of characters, representing the breadth and variety of American life. But this particular ensemble is most interesting for what it leaves out. The young people who are such an important part of *Easy Rider, Alice's Restaurant, Joe,* and even *Dirty Harry* simply do not exist in *Airport.* All the main characters are middle-aged and above, except for Gwen (Jacqueline Bisset), a young stewardess who is in love with pilot Vernon Demarest (Dean Martin). Blacks and other minorities are also absent; this is a film which deals with social change by avoiding it. The men in *Airport* are aggressive and self-confident, the women supportive and empathetic, and everyone is well dressed and well groomed. The cross-section of characters covers a wide range of occupations and personality types, but it is remarkably narrow in terms of age, race, and class.

The plot plays off individual tensions and rivalries against the drama of landing a damaged airliner in hazardous weather conditions. The main runway of Lincoln Airport—a fictitious airport in the Chicago area—is closed because a plane is stuck in the snow. Airport manager Mel Bakersfield (Burt Lancaster) diverts traffic to a second runway, even though this creates noise problems for nearby wealthy neighborhoods. The airport's board of directors wants Mel to shut down, but he brings in mechanic/technical expert Joe Petroni (George Kennedy) in an attempt to move the disabled plane and keep everything running. Meanwhile, Mel is fielding complaints from his society wife Cindy (Dana Wynter), who expects him at a formal dinner, and accepting the sympathy of Tanya Livingston (Jean Seberg), a beautiful airline supervisor. Mel's brother-in-law, Vernon Demarest, is on his case to keep the airport open so that a flight to Rome may take off. As this plane prepares for takeoff, we learn that the lovely Gwen (Bisset) is pregnant with Vernon's baby. Though *Airport* is a conservative, backward-looking film in many ways, it does revise the sexual mores of classic Hollywood (e.g., the Production Code's insistence that adultery was not normal and should be punished) to reflect more permissive times.

These melodramatic tensions are eventually rendered secondary by the discovery that D. O. Guerrero (the demolitions expert) has a bomb on board. A plan to take the bomb from Guerrero goes awry, and he explodes it in the rest room in the rear of the plane. The resulting loss of pressure creates a great deal of action and tension in the main cabin of the aircraft, but aside from Guerrero only stewardess Gwen is seriously injured. Now the drama becomes whether the damaged aircraft can be landed. Conveniently for the film, all airports from Detroit east are closed because of snow, so the plane must return to Lincoln. The main runway now *must* be cleared, because the damaged plane needs its additional length.

Can-do hero Joe Petroni frees up the stalled plane on the runway at the last moment, using an unorthodox maneuver that "the book says is impossible." Mel and the air traffic controllers direct the 707 to the main runway. It lands safely, and Vernon escorts Gwen to the ambulance. Also, at some point in the frenzied final hour, Mel's wife tells him that she is having an affair with a man who appreciates her, and she wants a divorce. So Mel is free to pursue the devoted Tanya (Seberg). Professional and personal crises come to a satisfying conclusion.

The last word in the film comes from Demarest's copilot: "Give my regards to Mr. Boeing." Underlying the human drama is the incredible durability of the Boeing 707, which survives a detonation in its tail section and lands safely. The skill of the pilots, the air traffic controllers, the airport manager, and the improvising Petroni, linked to the superior technology of American industry, has overcome a dangerous situation. The theme of *Airport* is that skill, courage, and technology can avert disaster and save the day. If we view the film metaphorically, the message is that the way to avert social breakdown is to trust the resources and structures we already have. Since William Boeing left Boeing Aircraft in 1934 and died in 1956, the copilot's thanks go not to an individual but to the entire pattern of corporate America.

Vincent Canby comments with some disgust that *Airport* is a very conventional, *Grand Hotel*–style movie and that everything in it could have been done thirty years earlier.[1] This is true except for the treatment of sexuality, which has been updated a bit in post–Production Code Hollywood. But is the backward-looking quality of *Airport* necessarily a weakness? It seems to me that *Airport*'s glossy conventionality suggests a surprising continuity in Hollywood film. Whereas some popular films of 1969–1970 present a radically changed social universe, *Airport*, the most popular film of 1970, presents a stable, middle-class, middle-aged social drama that could have been staged in 1950, perhaps even 1940. The film audience (or audiences) was evidently able to support both *Easy Rider*'s iconoclasm and *Airport*'s conservatism.

In *The Poseidon Adventure* (1972), the looming threat is a tidal wave bearing down on the luxury ocean liner *Poseidon*. This threat is heightened by corporate irresponsibility: the owners of the *Poseidon* have directed its captain to ignore safety problems and operate at full speed. However, as in *Airport*, the emphasis here is on survival, not on affixing blame. The wave hits the *Poseidon* in the middle of a New Year's Eve party; many passengers and crew are killed; the ship turns over and begins to sink. A surviving officer, the purser, urges the passengers to wait in the now upside-down ballroom for help, but a small group led by Reverend Frank Scott (Gene Hackman) decides to ascend to the ship's hull and seek a way out.

The small group of *The Poseidon Adventure* is quite a bit more varied than the group in *Airport*. Aside from clergyman Scott, the charismatic leader, the group includes Mike Rogo (Ernest Borgnine), a New York City cop; his wife Linda (Stella Stevens), an ex-hooker; Manny and Belle Rosen (Jack Albertson and Shelley Winters), retired Jewish shopkeepers; and businessman James Martin (Red Buttons), a widower. Young people are represented by Nonnie Perry (Carol Lynley), a singer in the ship's house band; teenager Susan Shelby (Pamela Sue Martin); and her younger brother Robin (Eric Shea). The members of Nonnie's band are youthfully stylish in hair length and clothing, but the music they play is bland and middle-of-the-road (probably accurate for a cruise ship band). Nonnie herself is shown as passive and dependent; she eventually forms a bond with the much older Mr. Martin (Buttons). Of the two Shelby kids, the boy is the more independent and self-reliant, but both kids are dependent on the experience and good judgment of the adults. So *The Poseidon Adventure* includes young people, but in subordinate and deferential roles.

As Nick Roddick notes, the film is suffused with religious imagery. The submerged yet burning *Poseidon* is an image of hell. The trip upward is "a long journey of redemption," a journey filled with "purgatorial tests and trials."[2] The Reverend Scott wins a battle for leadership with ex-policeman Rogo, representing secular authority. Scott is an unusual clergyman, preaching self-help and a distrust for established institutions, but he does have a deep faith in God and in human potential. Near the end of the journey, he sacrifices his own life so that the group can continue upward. The film suggests that faith plus self-help plus independent thinking can lead the group to safety; it is a somewhat different conservative message from *Airport*'s reliance on technology and existing institutions.

Looked at from a distance of twenty-five years, it is surprising how many films of the late 1960s and early 1970s have a religious dimension. No histories of Hollywood describe a religious revival in this period, but such diverse films as *Easy Rider*, *Alice's Restaurant*, *Dirty Harry*, and *The Poseidon Adventure* all draw on Christian themes and imagery. In *Easy Rider*, there are non-Christian religious elements as well. The explanation is most likely that religious imagery is one way to respond to moments of extreme social stress. The Christian imagery often remains at a very general level, so as not to offend portions of the audience. For example, the singing of "Amazing Grace" at Thanksgiving in *Alice's Restaurant* subtly connects the hippie commune to Christian tradition, without specifying any doctrinal or denominational links. Another example would be *The Poseidon Adventure*'s Reverend Scott, whose group includes the Jewish Mr. and Mrs. Rosen. Indeed, Belle Rosen is one of the heroes of the film; with her underwater swimming she saves Scott and gives up her life for the greater good.

In *Jaws* (1975), the threat to the group comes from one shark and is thus far more individualized than the tidal wave of *The Poseidon Adventure*. The plot of *Jaws* can be summarized very briefly. An enormous shark is feeding on swimmers and boaters off idyllic Amity Island, on the New England coast. Police Chief Martin Brody (Roy Scheider) wants to shut down the island's beaches, but the mayor of Amity insists on keeping them open. Further deaths are thus inevitable. When evidence of the shark becomes irrefutable, the beaches are closed, and a mismatched trio of shark hunters sets off into the ocean. They are Chief Brody, the young scientist Hooper (Richard Dreyfuss), and the grizzled fisherman Quint (Robert Shaw). The hunters manage to harpoon the shark, but this only begins an epic battle. After long struggle, Quint is killed by the shark, Hooper has disappeared underwater in diving gear, and Brody, perched on a sinking boat, improbably manages to kill the shark. Hooper reappears, and he and Brody slowly make their way to shore.

Like other disaster films, *Jaws* works well at the literal level. The shark is a mysterious and terrifying antagonist. It has certain general habits of behavior, including an attraction to irregular movement in the water (e.g., as made by human swimmers), but where or when it will strike is unpredictable. Director Steven Spielberg does an excellent job of controlling and channeling the threat of the shark. For most of the film it is rarely seen, but its presence is indicated by underwater camera shots (the shark's point of view) and a repeated musical motif. Images of struggle and death are also minimized during the film's first two thirds, though occasionally a terrifying moment bursts onto the screen (e.g., the image of a dead boater with an eye torn out of its socket). Then, at the end of the film, Spielberg finally shows us the shark, in its terrible majesty, destroying the boat and attacking the hunters. The shark used in production was actually a series of mechanical creatures, but it certainly looks convincing on screen.

Jaws UNIVERSAL PICTURES.
The tourists of Amity Island respond to a shark alarm. Courtesy of Museum of Modern Art /
Film Stills Archive.

Aside from the thrills and chills of the shark attacks, a secondary threat
in the film is the short-sighted venality of the mayor and city fathers of the
fictional Amity Island (the film was shot on Martha's Vineyard). They ignore
and deny the evidence that a shark killed a young woman in the film's opening moments, and by this denial they put the entire summer population of
Amity in danger. A funny-sad scene at the beach shows the mayor asking a
friend's family to go in the water. This prompts a mass movement of people
wading into the ocean, even though various lookouts and deputies suggest
a real danger from the shark. In search of profits, the mayor turns the tourists and residents of his town into prey for the shark. And after a few false
alarms, the shark does take the bait.

As Stephen Heath and Robert Kolker have noted, this secondary threat
may well be a representation of the Watergate cover-up, which would have
been fresh in the minds of many audience members in 1975.[3] The Mayor,

following a narrow version of self-interest, denies the threat of the shark and thereby greatly increases that threat. The moral issue involved in the "cover-up" is presented in the scene in which the mother of the second victim slaps Brody's face. Brody knew that a killer shark was in the water, yet he obeyed the mayor's order to do nothing. Remarkably, the film does not follow through on this idea of moral responsibility, nor does it place the blame squarely on the mayor. Instead, *Jaws* veers away from the social functioning of the town of Amity (with parallels to Watergate) to become a mythic tale of Man versus Shark.

Stephen E. Bowles makes the interesting point that the subplot about "the business ethic" is actually designed to "mislead or distract us."[4] In the vocabulary of the mystery genre, it is a "false lead." But this means that the metaphoric reference to Watergate in the film is quite superficial, like the similar reference to corporate ethics in *The Poseidon Adventure*. The primary problems raised by both films suggest that society's malaise can be solved by simple responses to physical threats. Watergate is displaced to a situation of physical combat, a situation which, moreover, fits easily within the genre expectations of the audience. The liberal, socially critical stance of *Jaws*'s first half and *Poseidon Adventure*'s first few minutes thus fades to insignificance.

Unlike *Airport* and *The Poseidon Adventure*, *Jaws* is filled with young people. Children and teenagers figure prominently in the story. Brody and his wife are fairly young (early thirties?) and have a young family. Hooper, the shark expert from Woods Hole, is also a young man. Quint, much older, represents the knowledge and experience of the older generation. In one mesmerizing moment, he tells of being in the water after the sinking of the USS *Indianapolis* in World War II. Sharks killed more than half of his shipmates. But Quint dies in *Jaws*, leaving the way clear for the younger generation. Similarly, in town politics, Sheriff Brody is seen as far more competent and trustworthy than the mayor and the "city fathers." *Jaws*, filmed by a very young director (Spielberg was twenty-six in 1974, when the film was in production), is a movie made by and for the post–World War II Baby Boom generation.

Robert Kolker describes a shrinking of community in *Jaws*. Though Brody has a general commitment to all residents and tourists on Amity Island, he is truly engaged only by his family, and later by the all-male

Jaws UNIVERSAL PICTURES.
The all-male group of shark hunters: Chief Brody (Roy Scheider), Quint (Robert Shaw), and Hooper (Richard Dreyfuss). Courtesy of Museum of Modern Art/Film Stills Archive.

fellowship on Quint's boat. Brody, a newcomer to Amity (he moved from New York City, seeking a better life for his family), is isolated from the "civil society" of town residents, and town government seems to be vestigial. So, in protecting the town, Brody is protecting first and foremost his family—a point made when his son is specifically threatened by the shark. In the climactic confrontation with the shark, the nuclear family is replaced by an all-male fraternity which might be called "the return of patriarchy." In times of crisis, social heterogeneity is replaced by the leadership of the Father. But which father? The tough, traditional Quint is inadequate; so is the expert Hooper, representing science and technology. Brody, intelligent and resourceful but with no special knowledge or talents, wins the day. He represents the triumph of the average man (the spectator), and the protective role of the literal father. The nuclear family is safe, the father is in charge.[5]

Jaws is a bravura, self-assured piece of filmmaking, an interesting transition between the backward-looking disaster movies and the neoconservative films of the late 1970s and early 1980s (e.g., *Star Wars, Kramer vs. Kramer, E.T.*). But it is also a film of some complexity, a film whose pleasure is not entirely an operation of transparent ideology. Consider, for example, the following quote from Spielberg: ". . . the third act was basically a man-against-beast tale. It could be called a celebration of man's constant triumph over nature—not necessarily for the good."[6] Spielberg's qualifier suggests an ecological awareness which, indeed, colors the entire film. Both Hooper and Quint have respect and even love for the shark, though they are resolved to kill it. Brody's pursuit of the shark is also an initiation to the sea. For the characters, and by extension the viewer, something of value is lost when the shark is destroyed. *Jaws* may be the "middle-class remake" of *Moby Dick*, but this somewhat derisive comment by Stephen Heath also points to the many-layered conflict/relationship between humanity and nature.[7] Even a conservatively middle-class *Moby Dick* may merit our attention.

Overall, the disaster movie of the early 1970s is a way to displace contemporary problems into simple, physical confrontations—for example, man versus shark, or airline crew versus hole in the tail section. These confrontations are generally resolved via old-fashioned virtues: hard work, individual initiative, group cooperation. The disaster movie is thus a conservative response which "solves" the 1970s malaise by drastically simplifying and reframing it.

Conspiracy movies of the 1970s differ from disaster movies in providing a more detailed and pessimistic vision of contemporary malaise. These films use the detective or mystery genre to offer an investigation of what is wrong with contemporary America. The conspiracy film's social critique is often muted by or in conflict with genre requirements, but the willingness to critique such institutions as capitalism and government gives these films a liberal or Leftist slant.[8]

Conspiracy films of 1974 (e.g., *The Conversation, The Parallax View, Chinatown*) are unusual in American cinema in their withholding of a happy ending. The explanation may be that the moment of the Watergate hearings was so grim that a few Hollywood films departed from the recuperative, happy ending tradition. By 1975 and 1976, however, conspiracy films such as *One Flew Over the Cuckoo's Nest* and *All the President's Men* end with a movement toward hope. Arthur Penn's *Night Moves* (1976), which belongs to the earlier, grimmer cycle of detective/conspiracy movies, reminds us that films do not always arrive in neatly separated periods.

The Parallax View (1974) is a somewhat abstract story of an assassination-for-hire conspiracy. Joe Frady (Warren Beatty), an obsessive and flaky reporter for a West Coast newspaper (perhaps Seattle or Portland), investigates the death of several witnesses to the assassination of Senator Charles Carroll, a liberal candidate for President. Carroll was killed at a reception on top of the Space Needle tower in Seattle—a location worthy of Hitchcock. Frady discovers the promotional literature of the mysterious Parallax Corporation, which appears to be screening for assassins via the use of multiple-choice personality tests. Using an imprisoned killer as his surrogate test-taker, Frady passes the first screening and goes to Parallax's Los Angeles office for further tests. He is accepted into the corporation, but later, when following one of the killers, he finds himself in a large convention center where a band rehearses for a political meeting. Another senator, this time a conservative candidate for President, appears at the rehearsal and is shot. As Frady gapes from the catwalks above the convention center floor, he is seen and accused of being the killer. He tries to escape but is killed by a Parallax assassin. The film concludes, as it began, with the statement of a committee investigating an assassination: no evidence of conspiracy; the killer (in this case, Frady) acted alone.

The film is based on a now-forgotten novel of the same name by Loren Singer.[9] In the novel, the force behind the assassination conspiracy is revealed to be an out-of-control government agency. This agency is committed to a senseless course of destruction, and it does destroy the novel's protagonist, whose name is Graham. However, Graham's death by highway accident looks suspicious to a policeman on the scene, and therefore the novel ends with at least the possibility that the assassination scheme will be discovered and stopped. Singer's novel is more explicit and more concrete than the film adaptation; indeed, one might cite Kafka's *The Trial*, with its insistence on *not* explaining, as another source of the film.

The Parallax View works on two registers which, unfortunately, are not

The Parallax View PARAMOUNT PICTURES.
Warren Beatty as a print journalist and Paula Prentiss as a TV journalist. Courtesy of Museum of Modern Art / Film Stills Archive.

always mutually reinforcing. First, there is the narrative line of a mystery, a reporter, an enormous conspiracy. This works well until the middle of the film, when the malevolent actions of the Parallax Corporation (a plane with a bomb on it, a boat blowing up in San Pedro harbor) start to pile up. Another problem is that we don't know much about the character Joe Frady, so it is hard to empathize with him as he takes on a vast, shadowy antagonist. The name Frady itself suggests a symbol, not a man; Joe Frady (as in "'fraidy-cat") may be the twentieth-century counterpart of Fielding's Squire Allworthy. Beyond this, the narrative is full of jumps and gaps; the elliptical technique serves a symbolic function but impedes the process of identification. For example, at one point TV reporter Lee Carter (Paula Prentiss), a witness to the first assassination, comes to Frady's apartment and says she's terrified. Another, younger woman appears from a back room and marches out the door, uttering not a word. The suggestion is that Frady has transient relations with a number of women (Lee Carter must be a former lover), but the scene is so truncated that we lack a firm sense of character. In general, the narrative starts strongly, loses momentum and conviction in the middle, and then picks up again at the end.

The visually expressive dimension of *The Parallax View* is more impressive. This film, like *The Godfather,* makes excellent use of dark images (Gordon Willis was the cinematographer on both). The commissions of inquiry which open and close the film are very, very dark. A panel of members, barely lit, stretches rectangularly across a hearing room or courtroom. The only colors are black and brown. In the first commission scene (at the end of the opening credits sequence), the camera zooms slowly in on the panel. In the second commission scene (at the end of the film), the camera zooms slowly out. The verbal content of the scenes is almost identical: in both cases, the chairman announces that the assassin acted alone and that he will take no questions at this time. These symmetrical scenes craft a convincingly paranoid vision from the stylized yet institutional mise-en-scène plus the verbal sense of tired routine. By being so thoroughly nonspecific, the chairman's reports throw doubt on all the assassinations of the previous eleven years, beginning with the death of John F. Kennedy in 1963.

Many other parts of *The Parallax View* are shot in almost total darkness, including various scenes in Frady's rented rooms, conversations between Frady and his editor in the newspaper office, and the shadowy, scary moments on the catwalks above the final assassination scene. The dark mise-en-scène suggests a darkness of the soul in both political and personal senses. Politically, a world of shadows is appropriate to a situation in which assassination by unknown groups for unknown reasons dominates the body politic. In personal terms, the darkness suggests that Joe Frady himself is unformed, mysterious, and that he, like all of us, is capable of violent acts. However, some distinctions can be drawn between the various darkly lit scenes in *The Parallax View*. The scenes in Frady's rented room in Los Angeles present an accumulation of cultural debris—wallpaper, old furniture—with no strong link to the character. Frady, undercover here as he tries to penetrate the Parallax Corporation, lacks a clear personality; he is a fragmented, postmodern man. The newspaper office, on the other hand, contains layer upon layer of personal meaning. The furniture, the lamp, the decorations, the unlocked desk drawer embody the coherent past and present of Frady's managing editor, Rintels (played by Hume Cronyn). According to director Alan J. Pakula, the newspaper office embodied

> much more simple American values, almost nineteenth century values. It represented a family, a man who was rooted, a whole American tradition that was dying, an anachronism, as compared to this totally cold and enormously bizarre world that Beatty goes after, and in comparison to his own character, which is the totally rootless modern man.[10]

The scenes on the catwalks present a third view of darkness—in this case modern, hard-edged, technological, dangerous. There is no personality, no history to the catwalks and corridors high above the convention center floor, and this makes them an apt setting for an assassination without apparent roots or motives.

The catwalk scenes are also the culmination of *The Parallax View*'s film-long play with modern architecture. Beginning with the Space Needle, the film presents glass-and-concrete twentieth-century architecture as abstract and soulless. In an early image, the abstract upward motion of the Space Needle is contrasted to the older, more iconic image of an American Flag. The scenes of the reception for Senator Carroll are shot in a disorienting, fragmented way, so that one does not get a sense of the dimensions of the room atop the Space Needle. An outdoor chase of the presumed assassin on the steep Space Needle roof adds to a discomfort with this space. Later in the film, the Parallax Corporation is connected with the clean lines and shiny surfaces of modern architecture. In a nicely understated moment, Frady finds the room number of the "Parallax Corporation, West Coast Offices" in an office building lobby with marble walls and a clean, clear design. It looks just like any other new, luxurious office building—which is the film's point. Frady's training for Parallax takes him to other new, geometric, abstract buildings, for example a hotel in Atlanta and the conference center of the film's final scenes. The visual argument seems to be that the coldness of modern architecture matches the amorality of assassination-for-hire.

The film expands this critique of contemporary urban environments to include the motion picture itself. At the Parallax offices, Frady is given a test which consists of watching a five-minute montage while his physiological responses are monitored. The montage involves still images under the headings "Love," "Mother," "Father," "Me," "Home," "Country," "God," and "Enemy." It begins with conventional imagery but soon moves to more violent and disturbed shots—e.g., "Dad" as threatening, "Mom" and "Me" as abused, "Country" as Hitler giving a speech. This sequence is not discussed or explained, but Frady evidently passes the test, for he is offered a job. Although the montage is simplistic, it does implicate film in the process of "training" violent, amoral human beings.

Who or what the Parallax Corporation represents is never made clear. Is it a strictly for-profit venture? Does it have a political affiliation? Is it primarily aimed at destabilizing the American system of government? The film shows no interest in answering these questions—nor will its narrative line stand up to sustained investigation. The film does work, however, as a visual impression of American paranoia and despair, circa 1974. Its dark images linger in the mind.

The Parallax View actually includes a sequence of Frady endangered by a water gate. Looking for clues to the supposed drowning of a journalist who witnessed the assassination of Senator Carroll, he finds himself held at gunpoint beside a stream as the sluice gate of a dam opens up. However, this episode cannot be credited as either a conscious or unconscious verbal-visual pun, since it exists in Loren Singer's novel, published in 1970, two years before the Watergate scandal began.[11] Rather, the threat from water is an archetypal symbol of the fragility of human existence, a common motif of other films of the period (e.g., *The Poseidon Adventure, Chinatown, Night Moves*) and of imaginative literature dating back to the story of Noah and related creation myths.

Chinatown, another film about water and dams, is a more fully realized paranoid vision and critique of American society than *The Parallax View.* The specific subject here is the politics of water in Los Angeles, and the given time period the 1930s. As screenwriter Robert Towne has noted, the film is to some extent an adaptation of Cary McWilliams's *Southern California Country,* a history of Los Angeles, with special emphasis on the chapter "Water! Water! Water!"[12] The Hollis Mulwray of the movie is loosely derived from William Mulholland, the engineer most responsible for building the elaborate Los Angeles water system. Noah Cross, the colossally rich antagonist of the film, could be a composite of several wealthy businessmen who manipulated water rights in Southern California for their own benefit. The dates in the film have been changed (the historical events took place before 1910), but some of the outrageous political and economic swindles of *Chinatown* are based on actual occurrences. For example, the water supply of Los Angeles really was privately owned for a number of years.

Chinatown is additionally a response to the Watergate scandal of 1972–1974, as well as a comment on American venality in general. Like *The Parallax View*, it tries to move from a concrete situation to a broader speculation on corruption, conspiracy, and human weakness. But whereas *The Parallax View* employed visual patternings, with corresponding narrative atrophy, to present a world infused by dark conspiracy, *Chinatown* builds to a generalized sense of evil by penetrating deeper into story and character. *Chinatown* does not need semi-abstract patterns of light and dark to signify evil; indeed, its Southern California of the 1930s is colorful and stylish (the director of photography was John Alonso). Instead, director Roman Polanski and writer Robert Towne have added multiple layers of symbolic resonance, both narrative and visual, to gradually suggest an all-encompassing evil. For example, there are both pagan and Biblical echoes in the story of a land that is barren because of transgressions by the rich and powerful.

Chinatown begins with self-assured private detective Jake, or J. J., Gittes (Jack Nicholson) showing Curly (Burt Young) pictures of his wife's infidelity. He then interviews a new client (played by Diane Ladd), who gives the name Evelyn Mulwray; this client also complains about a suspected infidelity. Gittes investigates the new case, takes some pictures of Hollis Mulwray with a young blonde, and then finds the pictures in the newspaper. Next, he receives a visit from a very angry Mrs. Evelyn Mulwray (Faye Dunaway)—the *real* Mrs. Mulwray—threatening a lawsuit. However, when Hollis Mulwray drowns, in the middle of a drought, Evelyn Mulwray hires Gittes to investigate.

The film begins with a false story and then moves slowly toward a perception of truth. As Virginia Wright Wexman notes, it follows the pattern of the hard-boiled detective story, as embodied by the novels of Dashiell Hammett and Raymond Chandler, and by the films *The Maltese Falcon* (1941) and *The Big Sleep* (1946). However, unlike the detectives of these works, who ultimately master (at least momentarily) a threatening situation, Gittes continually misperceives the situation and reacts in a bumbling way. Wexman rightly characterizes the superficially confident and masterful Gittes as "clownish."[13] And when Gittes finally does recognize a terrible truth, he has no power to change it.

Gittes finds that someone has been manipulating the Los Angeles water supply, dumping large quantities of water into runoff channels at night and claiming drought. Also, the orange groves of the San Fernando Valley are totally without water, and thousands of acres have changed hands very recently. Gittes is threatened and beaten up as he investigates this conspiracy—in fact, he has his nose badly cut by a switchblade wielded by Roman Polanski, the film's director playing a small-time hoodlum. Gittes suspects that Mulwray was killed because he knew too much about the water conspiracy, but Gittes keeps getting distracted by the unexplained matter of the young blonde. Was the cause of Mulwray's death personal (connected with the blonde) or political (connected with the water conspiracy)?

It turns out to be both. The deus ex machina behind the convoluted plot is Noah Cross (John Huston), Evelyn Mulray's father and Hollis Mulray's former business partner—they owned the water system of Los Angeles together. Cross, an amazing picture of businessman as user, businessman as exploiter, still acts as though he owns the water system. He is creating the drought to buy up the San Fernando Valley. When questioned about his motives he denies simple greed and talks about "The Future! The Future, Mr. Gits!" (a mis-speaking of Gittes). Cross accepts no limits to his aspirations, and he honestly (if that is the right word) thinks he is doing Los Angeles a favor by dominating and manipulating its water and therefore its growth. But Cross is not just an impassioned businessman. His acquisitive, exploitative nature extends to incestuous relations with his daughter Evelyn, which he now seeks to extend to *her* daughter Katherine (the young blonde in the photographs). Gittes the worldly detective has consistently missed this aspect of the story, because he is really Gittes the innocent, Gittes the rube (another American archetype). And when Gittes finally does discover the shocking truth, he can do nothing to protect his lover Evelyn, nor the young and innocent Katherine. Evelyn wounds Cross and is shot down by the police, and the evil father/grandfather ends up comforting the innocent Katherine.

Meanwhile, the stunned Gittes is led away by his associate Walsh, who

Chinatown PARAMOUNT PICTURES.
Confident detective J. J. Gittes becomes Gittes the clown. Courtesy of Jerry Ohlinger Archives.

utters the film's signature line, "Forget it, Jake, it's Chinatown." Chinatown is the scene of the final action. It is also the place where Gittes, as a young policeman, failed to protect someone he loved. It is additionally a zone of the city beyond police or government control—but all of the city seems to be beyond control, so "Chinatown" is perhaps a synecdoche, a part which stands for a whole. Finally, "Chinatown" is certainly an example of "orientalism," as defined by Edward Said,[14] with the inscrutability of things Asian extended to cover human existence in general. Towne and Polanski start from a Hollywood cliché of the 1930s and 1940s, a cliché which presents the Chinese as less-than-Western, but this cliché eventually becomes a metaphor for human limits in general.

Chinatown PARAMOUNT PICTURES.
The sensual pleasures of a world in which the knight cannot save the lady. Evelyn Mulray (Faye Dunaway) and Jake Gittes (Jack Nicholson). Courtesy of Jerry Ohlinger Archives.

Herbert J. Gans, a noted sociologist who for several years reviewed films for the journal *Social Practice*, suggests that *Chinatown* is "an anticapitalist detective story."[15] The film's key political insight is that the specific mechanisms of government do not matter; wealth and power matter. In a sense, Noah Cross still owns the Water Department because he can manipulate it to his own ends. This narrative of government activity for private gain is substantially consistent with Marxist theory, which holds that economic power always controls and determines the political superstructure. The major difference between *Chinatown* and the Marxist view of capitalism is that *Chinatown* holds out no hope for reform or revolution. No alternate nexus of social power is identified which could change things for the better. Instead, the film concludes with Noah Cross dominating not only the world of wealth and power but also the intimate/personal/sexual lives of Jake, Evelyn, and Katherine. *Chinatown* is, among other things, an Oedipus story where the dominating Father wins.

In preparing the film, screenwriter Towne and director Polanski had a falling out on the question of whether the Father should prevail. Towne wanted Evelyn Mulwray to shoot and kill Noah Cross at the end of *Chinatown*. This ending would have sustained a belief in the efficacy of human action. Even though Evelyn would have been arrested and sent off to prison, at least she would have struck down the evil Father.[16] This ending suggests a bittersweet variety of Hollywood populism, with the hero's lover sacrificed for the greater good. Towne's ending could even be construed as enacting a successful class alliance, with the middle-class detective and the aristocratic Evelyn (and possibly even working-class Curly)[17] uniting to slay the plutocratic Mr. Cross. Polanski's ending has the virtue of underlining the seriousness and omnipresence of capitalist domination. If Cross is killed and the threat is ended, then *Chinatown* becomes simply a genre piece where evil is overcome by good, as in the Western, the detective story, and other genres. But if Cross wins, then the conspiracy of the rich, the conspiracy which runs America, is presented as all-encompassing. This is a terrifying vision, a vision appropriate to the dark moment of Watergate.

However, Roman Polanski's ending has its weak point as well. The last thing Jake says is "As little as possible," the motto he remembers from police work in Chinatown. Nothing can be done, the knight cannot save the lady. But this brings us back to the surface of *Chinatown*, to the pleasures of sight and sound and taste and sex. If action is futile, we are left with the self-indulgent passivity of a stylish yet empty Los Angeles.

Chapter 4

Nashville

Shampoo

The End of the Sixties

Between the Lines

The Return of the Secaucus Seven

The Big Chill

The mixture of political activism and popular culture often labeled "the sixties" in American social history had little impact on the Hollywood film industry during the decade of the 1960s. *Bonnie and Clyde* (1967) was adopted by young audiences as an allegory of their feelings of alienation, but this film was a heavily disguised version of contemporary tensions. *The Graduate* (1968) is another example of youthful alienation, but Benjamin Braddock, protagonist of that film, is hardly an example of radical perception or activity. Though *The Wild Bunch* (1969) is about an outsider group, a film about aging gunslingers cannot be considered allegorical of youth in revolt. The film industry began to explicitly document youth culture and antiwar activism only in 1969–1970, with films such as *Easy Rider, Midnight Cowboy, Medium Cool, Woodstock,* and *M.A.S.H.*

Even with this group of films, however, one gets a sense of isolated changes rather than a broad movement of social change. The various moments of social conflict and change in these movies are transitory or ephemeral. One sees anger against the Establishment, against the way things are, but not a broad movement of social change. *Easy Rider* does present a set of alternative lifestyles, but none of these appears successful or stable. For example, in the emblematic commune scene, the city kids turned farmers seem to be planting bone-dry fields, even though a canal runs through their property. Wyatt (Peter Fonda) declares of the commune "They're going to make it," but for more-or-less objective viewers it's clear that this experiment is not going to last. In *Midnight Cowboy*, Joe Buck and Ratso Rizzo fail to establish an alternative lifestyle in New York City. *Medium Cool* and *Woodstock* are both about transitory events, and in *M.A.S.H.* the anti-establishment doctors played by Elliott Gould and Donald Sutherland leave Korea after one tour of duty.[1] In all these cases, the 1960s are presented as a moment of revolt, not as a set of long-lasting changes.

Paradoxically, although there is a dearth of high-quality films about the promise of the sixties, many noteworthy films have been made about the death of the sixties. As we have seen, *Easy Rider* already recounts the failure of an alternative vision (softened by the union with nature implied by the film's final shot). The "death of the sixties" became a prominent theme in American films in 1974–1976, when the catastrophic events of Watergate and the OPEC oil shock as well as the apparent lack of social change in the United States strongly suggested that the moment of social optimism was over. Numerous films—*Chinatown, Nashville, The Parallax View, Night Moves, Shampoo, One Flew Over the Cuckoo's Nest*—described a loss of idealism and an omnipresent sense of social and political corruption. The sixties were regretted in a series of memorable films. The trend then continued, with films from the late 1970s and into the 1980s documenting and critiqueing the 1960s counterculture.

Chapter 3, "Disaster and Conspiracy," has already dealt with a few of the "end of the sixties" films (notably *Chinatown*) in sketching out the "conspiracy/mystery" cycle of films as a reaction to disillusion and social crisis. This essay discusses five films dealing in a more direct, less genre-driven way with the end of the sixties. The films to be covered are *Nashville, Shampoo, Between the Lines, The Return of the Secaucus Seven,* and *The Big Chill*. Please note that the distinction between "more direct" and "genre driven" is descriptive rather than evaluative. *Nashville* does not readily fit into any generic category; *Chinatown* is a detective story and a mystery. This difference does not in itself make one film superior to the other.

The five films under discussion in this chapter can be divided into three groups. *Nashville* and *Shampoo* are about failures of vision and community: the inability to translate "youth culture" and related movements into meaningful social change. *Between the Lines* and *The Return of the Secaucus Seven* take an opposed position, pointing out a quiet social activism which persists into the seemingly conservative late 1970s. Finally, *The Big Chill* posits an almost seamless transition from 1960s radical to 1980s yuppie; social activism was just youthful good spirits which naturally gave way to more grown-up hedonism and careerism.

Nashville is Robert Altman's first great ensemble piece, the precursor to 1993's *The Player* and 1994's *Short Cuts*. An ambitious fresco of life in the country music city, it features twenty-four characters and about thirty songs. As a "taking stock" of America in 1975, the film encompasses many social and cultural issues of the sixties, including sexuality, racism, the Vietnam War, the influence of the media, the decline of electoral politics, and the need for a new, participatory culture.

Nashville presents failures of the imagination in music, in politics, and in personal life. A third-party campaign for President, slickly organized by John Triplette (Michael Murphy), intersects with the lives of several prominent Nashville musicians. Candidate Hal Phillip Walker, represented by Triplette and an omnipresent sound truck, seems to stand for many changes but no specific philosophy or program. Meanwhile, the musical numbers range from patriotic ("We must be doing something right to last two hundred years") to personal ("I'm Easy") to self-consciously inept ("Let Me Be the One").[2] The film gains a good deal of energy from its large and diverse set of characters (hippies, would-be singers, business managers, a soldier on leave, and so on), but almost all of them are motivated by a narrow self-interest. Even the seemingly saintly Linnea Reese (Lily Tomlin), who sings gospel music, is easily seduced by Tom (Keith Carradine), a folk music Don Juan. The film concludes with a benefit concert for the third-party candidate where Barbara Jean (Ronee Blakley), the biggest star in Nashville, is assassinated. To quiet the crowd after the assassination, a country music wannabe (Albuquerque, played by Barbara Harris) jumps onstage and leads a collective singing of "It Don't Worry Me." Popular culture, like politics, is out of control, and the USA lurches into its third century.

Part of *Nashville*'s uniqueness is that it is a brilliant group project about the impossibility of cohesive and effective groups in the America of 1975. The project starts with director-producer Altman and screenwriter Joan Tewkesbury, but many of the songs and speeches were written by the actors. Ronee Blakley, Henry Gibson, Keith Carradine, and Karen Black all wrote their own songs. Blakley added a key monologue (in the scene where her character, Barbara Jean, breaks down on stage), and Geraldine Chaplin wrote or improvised the often inane comments of her character, "Opal from the BBC." Most striking of all, the Hal Phillip Walker campaign was designed by a political consultant, with little or no input from director or scriptwriter. Altman functioned something like the leader of a jazz band, choosing the theme and the tempo but leaving his collaborators room to stretch. But if the film's making presents a model of individual and group working together, the film's diegesis suggests a huge chasm between citizen and social life.

The first Hal Phillip Walker speech via the sound truck makes two points: (1) "We are all involved in politics, whether we know it or not, and whether we like it or not." (2) "We can do something about it." These points could be agreed on by the New Left, the Far Right, and all political activists in between. However, in the film we see no interest in political ideas or positions; even Triplette is purely a deal maker. Other areas of social life have broken down as well: the family, the romantic couple, the news media (as objective observer), and basic relations of civility and trust. L.A. Joan (Shelley Duvall) is too busy chasing men to see her aunt in the hospital. Sueleen Gay's (Gwen Welles) humiliating striptease is part of everyday American culture (woman as object), and so is the promise of celebrity that motivates Sueleen. Linnea sleeps with Tom, while Del Reese (her husband, played by Ned Beatty) tells the hapless Sueleen he wants to "kiss her all over." So much for the couple. Spontaneous, energetic Opal, the news reporter, distorts everything she sees and hears. She is unconsciously racist and very consciously a celebrity hound and groupie. Opal is one of several characters in the film who cherish celebrity more than other human values.

In this debris of a society, this void created by twenty-four characters, the assassination of Barbara Jean does not come as a major surprise. For one thing, if Altman is summing up the America of recent times, then assassination is certainly part of the equation. And in the absence of values, anything is permitted. As Helene Keyssar notes, Altman and company have some

Nashville PARAMOUNT PICTURES.
Opal from the BBC (Geraldine Chaplin) meets country singer Tommy Brown (Timothy Brown).
Courtesy of Jerry Ohlinger Archives.

mordant fun with the assassination by rousing our suspicions of a young
soldier obsessed with Barbara Jean.[3] Then the quiet and troubled Kenny,
a nondescript young man seen throughout the film, turns out to be the
assassin. As Keyssar further notes, Barbara Jean's murder *is not* explained.[4]
Assassination is in the air, part of the culture.

The assassination scene and its aftermath can suggest some of the complexity of *Nashville*. Almost all of the characters gather for a free concert
at the Tennessee capital's Parthenon (homage to Athens or mockery of
Athens?), the centerpiece of a Nashville park. Kenny pulls a gun from a
violin case, and thus becomes a kind of star—"stardom" being a major theme
of the film. Singer Haven Hamilton (Gibson) shows some strength in talking
to the crowd, then gives the mike to the unknown Albuquerque (Barbara
Harris). Albuquerque, who has been waiting throughout the movie for a
chance to perform, turns out to be an original, bluesy singer. So many

characters sing in *Nashville* that one is tempted to speak of a democratic, participatory culture, with music creating a shared bond.[5] But the song Albuquerque sings is "It Don't Worry Me," which Robert Kolker aptly describes as "the great anthem of passivity."[6] We are back to the star system and consumerism. The assassination scene, like *Nashville* as a whole, is a creative, energetic view of a society gone awry.

It is worth underlining that the young people in *Nashville* are every bit as selfish and short-sighted as their elders. The youth culture characters (L.A. Joan, Opal, Tom, the motorcyclist played by Jeff Goldblum) offer no special insight, so the spectator cannot take comfort in a countercultural perspective different from that of the majority culture. If "you're either part of the problem or part of the solution," according to the sixties maxim, then these characters are part of the problem. Those few characters who show a glimmer of self-knowledge and courage (Haven Hamilton, the black dishwasher, perhaps Albuquerque) are middle aged and middle American. Altman and Tewkesbury are clearly not impressed by stylish hippie chic.

Shampoo, released in 1975, takes place on election day 1968 and thus offers both an immediate and a distanced view of the sixties. George (Warren Beatty), a Beverly Hills hairdresser, is trying to open his own shop. But George is mainly interested in the ladies; he admits, late in the film, that he chose his career as a way to seduce women. George's alter ego in the film is Lester Karp (Jack Warden), a hugely successful businessman and Republican political kingpin. In the course of the movie George sleeps with Lester's wife Felicia (Lee Grant), his mistress Jackie (Julie Christie), even his teenage daughter Lorna (Carrie Fisher), while trying to be attentive to his own "steady girlfriend" Jill (Goldie Hawn). But Lester retains the real power in the film. Lester and his graying Establishment friends dominate business and politics. Lester also controls women, despite being multiply cuckolded. At the end of the film George proposes to Jackie, but she has already committed to going to Acapulco with Lester. Lester plans to divorce his wife and marry Jackie, and this offer of wealth and security leaves George alone and pensive as the film fades out.

Shampoo is a light comedy/bedroom farce which does not have *Nashville*'s density of meaning. But *Shampoo* does have an acute point of view on the political and social choices of the 1960s. The political angle enters via an election-night party held by Lester. George is there as a supposedly gay

Shampoo COLUMBIA PICTURES.
Hairdresser George (Warren Beatty) with Jackie (Julie Christie), one of
several women in his life. Courtesy of Jerry Ohlinger Archives.

escort for Jackie. Via this device we hear political speeches and reports
throughout the evening, including Spiro Agnew talking about the moral
tone a President can provide, and Richard Nixon promising to "bring us
together." Both statements are thoroughly ironic, since in 1975 we know
that Agnew and Nixon have resigned in disgrace. Also, in 1968 it is clear that
long-haired George and Republican businessman Lester are *not* together.
The idea of these two becoming partners in a beauty salon, which is discussed through much of the film, is simply ludicrous. Reduced to basic
terms, Lester is a "have," George is a "have-not."

From the distanced, 1975 perspective, *Shampoo*'s theme is that the countercultural attitudes of the 1960s do not necessarily lead anywhere. George is longhaired, handsome, conventionally unconventional, a doer rather than a thinker. But, in the film's key move, he is very specifically located in society as a Beverly Hills hairdresser; he is not a free-floating hippie à la *Woodstock*. As a hairdresser, he has access to rich and beautiful women, but he lacks the economic and social power to interact with them as equals. The filmmakers at times show George's sexual adventures (e.g., going to bed with Lorna and then with Felicia) as difficult, exhausting work. More seriously, George realizes that he does not have the resources to "take care of" Jill or Jackie.

Though George does go to the bank in search of a business loan (his interview is disastrous), he usually responds to only the most immediate stimuli. We typically see George in frenetic motion: racing around town on his motorcycle, doing ten things at once in the beauty salon, rushing to please the latest woman who wants something from him. In his own words, George is always "trying to get things moving." But this claim of purposeful activity is punctured by Jill, who responds: "Oh, grow up. You never stop moving, you never get anywhere. Grow up, grow up!" This verbal description is beautifully translated into visuals when George, Jackie, Jill, and Lester wander into a hippie party after the political party. Lester and Jill happen across George and Jackie sexually intertwined in a room near the tennis courts. Jill runs away to her car, and George chases after her. As Jill pulls away in her car, George next runs to where he left Jackie. Then he runs back to the driveway, to see Jackie pull away. Perpetual motion, no sustained purpose. Perhaps this description could be extended from the character of George to the young hedonists of the sixties.

Shampoo is not, however, a thoroughly negative critique or satire of the sixties. The film has another, more immanent theme as well. George is a nobody going nowhere, but he does manage to have a good time. Though usually inarticulate and even self-deceiving, he finally does reveal himself at the end of the film. Jill presses George about how many women he has had sex with. He hems and haws, then says: "Let's face it, I fucked them all. . . . Maybe that means I don't love 'em. Maybe it means I don't love you. I don't know. Nobody can say I don't like 'em very much." George has systematically been deceiving Jill, and Felicia, and other women in his life. But in a bedroom farce, deceit is common and expected, and thus morally almost neutral. George spends his days with women, he listens to them, he tries to please them in immediate ways. George certainly understands women better than Lester—Lester understands only power. Given the generally sympathetic treatment of George, *Shampoo*'s overall attitude might be stated as follows: The sixties are gone, and they didn't change much. But oh, we had fun while they lasted.

Both *Nashville* and *Shampoo* stress physical and emotional realities and underplay intellectual analysis. Their characters are inarticulate, frustrated, unformed. These films present the failures of the sixties via the chaotic, irrational lives of a group (*Nashville*) or an individual protagonist (*Shampoo*). By contrast, *Between the Lines* (1977) and *The Return of the Secaucus Seven* (1979) are calmer, more rational films about the survival of 1960s ideals in the politically and economically conservative late 1970s.

Between the Lines (1977), Joan Micklin Silver's second feature film, is a comedy about a Boston underground newspaper. Based on a script by Fred Barron, it was independently produced by Raphael Silver (Joan's husband). The story presents the struggle of the *Back Bay Mainline* newspaper, founded in the countercultural excitement of 1969, to maintain a viable identity some years later. The paper is being bought out by a media entrepreneur, and there is considerable uncertainty about what happens next. Lynn the receptionist quits, Harry the award-winning investigative reporter is fired, and reporters Michael and Laura prepare to leave for New York. However, the film ends with the sense that the ideals of the newspaper live on with the individuals and not necessarily with the institution.

An ensemble piece with twelve important roles, *Between the Lines* becomes at times a collage of moments about resistance to the end of the sixties and adjustment to the end of the sixties. Michael J. Pollard, an icon of sixties youth culture since *Bonnie and Clyde* (1967), plays a long-haired newspaper hawker who continues selling papers through the entire film. Lynn (Jill Eikenberry), the good-hearted receptionist who is the "spirit" of the paper, quits rather than work for new management. On the other hand, apprentice writer David (Bruno Kirby), younger than the others, proves himself as an investigative reporter and reaffirms the ideals of the group at the moment when everything is falling apart. Max (Jeff Goldblum), the longtime rock critic of the *Mainline*, provides a subtle example of resistance *and* adjustment. Max is frustrated by writing for a small, demographically limited audience. He can captivate teenage girls or cadge a drink from a longhaired young man, but he has no room to grow, to reach a different audience, to get beyond minimal wages. Max complains a lot and holds tightly to what he has. He also tries to live in the moment; a defining image shows him dancing the night away with two young female admirers.

Though this is a group comedy with a majority of masculine roles, Silver's sensitivity to women's issues shows up in two subplots involving couples. Abbie (Lindsay Crouse) and Harry (John Heard) are friends and occasional lovers. Harry is jealous and possessive and wants a more permanent arrangement, but Abbie wants to protect her personal and professional freedom. She is a fine photographer and is beginning to get recognition for her work. At one point she tells Harry that she doesn't want to stay home and bake bread while he writes a novel. Michael (Steven Collins) and Laura (Gwen Welles), on the other hand, are heading toward a very conventional version of the middle-class couple. The egotistical Michael has sold a book about the end of the sixties to a publisher and is moving to New York to do rewrites. He assumes that his live-in lover is coming along, too. In a moment of revolt, Laura sleeps with Harry, and reminisces about the old days of community and social commitment. She later agrees to go to New York with Michael, even though she realizes he is selfish and borderline abusive. Silver and Barron have sympathy for Laura, but the film clearly favors the independent spirit of Abbie. In the final scene, Abbie and the just-fired Harry leave a bar together, happy but with no promise of permanence. The suggestion is that an alternative, independent approach to life, including a new flexibility of gender roles, is something that must be chosen and lived every day. This redefinition of the sixties counterculture can survive the decline or dissolution of the newspaper; it persists "between the lines."

The Return of the Secaucus Seven (1979),[7] written and directed by John Sayles, is another modest film which lucidly presents the survival of 1960s ideals into the inhospitable late 1970s. Several old friends who were anti–Vietnam War activists during college get together for a summer weekend in a small New Hampshire town. They are the "Secaucus Seven" in the sense that they were arrested on a trumped-up charge in Secaucus, New Jersey, while on their way to a demonstration in Washington. In the present, none is wildly successful, but most have retained some tie to their former activism. Katie (Maggie Renzi) and Mike (Bruce McDonald) are high school teachers,

Jeff (Mark Arnott) is a drug counselor in Harlem, Maura (Karen Trott) has just left an inner-city children's theatre, Irene (Jean Passanante) is the aide to a liberal senator, J.T. (Adam Lefevre) is a struggling folk singer. During the weekend, they talk, they play, they start (or resume, or end) sexual relationships. They also interact in a friendly way with working-class young adults in the small town; this film both acknowledges and tries to overcome class differences in the United States. At the end of the film the visitors depart, friendships renewed, to face the uncertainties of daily life.

The characters in *The Return of the Secaucus Seven* are more practical than utopian, yet they do have a commitment to social change. John Sayles describes his characters as "downwardly mobile" (in contrast to the upwardly mobile characters in *The Big Chill*),[8] which allows them to remain true to their beliefs. The two exceptions to downward mobility are Frances (Maggie Cousineau), a medical student disgusted by the values of her fellow students, and Irene, who writes speeches for a senator. There are only a few specifically political conversations in the film. Most prominent is an ongoing discussion of whether Irene and her boyfriend and fellow speechwriter Chip (Gordon Clapp), who is meeting the group for the first time, can have a positive effect on mainstream politics. Otherwise, *The Return of the Secaucus Seven* tends to be a film about friendships within a particular group. The subcultural tone is set by Katie, who says she likes having people around who understand her jokes.

John Sayles meticulously planned *Secaucus Seven* as a low-budget film which could present ideas and characters important to him and at the same time function as an "audition piece" for the studios.[9] The multicharacter format, which Sayles borrowed from *Nashville*, was a way to keep the story moving in the absence of violent action or distinctive locations. The characters were people just turning thirty because the director knew non-Union actors in that age group. A few action scenes (a basketball game, nude diving at the local swimming hole) were added to show that Sayles could handle visually dynamic material.[10] Sex scenes, though without explicit nudity, undoubtedly added to the marketability of the project. The resulting film is a bit like *Nashville* and *Shampoo* in its physicality, but more akin to *Between the Lines* in its message. *Secaucus Seven*, like *Between the Lines*, suggests that the 1960s did not die. Instead they continue, in the everyday actions of everyday people.

Which brings us to *The Big Chill*, writer-director Lawrence Kasdan's 1983 film about the "death of the sixties." In this case there really is a death: Alex, a genius science student who deserted physics for the anti–War movement, has killed himself in the early 1980s. Alex's friends from his University of Michigan days gather for his funeral. But these are not ordinary people— Sam (Tom Berenger) is the star of a TV series; Michael (Jeff Goldblum) is a writer for *Us* magazine; Harold (Kevin Kline) is the founder of a successful running shoe business; Sarah, Harold's wife (Glenn Close), is a doctor; Meg (Mary Kay Place) is a corporate lawyer; Karen (Jo-Beth Williams) is the wife of an advertising executive. Only one of the friends, Nick (William Hurt), is an unreconstructed 1960s character, a Vietnam vet now supporting himself as a drug dealer. These characters and more spend a few days at Harold and Sarah's summer house in South Carolina.

In *The Big Chill*, the 1960s seem to be about friendship, music, and sex. The sexual theme culminates in an evening where Harold sleeps with Meg, with his wife's blessing; Sam sleeps with Karen; and Nick starts a liaison with Alex's (much younger) lover Chloe, even though Nick was injured in the war and warns her, "I don't do anything." In this version, the sixties was a kind of wild carnival, reinvented for one night. Political action is remembered with pride and perhaps a little guilt, but seems completely unconnected with current actions. In this regard, Kasdan's decision not to show a living Alex (in flashback or otherwise) becomes important. Alex is at least potentially the conscience of the group, the one who never compromised. With Alex gone, Yippies (the Youth International Party of 1968) can become yuppies.

According to Joe Klein, an alternate version of the film with concluding flashback scene (Kevin Costner as Alex) was shown at the first screenings. Klein found the final scene "something of an embarrassment . . . bad wigs, bad makeup, the presence of Alex, who should have remained a specter. The actors—who are marvelous in the rest of the film—seemed strained, clearly acting."[11] Klein concurs with the decision to cut the flashback. As written in the first draft script, however, the flashback sequence is fascinating.[12] It begins with a dissolve from one scene of cleaning up in the kitchen (in the present) to another (Thanksgiving dinner, 1969). The great friends of the early eighties are, in 1969, bickering about career plans. Some nice touches of character development are added (e.g., Karen's comment about Sam: "How do you make a living out of charisma?" The answer: Sam becomes a

TV star.) Alex says of his decision to give up proton physics: "Every fuck-ing job in the field is in the military-industrial complex." The sequence concludes with good friends settling down to dinner and Alex bringing the turkey into the dining room. In other words, politics recedes, and the film ends with Alex and the others in a warm, supportive environment. Rather than confronting the careerist 1980s with the politics of 1969, the flashback scene is consistent with the rest of the film in stressing personal relations.

A few commonalities can be taken from this group of films. First, all of the films agree that the sixties are associated with a freer sexuality. *Nashville*, *Shampoo*, *Secaucus Seven*, and *The Big Chill* move from bedroom to bed-room, and even the slightly more staid *Between the Lines* includes two un-married couples and a scene of two friends spending a night together. The films disagree, however, on the meaning of this freer sexuality. In *Nashville* and to some extent *Shampoo*, sexual license leads to distance and deception between people, not to closer, more authentic bonds. In *Between the Lines* and *Secaucus Seven*, on the other hand, sexual freedom is compatible with friendship and idealism. *The Big Chill* seems to fall between these two posi-tions, with Sam and Karen's liaison based on deception seen as alienating, whereas Harold's attempt to impregnate Meg (with Sarah's support and ap-proval) is presented as an affirmation of friendship.[13]

A second point of commonality is that the sixties experience seems to be about community. Four out of the five films feature multicharacter en-sembles; only *Shampoo* emphasizes an individual hero. And one could say that all of the films debate the meaning and import of social groups. *Nash-ville* creates a set of pseudo-groups, based on very narrow common inter-ests: the entertainment stars and wannabes, the unformed and uninformed electorate. *Shampoo* debunks the cool, hip Los Angeles "in-group" as the defining factor in George's life by insisting on the crucial importance of money and power. In *Between the Lines* an idealistic community based on the newspaper is slowly dissolving, whereas in *The Return of the Secaucus Seven* a looser community of like-minded friends seems to be sustaining itself. Finally, *The Big Chill* suggests that the sixties group was and is about friendship and shared culture, nothing more.

Michael Ryan and Douglas Kellner propose that the value of groups in 1970s cinema varies according to whether the film takes a feminine or a masculine point of view. They argue that because of "real socialization patterns," films directed by women tend to present "parallel, contiguously connected relations," whereas films directed by men show "more autonomous, less dependent" characters.[14] Ryan and Kellner see this difference in *Between the Lines* (directed by Joan Micklin Silver) versus *The Big Chill* (directed by Lawrence Kasdan), but I am not convinced. For one thing, these two films are very similar—both are about groups of sixties friends who are slowly drifting apart. Also, the notion that *The Big Chill* "establishes a male center around which the other characters revolve"[15] is a reductive view of a film which remains committed to an ensemble approach. I would counter that if the group in *Between the Lines* is nonhierarchical, whereas the group in *The Big Chill* is beginning to be hierarchical, this is because of political rather than gender-based reasons. The nonhierarchical groups in *Between the Lines* and *The Return of the Secaucus Seven* represent a continuing belief in the voluntary association of like-minded activists. On the other hand, the beginnings of a hierarchy favoring Harold in *The Big Chill* shows the group adjusting (but with countermovements as well) to the politics of wealth and power.

Overall, the five films profiled in this chapter do not agree on the meaning and current status of the sixties. In *Nashville* the sixties clearly are dead, and by any standard society is dystopic. *Shampoo* shares *Nashville*'s social pessimism but presents George as a character achieving at least momentary happiness. *Between the Lines* and *Secaucus Seven* suggest a link between the political values of the 1960s and character actions in the late 1970s. *The Big Chill*, on the other hand, contests the relevance of such a link in the early 1980s. These films and others demonstrate that the sixties, like the Vietnam War, is a continuing locus of cultural debate. We continue to negotiate what we mean by "the sixties" and whether they really are dead.

The authentic environment of an utterance,

the environment in which it lives and takes

shape, is dialogized heteroglossia, anonymous

and social as language, but simultaneously

concrete, filled with specific content and

accented as an individual utterance.

—Mikhail Bakhtin, "Discourse in the Novel"

Let a thousand movies bloom.

—James Monaco, *American Film Now*

Part

2

Chapter 5

OR ART,

SEX,

AND

HOLLYWOOD

Last Tango in Paris

Last Tango in Paris is a hybrid film, part American star vehicle, part European art film. This film by an Italian director featuring two languages, English and French, is an excellent example of what I have elsewhere called the "Euro-American cinema."[1] It combines elements of the American commercial cinema and the European art film in order to reach a broad audience and to represent a "between cultures" experience. The experience of cultures meeting and often conflicting can express both the new realities of modern transportation and communication and the subjective impression of being at home nowhere. *Last Tango in Paris* is included in this study of American cinema of the 1970s for two reasons. First, it is emblematic of an important cross-fertilization of European and American film in the period covered by this book. Ideas and talent flowed back and forth across the Atlantic; for example, Vittorio Storaro worked as cinematographer for both Bernardo Bertolucci (*The Conformist, Last Tango in Paris*) and Francis Coppola (*Apocalypse Now, One From the Heart*). Second, *Last Tango in Paris* had an enormous impact on American audiences. It earned about $40 million in the United States (an astonishing figure for an art film), and it was hotly debated in both the popular and the specialized press.

Pauline Kael's famous rave review of *Last Tango in Paris* begins by comparing the New York Film Festival showing of the film in 1972 to the opening night of Stravinski's "Le Sacre du Printemps" in 1913. Both works are erotic and scandalous: "*Last Tango in Paris* has the same kind of hypnotic excitement as the 'Sacre,' the same primitive force, and the same thrusting, jabbing eroticism." The film, like the ballet, hit the audience (per Kael) with astounding force: "This must be the most powerfully erotic movie ever made, and it may turn out to be the most liberating movie ever made, so it's probably only natural that an audience . . . should go into shock."[2]

Kael's tone is hyperbolic, but the comparison to Stravinsky is apt. As André Boucourechliev points out about "Le Sacre du Printemps," an audience can be shocked by a work of art only if it has a ground for understanding that work. If, on the other hand, an artwork is so original that the audience has no ground for understanding, scandal will not be possible.[3] The achievement of *Last Tango in Paris* is therefore not to venture into completely unknown territory, but rather to present shocking images and ideas in a graspable idiom. By 1972, eroticism in film was well established in the avant-garde (Anger, Brakhage, Schneemann, Warhol), in the European art film (Fellini, Bergman, Godard), and in a range of pornography. *Last Tango* transposed the erotic to an intelligible, mass audience context by blending the European art film with the American popular cinema.

From its very beginning, *Last Tango in Paris* indicates that it will challenge film genres and conventions. It opens with a credit sequence featuring two paintings by Francis Bacon, showing first a man, then a woman seated uncomfortably in the corner of a room (the paintings are "Double Portrait of Lucien Freud and Frank Auerbach" [1964] and "Study for a Portrait" [1964]). The man seems to be wounded, in pain; the woman seems to be depressed. Both paintings, with their bright colors but fiercely unhappy subjects, suggest a context of masochism and desperation. The style is generally representational, yet the figures are distorted and twisted in powerfully expressive ways. Michel Leiris, in a description of Bacon's mature works, says that the deformed figures are shaped by the painter's instinct and that they address the spectator with unusual directness.[4] The two paintings are accompanied by Gato Barbieri's harsh saxophone, which dominates the musical track. Though not as striking as the Bacon paintings, the music is far removed from the clichés of "movie music." This introduction—paintings, music, and credits—already suggests that *Last Tango* will transgress the normal boundaries of the Hollywood film, where emotions are standardized and unhappiness is present only in extremely conventional forms.

The first live image we see is of Paul (Marlon Brando) standing under the elevated Metro line at Passy and screaming "Fucking God!" as the Metro train passes overhead. This image is both reassuring and off-putting; reassuring because we are introduced to a recognizable Hollywood star, off-putting because the emotional content of the scene is so strange. The first sequence proceeds to juxtapose Paul with another character, Jeanne, the young woman played by Maria Schneider. They are connected in various deep focus shots, both outdoors and in a cafe, but always with some visual tension (e.g., the two characters at opposite corners of the frame). They soon meet when both go in to look at an apartment for rent. This leads to a violent and anonymous sex scene—not a rape because Jeanne is a willing participant.

One of the odder subtexts of *Last Tango* is the American screwball comedy. Paul and Jeanne "meet cute" by going separately to look at the vacant apartment. They are both marked as "screwballs" by eccentric appearance and behavior. Paul wears an elegant, 1940s-style overcoat, but his hair is unkempt and his face worn and pinched. He screams an obscenity in English over the roar of the Metro. Jeanne wears a plush white coat with fur collar, a very short tunic dress, and knee-high boots. She seems to be a young, rich French girl experimenting with an unconventional look. The two are separated by age, nationality, and (most likely) social class, but following the pattern of screwball comedy they meet, banter, fight, and become a couple. Of course, there are breaks in the pattern as well. The mood is somber, the sexual relationship is consummated right away (instead of after the film's end, as in screwball comedies of the 1930s), and the strength of the couple deteriorates instead of gradually building. Also, the relationship Paul-Jeanne exists only within the space of the apartment.

When the two protagonists leave the apartment after the first meeting, we discover their "other" lives. Paul, we learn, is a man devastated by the very recent suicide of his wife, Rosa. Rosa, the owner and manager of a small Paris hotel, killed herself in the bathtub of one of the guest rooms. She left no note, no explanation. A gruesome scene shows a maid cleaning blood from the bathtub and shower curtain as she and Paul discuss Rosa's death and the police investigation. The maid wears a red turtleneck which visually echoes the bloody bathroom. This sequence matches the mood and color scheme of Bacon's paintings; *Last Tango* is, overall, a film of red, orange, brown, and gray. Jeanne, on the other hand, rushes to the train station to meet her boyfriend, Tom (Jean-Pierre Léaud), a filmmaker, and finds to her amazement that she is being filmed. Tom has sold a film called "Portrait of a Young Woman" and is therefore filming her *cinéma vérité*–style. The idea here seems to be the naïveté of most cinema, which claims to be showing the truth of a human interaction while presenting only a clichéd and super-ficial view. Tom accepts Jeanne's playacting ("I thought of you day and night, and I cried") as an immanent truth; instead, it is the mask of a more complicated reality.

The film cuts back and forth between Paul and Jeanne meeting in the apartment and other scenes—Paul in the hotel, Jeanne with Tom, Jeanne with her mother, and so forth. The apartment seems to be a space of fantasy (the address is "Rue Jules Verne"), but also of research. Paul and Jeanne try to meet without names, without histories, without all the limits and repres-sions of the social order. I use their names in this essay, for convenience, but the absence of names in the apartment establishes an atmosphere of danger, of the unknown. The quest for an absolute relationship provides at least a chance for knowledge of self and knowledge of Other. The sexual relation-ship as research partially resembles Godard's *Le Gai Savoir*, although the young people in Godard's film limit their research to words, images, and sounds. The sexual relationship in the apartment also partially mirrors the American musical, where the dance scenes typically present a more vivid, more emotional, truer image of the characters and their love than the fram-ing dramatic scenes. Bertolucci's film, however, cuts through the sublima-tions of the musical comedy to present the dance of sex.

The idea that sex is (can be?) liberating is central to *Last Tango*. To quote Pauline Kael once again, "It may turn out to be the most liberating film ever made." Bertolucci himself says "In the film, sex is simply a new kind of language that these two characters try to invent in order to communicate. They use the sexual language because the sexual language means liberation from the subconscious, means an opening up." Since Bertolucci is a disciple

Last Tango in Paris UNITED ARTISTS.
Marlon Brando and Maria Schneider as the couple without names or histories. Courtesy of Museum of Modern Art/Film Stills Archive.

of Marx as well as Freud, he links social liberation to the psychological
change: "Brando, initially rather mysterious, manages to upset the girl's
bourgeois life-style."[5] The theme of sex as personally liberating is very
much in line with ideas circulating in the United States in the 1960s and
1970s, from Herbert Marcuse to pop psychology.[6] It is exemplified by the
pleasurable moments of sexual play, dialogue, and appearance in the film's
first half. In one scene Paul and Jeanne sit on the floor with legs side by side
and Jeanne says "Let's try to come without touching." In another scene, the
two wash up in the bathroom and Paul says, "I think I'm happy with you."

Paul ends an argument by putting Jeanne on his shoulder and spinning her around, causing an amusement park–like pleasure. There is a good deal of play involving animals: Paul and Jeanne enact the story of Little Red Riding Hood; they invent animal-grunt-and-squeal names for themselves; Jeanne enters the apartment on all fours, grunting, only to meet an embarrassed workman delivering furniture. Jeanne tightly curls her hair after the first day of sex, a gesture toward "natural" style which eventually became a film cliché (see Jane Fonda in *Coming Home*). Sexual play in these early scenes seems to have a utopian potential, although it remains limited to the "laboratory space" of the apartment.

However, the theme of liberation and utopia is undercut by a series of analogies within the film questioning any possibility of happiness or fulfillment. These analogies have two main subjects: the couple and the body. In a logical but nonlinear (and non-Hollywood) fashion, all the couples in the film are mutually illuminating. The main couple, Paul and Jeanne, presents a new start, a reaching out to another person via very basic physical and emotional responses. This couple is mirrored/questioned by several established and unsuccessful couples: Paul and Rosa, a relationship ending in disaster; Jeanne and Tom, the superficial couple of "pop" culture; Rosa and Marcel, a lover whom Rosa has fashioned into a bad copy of Paul (same bathrobe, same whiskey, etc.); Rosa's mother and father, a couple of conventional pieties and conventional miseries; Jeanne's mother and her deceased father "the Colonel," a relationship reduced to a few narrow fetishes.[7]

The implication of all these parallel couples is that the main couple, too, will fail. Paul and Jeanne start out with a meeting of bodies, a magical few moments of happiness, but they cannot escape the burdens and repressions of the world. Paul brings a fearsome anger to the relationship, which eventually expresses itself in sadism and masochism: first, the anal near-rape of Jeanne; then, the scene where Jeanne's fingers penetrate him anally. Jeanne is impatient with the no-names, no-histories rule established by Paul, but as the rule breaks down she loses interest in this middle-aged man of no particular distinction. Jeanne's disillusion is well presented by her attitude toward a large, shrouded object in the apartment which she calls "monster" and associates with Paul. At the beginning of the film the monster is mysterious, sculpturelike, never investigated too closely. At the end of the film, on her last trip to the apartment, Jeanne removes the white sheet from the monster and discovers some boards, some fragments of furniture, etc. The mystery of the monster—and of the man—is over.

Bertolucci has made two generalizing comments on the theme of the couple in *Last Tango in Paris*. The first, tragic and absolute, is that "every sexual relationship is condemned."[8] There is no way to sustain the happiness of the couple's first meetings. The second statement, more nuanced, is that "I believe that in an adult relation, one reaches complete sexuality when what we call 'perversions' in psychoanalysis are abandoned. But after all, who is interested in this mature sexuality? It exists in laboratories, but who knows if it is true in reality?"[9] In the absence of "complete sexuality," we must settle for incomplete and distorted versions.

Adding to the misery of the couple in *Last Tango in Paris* is the misery of the body. It goes without saying that every body is condemned, that hiding behind life is death. As with the unsuccessful couples, evidence of the frailty of the body accumulates throughout the film. We see it in the very first sequence when, before Jeanne and Paul meet, an old lady washes her false teeth in the cafe bathroom. The bloody bathtub and Rosa in her funeral bed are grim reminders of mortality. Rosa's proper mother dressed in black and Jeanne's mother still devoted to her dead husband are evidences of absent sexuality and the hold of death over life. Even the two protagonists suggest the ravages of the aging process. Marcel mentions to Paul that he must have been an extremely good-looking young man, and we know from film history that Brando was once a model of male beauty. Now his hair is thinning, his face is lined, he's developing a belly. Jeanne, on the other hand, is young and lovely in the movie, but Paul tells her that "in ten years you're going to be playing soccer with your tits." Aging and mortality spare no one.

The impossibility of the couple and the frailty of the body are reemphasized by the film's ending. Paul meets Jeanne on the street, talks about his age and circumstances, and asks Jeanne to marry him. She rejects him: "It's over!" she says. Their difficult conversation continues in a ballroom hosting a tango contest, with the extremely stylized movements of the dancers contrasting with the earlier, freer lovemaking scenes in the apartment. Then Paul follows Jeanne to her family's apartment and forces his way in. He puts on the military cap of Jeanne's father in jest. Jeanne responds by shooting and killing him. As Paul dies, Jeanne rehearses her story for the police: "I don't know who he is. . . . He tried to rape me. . . . He's a madman. . . . I don't know his name." The disastrous end of Paul and Rosa finds an echo in the disastrous end of Paul and Jeanne.

Last Tango is a film about liberation and utopia, and a film about misery and death. It makes no univalent statement about the value of the couple, of sexuality, of love. Certainly, the film's complexity separates it from the discourses of pornography and links it to the ambiguous discourse of the European art film. However, the framing of ambiguity in this film is compatible with a traditional device of the American cinema described by Robert B. Ray.[10] In the "certain tendency of the Hollywood cinema" discussed by Ray, films refuse to choose between seemingly incompatible options. One of Ray's examples is *Meet Me in St. Louis,* which "overcame the opposition inherent in the myth of the family (encouraging contentment and permanence) and the myth of success (encouraging ambition and mobility)."[11] Another example would be the Hollywood gangster film. The spectator is invited to empathize with the gangster and his quest for individual fulfillment, and/or to feel reassured as the gangster's threat to social welfare is put down. Most viewers probably feel pulls in both directions.[12] *Last Tango* has something of the same pattern, though the ground of the adventure is now sexual experiment. The spectator can focus on the joys of the moment, with their utopian subtext; or the spectator can concentrate on the deterioration of the main couple and the surrounding images of unhappiness. The film chooses not to choose. Although Hollywood cinema is commonly labeled linear and nonambiguous, *Last Tango in Paris* utilizes a type of ambiguity that is familiar and comfortable to the viewers of Hollywood films.[13]

Last Tango does not, however, simply copy the classic Hollywood device described by Ray. In *Meet Me in St. Louis,* the narrative reconciles the conflict between success and family. Mr. Smith can have both, because the dynamism of St. Louis as a modern city (shown in the concluding World's Fair sequence) allows him to achieve success while staying at home. In *Last Tango,* on the other hand, the conflict "joy of the couple"/"horror of the couple" is suspended rather than reconciled. The evidence of the film is mixed: there is joy, there is horror. The concluding murder does not resolve all questions and needs.

Performance and character add another set of concerns to *Last Tango in*

Paris. Although the film was scripted in advance, much of the detail of individual scenes was improvised by the actors. Bertolucci talks about *Last Tango* as a personal, confessional kind of film: "With Brando and Maria my subconscious relationship was extremely intense, but I think I managed not only to drop most of my defenses, but that I helped them drop theirs as well." [14] This kind of confessional works extremely well with Method Actor Marlon Brando. In several intense scenes, Brando rails at his dead wife, remembers the humiliations of his childhood, and gives Jeanne long speeches on the horrors of existence. The most controversial of these speeches is Brando's diatribe against the tyranny of the family, illustrated (if that is the right word) by the anal rape, or near-rape. Paul talks about torture and repression as he commits a violent act. A less controversial but similarly intense moment, occurs when Paul talks about his dominating father, his poetic drunken mother, the embarrassment of going on a date with shoes smelling of cow manure. Here Vittorio Storaro's camera stays in close-up, unmoving, as Paul/Brando recounts scenes from Brando's childhood. Actor and character merge, for a moment.

The excitement of these scenes stems in part from the involvement of a major Hollywood star, but more than the audience's appreciation of celebrity is involved. Brando's confessional scenes are explosive because they break Hollywood taboos; they talk very directly about sex and anger and the ravages of the past. The language is obscene, the emotions harsh, the reactions extreme. In one scene, Brando cries in grief and frustration. Brando had pioneered a new, more expressive visual language of film acting in the 1950s; now, in the post–Production Code atmosphere of 1972, he adds the language of scatological confession to Hollywood's repertoire.

Maria Schneider, a nineteen-year-old playing her first major screen role, does not fare as well in Bertolucci's improvisatory style. Schneider does show intelligence, balance, and courage in the role of Jeanne. Jeanne enters into the agreement of a love affair without names fully and without regret, and she holds to it longer than Paul. She quite correctly points out to Paul, late in their three-day affair, that "Your solitude is not generous." Jeanne is an interesting movie heroine, but her "presence" on screen is overwhelmed by the power of Paul's confessions. Jeanne's memories of her own childhood have no such force. She remembers childhood as being "beautiful," and though she talks freely about sexuality, she does not show the corrosive insight of Paul. Jeanne is also hindered by a mise-en-scène inflected by star power and sexism. The film is organized (in marketing, but also in construction) around a new departure for a major star: Marlon Brando in an X-rated movie. Brando's character Paul has more history, more psychological development, more emotion than Schneider's Jeanne. Also, despite the film's theme of liberation, Schneider is the only cast member who appears nude on screen. She thus becomes, at least in part, the traditional object of the male gaze.

Tom, the third major character, is used for purposes of comic relief and parody. Tom prefers making a documentary to interacting with the real, flesh-and-blood Jeanne. His movie attempts to capture the truth of Jeanne by simply being present, but in fact he misses everything important that's going on in the film. Jeanne expresses the relative importance of Tom and Paul in her story about marriage and love. After Tom has proposed—or, rather, announced their pending marriage—Jeanne tells him that marriage is "pop" (superficial, conventional, commercial). Love, on the other hand, is not "pop." Love, she says, involves workers who meet in an empty apartment, take off their overalls, and become human beings. Tom is in the story in part to break the enormous tension of the film's other narratives—the death of Rosa, the meeting of Paul and Jeanne. He also exposes the pretension of filmmakers who attempt to probe human nature via a highly contrived form. The use of Jean-Pierre Léaud suggests a parody of the French New Wave, but Tom could be Bertolucci's self-parody as well.

The character relationships of *Last Tango* clearly form a romantic triangle, a pattern found in Hollywood films, in European art films, in almost any form of drama. Bertolucci's innovation is to develop the characters in widely different ways. Paul has a thoroughly developed "backstory," a history and pattern of life that gives his character a great deal of depth. Paul's character also merges, to some degree, with the background of Brando the actor. Jeanne has a backstory as well, but it is limited to conversations with Tom and her mother plus a few memories of childhood. Whereas Paul's actions have a psychological consistency, we do not know enough about Jeanne to explain her actions. Why does she enter into a violent sexual relationship with a stranger? Why does she keep coming back to the apartment? The third point of the triangle receives even less explanation. All that we know about Tom is that he withdraws from life to celebrate cinema. He creates Jeanne as a movie heroine instead of dealing with the give-and-take of everyday existence.

The lack of character development is most troubling at the end of the film, when Jeanne "resolves" the problem of the couple by shooting Paul. Jeanne has managed to sustain an intimate relationship with Paul for three days, so why does she suddenly take fright? The ending has a theoretical justification as an indication of the tenacious and violent rule of the dominant class (the bourgeoisie) over Paul and Jeanne. Paul is killed when he threatens Jeanne's home and therefore her self-definition as bourgeoise. But Jeanne, in the course of the film, does not seem bound to class strictures; indeed, she recognizes the class prejudice and racism of other characters as a kind of delusion. So it seems contrived and formulaic for Jeanne to become the unthinking instrument of her social class.

Feminist critics of *Last Tango in Paris* have justly pointed to the character of Jeanne as a weakness of the film. E. Ann Kaplan states the problem as follows: "Since we never know what Jeanne is thinking or why she is even bothering with Paul, her actions in the last part of the film are incomprehensible. . . . Nothing in the rest of the film prepares us for her suddenly turning into an archetypal bitch." [15] Bertolucci could have presented Jeanne as a character holding onto bourgeois attitudes while being temporarily fascinated by Paul.[16] Maria Schneider starts in this direction in one of her first speeches in the apartment: "I love these old houses. I find them fascinating" (my translation from the French). As spoken, the speech expresses a kind of ownership: such houses belong to *me*, as an upper-middle-class person. But Jeanne enters fully into the "research" with Paul in the apartment, becoming a hippie/bohemian girl rather than a calculating bourgeoise. Kaplan comments that "Bertolucci throws in the bitch image simply because it fits what he wants to do with Paul." [17] Jeanne changes because the director wants a tragic ending, and an original film narrative lurches to a formulaic close.

I see the merit of the above critique, but I would defend *Last Tango*, at least to a degree, on two interrelated formal grounds. First, a semi-improvised film like *Last Tango* will often have incongruities and lacunae. Some characters will come to life, others will remain stiff and undeveloped.

Some scenes will string together like beads on a chain, others will go wildly astray. The unevenness can be seen as a strength as well as a weakness. For by leaving things out, by underdetermining certain elements, the filmmaker creates a space for the spectator to interrogate the film. This device is quite familiar from modern painting, where a rough, unfinished surface allows the viewer to become aware of the materials and the process (mental and physical) of the work. Francis Bacon comes to mind again, but the device goes back at least to Matisse and the Fauves. A second argument would be that the contrast between an open, semi-improvised film style in the body of the film and a closed, melodramatic ending similarly creates a space for the spectator's thinking. The wrench of the conclusion (which is still objectionable, in Kaplan's terms) may lead the spectator to rethink the film.

One piece of evidence which supports this hypothesis is that *Last Tango* has stimulated a lively and impassioned critical debate. The film may be sexist, but it is open to discussion. I find it particularly revealing that several critics suggest alternate developments the film *should have* explored. Kaplan feels that Jeanne, not Paul, should have been the focus of the triangle and the center of the film.[18] Joan Mellen proposes a middle-aged, experienced woman for the main role; her ideal casting would be Simone Signoret opposite a "charming if unknown boy actor."[19] Claretta Micheletti Tonetti laments that *Last Tango* "could have been a sophisticated inquiry into the transpositions of the feminine and the masculine roles."[20] Finally, both Ingmar Bergman and John Simon maintain that the "film makes sense" as a disguised homosexual romance, with "Jeanne" a screen for "Jean."[21] All these alternatives suggest that *Last Tango* is an unusually open text.

The uneven quality of *Last Tango*, as highlighted by the film's conclusion, could be seen as a further mixing of film styles. The collective creation of avant-garde narrative, one option of the European cinema, yields to a violent, conventional Hollywood ending. A spectator used to closure gets closure, and can struggle to put together narrative and thematic elements that will explain Paul's death. A spectator comfortable with ambiguity gets ambiguity, and can reject the ending and rethink the film. By juxtaposing different heroes (Paul and Tom), different genres (screwball comedy, sex film, Hollywood musical, European art film, Godardian research, melodrama), and different visual styles (intensely focused with Paul, floating around Paris with Jeanne and Tom), the film allows for at least two possible responses.

Last Tango in Paris is a flawed but extraordinary experience. The intense subject matter and the unconventional stylistic treatment create a highly participatory film. This film located *between* genres and *between* national film styles encourages the viewer to throw off old habits of film viewing and to actively interrogate the film.

Chapter 6

American Graffiti

Cooley High

Teen Films

Animal House

Diner

Fast Times at Ridgemont High

The teen film genre first flourished in the 1950s, when Hollywood discovered that its slimmed-down, post-TV audience consisted primarily of teenagers and young adults. The leading writers, directors, and producers of the fifties were middle-aged and beyond, but nevertheless the film industry began to make teenpics. Notable titles of the period include *The Wild One*, *Rebel without a Cause*, *The Blackboard Jungle*, and *Rock around the Clock*, as well as the films of Elvis Presley and Frankie and Annette. Though ostensibly about antisocial rebellion, the teen film is usually pulled between a desire for independence and a need to belong. For example, the "rebel without a cause" in Nicholas Ray's 1954 film turns out to be searching for the guidance of a strong, patriarchal family. As Jon Lewis puts it, "The cultural function of the teen film has always been primarily one of reassurance." [1]

With *American Graffiti* (1973), George Lucas set off a new round of teen films, this time in a nostalgic mode. The films of the 1950s are a take on contemporary reality, but Lucas's film looks back from the early 1970s at a simple, idealized "teen culture" set in 1962. This date is significant as the last possible year of teenage innocence before the assassination of President Kennedy, the beginnings of the Vietnam War, and the various social movements of the 1960s. The year 1962 is really the tail end of the fifties, in social and cultural terms, and so Lucas is looking back at the original period of the teen film and reshaping it in a wistful, nostalgic way. This formula was soon adopted by a wide variety of 1970s teen films, including *Cooley High* (1975), *Grease* (1978), and *Animal House* (1978).[2]

The story of *American Graffiti* focuses on a fifteen-hour stretch — a night and a morning — in the lives of a group of friends in Modesto, California.[3] Steve (Ron Howard) and Curt (Richard Dreyfuss) revisit their high school for the beginning-of-school dance; both are due to take off for an East Coast college the next day. Steve pushes his steady girl Laurie (Cindy Williams), a high school senior, to have sex with him just once before he leaves, though he is too embarrassed to say exactly what he wants. Laurie rejects him, and they break up. Steve loans his old Chevy to Terry the Toad (Charles Martin Smith) for the school year, thus immediately making Terry a person of some substance in the teen culture. Terry proceeds to pick up Debbie (Candy Clark), a pretty, blonde girl from a neighboring school. Curt, a brainy kid, visits with an English teacher, sees an old girlfriend, and then gets entangled with a local gang, the Pharaohs. All of the characters eventually are drawn to the Friday night ritual of "cruising" (a promenade of cars down a specific street in town). Chief among the cruisers is John Milner (Paul Le Mat), the local drag racing champ, who will eventually take on the visiting Falfa (Harrison Ford) in a race.

The film economically develops a series of teen stereotypes, including the good boy (Steve), the good girl (Laurie), the brain (Curt), the nerd (Terry), the bad girl (Debbie), the bad boy (John), and the gang (the Pharaohs), but treats them with a rare egalitarianism. Steve the class president hangs around with nerdy Terry; Milner finds himself driving around with thirteen-year-old Carol (Mackenzie Phillips); Curt passes the Pharaohs' initiation by pulling the rear axle off a police car. Everything intertwines, and the teenage scene acquires a surprising density; it seems to be a complete world, if only for fifteen hours.

Much of this density is created by a rock-and roll score of about forty songs, taken from the period. All of the characters are listening to the same radio station, and this station is playing "Rock around the Clock," "Ain't

American Graffiti UNIVERSAL PICTURES.
Steve (Ron Howard) and Laurie (Cindy Williams), the nostalgic teen couple of the early 1960s.
Courtesy of Museum of Modern Art / Film Stills Archive.

That a Shame," "See You in September," "Smoke Gets in Your Eyes," "Why
Do Fools Fall in Love," "Do You Wanna Dance," and so on. The disc jockey
is Wolfman Jack (playing himself), who becomes a kind of sage of the teenage culture — in fact, Curt visits the radio station in the early morning hours
to consult the Wolfman. The music was, from the start, crucial to the film's
conception; George Lucas was confident that the musical selections would
establish the setting and involve the audience.[4] The carefully chosen, wall-
to-wall rock score is similar in impact to the score of *Easy Rider,* but there
is one important difference. In *Easy Rider,* the score at times suggests a
transcendence, a religious dimension of experience which goes beyond the
joys and travails of the moment. In *American Graffiti,* on the other hand,

the musical score stays focused on the joys and rituals of the nostalgically re-created teen culture.

Permanence/impermanence is actually the central motif of *American Graffiti* and of most (perhaps all) teen films.[5] One dynamic of the film is that both Steve and Curt are very reluctant to leave the town, their friends, and (by extension) their adolescent years. Through most of the film Steve is steadfast about leaving, whereas Curt hesitates. Contributing to Curt's befuddlement is the fleeting vision of a blonde (Suzanne Somers) in a white Thunderbird, a materialization of the yearning and promise of the teenage years. Eventually Curt the brain finds the independence of spirit to leave, whereas Steve cannot break his ties to Laurie. But clearly, this teenage world itself is fleeting and now vanished, as the 1962 setting makes clear. According to Dale Pollock, the title *American Graffiti* is meant to evoke "memories of a bygone civilization."[6] Within the film, John Milner, slightly older than

American Graffiti UNIVERSAL PICTURES.
College-bound Curt (Richard Dreyfuss) hangs out with the hoodlum gang the Pharaohs. Courtesy of Museum of Modern Art / Film Stills Archive.

the other characters, suggests that the golden age has already passed. Milner remembers when the cruising strip was much longer, and he visits a car graveyard full of totalled dragsters. Also, the day of leaving for college is a major turning point; either you break away, or you don't. To all these metonyms of impermanence, one must counterpose the film itself. In a certain sense, it is still and always 1962 (or Lucas's idealized version of 1962), as long as people are watching *American Graffiti*.

American Graffiti is also a reaction to the new emphasis on sex, violence, and profanity in Hollywood movies which began in the late 1960s. The American studios met a challenge from foreign competition and catered to the "new morality" of their increasingly young audience by relaxing the standards of acceptable conduct on screen. The scrapping of the Hollywood Production Code in 1968 is more an effect than a cause of these changes. But there is no explicit sexuality and very little violence in *American Graffiti*. Further, teenage rebellion in this film is decidedly muted: Terry the Toad's drinking episode with Debbie ends in embarrassment, tough guy Milner is saddled with a mouthy teenybopper, and even the law-breaking Pharaohs don't do any serious harm. Despite its emphasis on change and decision making, *American Graffiti* ends with very little alteration to the teenage culture. Steve will stay, Curt will go, and otherwise life goes on.

This conclusion is modified by printed titles which tell us what happened to some of the characters after the film. Steve became an insurance agent in Modesto; Curt moved to Canada (presumably to escape the draft) and became a writer; Terry was missing in action in Vietnam; Milner was killed by a drunk driver. Things did change in important ways for these characters, but not on-screen. Nineteen sixty-two was, indeed, a fleeting moment. Curt is the only one who successfully manages to leave Modesto and establish a new life; this is prefigured in the film's last images, where Curt looks down from his plane (he's flying "Magic Carpet Airlines") at the receding California farmland and highway. Conventional, weak-willed Steve ends up in a conventional profession; whether he marries Laurie is left to the viewer's imagination. Milner's death, arbitrary though it may be, suggests the limited horizon of a small-town drag racer. Terry's (presumed) death, on the other hand, brings the teen culture of *American Graffiti* into contact with the broad social issues of the later 1960s.

In a decision Lucas was later to regret, none of the women characters in

American Graffiti is given a postfilm trajectory. Scriptwriters Gloria Katz and Willard Huyck argued that the women should be included, but Lucas maintained that "It's a movie about the four guys" and that an additional title card would slow down the film.[7] The relegating of the women characters to secondary status may be justified for Debbie and Carol, for each appears in mid-film as an adjunct to a male character (Terry and Milner, respectively). However, Laurie is in the film from beginning to end, she is Curt's sister as well as Steve's girlfriend, and she is featured in several scenes without Steve. Further, Laurie is clearly smarter and more strong-willed than her romantic partner, a point interestingly anticipated by the film's casting. Ron Howard was eighteen when the film was made, with a background as a child actor; Cindy Williams, on the other hand, was twenty-five, an adult in bobbysoxer clothing! Laurie deserves a title card of her own — for example: "Laurie Henderson moved to San Francisco and became a TV news reporter."

American Graffiti provided a number of important plot conventions for teen films that followed: adults are either absent or ineffectual; the story is compressed into a short period of time; the story involves several characters of more or less equal importance; the film cuts back and forth between subplots; long-term outcomes are presented via end titles; the story focuses on a nostalgic, even mythic, vision of teenage years. *American Graffiti* did not invent any of these conventions, but its highly successful synthesis of elements was much copied, by numerous feature films as well as by television shows such as *Happy Days* and *Laverne and Shirley*. One should not forget that *American Graffiti* was highly successful in a commercial sense: production budget of $500,000, box office return of $50 million. This kind of return was in itself enough to set off a new cycle of teen films.

Cooley High (1975) is a high school film with an ensemble cast set in Chicago in 1964. Produced by B-movie company American International Pictures, it is to some extent derivative of *American Graffiti*. The film chronicles the high school experience, with a great deal of action crammed into a short period of time — several days, in this case, instead of *American Graffiti*'s less than twenty-four hours. The teenage world of *Cooley High* includes school, parties, pranks, even a high school hangout — Martha's soda fountain (equivalent to *American Graffiti*'s Mel's Drive In). The musical score is mostly Motown, including songs by the Four Tops, the Temptations,

Stevie Wonder, and so on. Motown is a wonderful choice, for two reasons: (1) it strongly evokes the mid-1960s; and (2) Motown's black/urban sound was appreciated, even loved, by a broad spectrum of Americans. The *American Graffiti* influence should not be overemphasized, however; the link between the films may be more commercial packaging than primary inspiration. *Cooley High* was based on an autobiographical script by TV and film writer Eric Monte (creator of the television series "Good Times"), who had attended Edwin G. Cooley Vocational High School in Chicago.

Cooley High is about a group of four high school boys, but only two, Preacher (Glynn Turman) and Cochise (Lawrence Hilton-Jacobs) are truly the focus of the action. Preacher is a bright, mischievous boy who writes poetry for fun but rarely comes to class. Cochise, a handsome basketball star, is more concerned with partying and girls than with school. We see them through a variety of pranks, including skipping school to go to the zoo, impersonating vice cops to get spending money from two whores, and joyriding in a stolen car. The seemingly harmless joyriding eventually gets Cochise killed. The film ends with a drunken Preacher speaking a soliloquy over his friend's grave.

Though *Cooley High* is not a great film, it provides a fascinating rearrangement of the conventions of seventies teen comedies. For example, in *American Graffiti* parents and home life are almost entirely absent (Curt's parents appear in a short scene at the airport). In *Cooley High,* we see scenes of Preacher at home with his Mama, who works long hours to support the family,[8] and two younger sisters. We discover, in these scenes, that Preacher is poised uncomfortably between childhood and adulthood; the teenage years here do not have the autonomy and completeness of other teen films. For example, the question of who will take care of the youngest causes lots of bickering and childish behavior in the Jackson household. Also, in a lovely scene, Mama comes home from work late one night and tells Preacher to go upstairs and get the belt. She's going to punish him for some serious misdeeds (including an arrest). But when Preacher comes downstairs with the belt, Mama is asleep in a kitchen chair. The cocky, mature Preacher kisses his Mama's hair and goes to bed; in some ways he's still a kid.

Another clear difference between *American Graffiti* and *Cooley High* lies in the area of sexuality. In *American Graffiti* the boys are looking for sex, but the film's rituals—the high school hop, cruising—are sublimations of

Cooley High AMERICAN INTERNATIONAL PICTURES.
Cochise (Lawrence Hilton-Jacobs) with one of his many female admirers. Courtesy of Museum of Modern Art / Film Stills Archive.

that impulse. This film's teenage world is exciting and complete without the exploration of adult sexuality. *Cooley High*, on the other hand, presents a far different picture. Ray, a slightly older friend of Preach and Cochise, cheats a white man looking for a black whore. Preach and Cochise rob the two streetwalkers. Cochise the basketball star is often embracing a female admirer, and he has sex with Preacher's ex-girlfriend. Preacher's big sexual moment involves the seduction of the beautiful Brenda in his own bed. But even here, Preacher's boy-man quality comes into play when he and Brenda are caught (after the act) by his two younger sisters. This is one of the transgressions prompting Mama to say "get the belt."

A third difference between *American Graffiti* and *Cooley High* lies in the consequences of teenage pranks. Curt in *American Graffiti*, guided by the Pharaohs, attaches chains to the underbody of a parked police car. When the Pharaohs then come speeding by, the police car pulls out at full power . . . and loses its rear axle. This prank seems to be free of consequences; no one is hurt, and the police do not reappear. In a similar scene in *Cooley High*, Preach and Cochise go joyriding with two friends, Stone and Robert, who have stolen a big, late-model car. Preacher brags about his driving prowess and is given a chance at the wheel. His unskilled, erratic driving attracts a police car, leading to a high-speed chase. The chase ends when Preach drives over the arms of an in-use forklift, and the police car gets caught in the forklift's upward movement—no one is hurt, but the police car is left dangling in the air. However, this prank has real consequences. Preach, Cochise, Stone, and Robert are arrested. Preach and Cochise are released because of the intervention of Mr. Mason, a teacher at Cooley High. But this release suggests to Stone and Robert that their friends must have ratted on them. When Robert and Stone make bail, they come after Preach and Cochise. They beat Cochise to death, destroying his chance at a college scholarship and a bright future.[9] In the inner-city world of *Cooley High*, adolescent pranks can have tragic consequences.

In technical terms, *Cooley High* has the rough look and feel of a "B movie." The cinematography is sometimes garish, the acting is uneven, and the editing lacks George Lucas's unerring sense of pace in *American Graffiti*. As a cultural document, though, this is an interesting film. *Cooley High* adds, or restores, to the teenfilm recipe family context, sexuality, and real consequences. And via these additions, it shows that the *American Graffiti* formula can be adjusted to fit a social milieu that is far removed from small-town California.

Animal House is another film at least slightly influenced by *American Graffiti*, though a more obvious influence would be the TV show "Saturday Night Live." *Animal House* takes place in the "innocent" year of 1962, and it ends with supered titles describing the characters' futures. The setting has shifted from high school cruising to college, but we are still involved in highly organized rituals that separate youth from the adult world. *Animal House* uses the format of ensemble cast (featuring the men) with several interlocking subplots, and in this film parents are entirely absent. One convention *Animal House* does dispense with is the tight time scheme. The film takes place over several weeks of the fall semester.

The plot of *Animal House* is both silly and crammed with events, so it need not be summarized at length. The primary plot involves a conflict between a nasty dean (John Vernon) and the dissolute Delta house, a fraternity characterized by drinking, rowdiness, and abysmal academic performance. The dean eventually closes the fraternity and expels its members, and they respond by disrupting and destroying the college's homecoming parade. Among the subplots are: (1) Larry (Tom Hulce) and Flounder's (Stephen Furst) transformation from nerdy pledges to full members of the fraternity; and (2) the conflict between Delta house and the militaristic, "all-American" Omega fraternity.

Animal House is less concerned about plot, however, than about modeling behavior. It is, quite frankly, in favor of sex, alcohol, marijuana, and rock and roll. Where *American Graffiti* was about creating a complete teenage world, *Animal House* is about having fun. Some of this fun is trivial and forgettable—e.g., the food fight—but the toga party is genuinely inventive. Young men and women dress up in variously wrapped sheets (with laurel wreaths, ties, and other accessories) and dance the night away. Otis Day and the Knights [10] whip the crowded dance floor to a frenzy—at one point, all the guys are writhing on the floor. Ancillary action takes place in a couple of bedrooms. Larry decides not to rape the young town girl he has invited, and Otter (Tim Matheson) gets erotically tangled up with the dean's wife. *Animal House* reminds us that the teen film is at least potentially Dionysiac.

Bluto, played by John Belushi, is the leader of the revels.[11] After seven years in college, his midterm average is 0.00. His interests seem to be drinking, eating, breaking things, and spying on sorority girls. In a second-story Peeping Tom scene, Bluto pauses to turn and raise his eyebrows at the spectator before falling, awestruck by the vision in front of him. Bluto is an unrestrained, carnivalesque spirit—he does what he wants, when he wants, with whomever he wants. But the end titles identify Bluto and the sorority girl he kidnaps from the parade as "Senator and Mrs. John Blutarsky, Washington D.C." Though wildly unlikely (and poking fun at the end title convention), this outcome suggests that the teen and college years are not necessarily predictive of later success. Spectators looking for an alternate outcome can recall that the actor John Belushi died of a drug overdose at age thirty-three.

As a college professor, I suppose I should be outraged about the drinking and destructive behavior of *Animal House*. Binge drinking, a very real problem on college campuses, is glorified here. Partying becomes the be-all and end-all of college life; the few brief classroom scenes are introduced only to make fun of classes, teachers, and tests. Property is destroyed, the surrounding community is disrupted, and so on and so on. But *Animal House* is a satire; it takes the privileged hedonism of college life and magnifies it to the nth degree. Its simplest message to anxious young people is "Relax; have a good time."

If we go beyond this level to investigate commission and omission, originality and stereotype, then the message of *Animal House* is mixed. On the one hand, the community of Delta Tau Chi really is more accepting and more flexible than the big-man-on-campus fraternity. The Deltas welcome overweight and anxious Flounder (his "fraternity name," given by Bluto), after he has been embarrassed and rejected by the Omegas. They really do have a functioning community which helps Larry and Flounder grow from high school boys to college men. The desirability of the hard-drinking, party-all-night college stereotype is another matter. On the other hand, the positive aspects of socialization in *Animal House* apply almost entirely to men. College women in the film are sexually provocative, easily disrobed, and without distinctive personalities. The sexism of *Animal House* prepares the way for the teen chauvinism of *Porky's*. But even on this point there is an exception. Katy (Karen Allen), the on-again off-again girlfriend of Boon (Peter Riegert), a Delta senior, finds the fraternity house parties juvenile and predictable. She disapproves of her boyfriend's habitual drunkenness, not for moral reasons but because of a sense of waste. Katy also sleeps with a charismatic English professor (played by Donald Sutherland, in a cameo role), as a gesture of independence. The character of Katy suggests that *Animal House* is not entirely an exploitation-of-women film.

Like some other teen films of the late 1970s, *Animal House* is unusually direct and participatory. *Animal House* invites its young audience to have fun, get high, throw a toga party. *Saturday Night Fever* (1977) both responds to and fuels the disco craze; it advocates a style of dress, dance, and behavior. *Grease* (1978) brings back the fifties in a simple, glossy, easily digested form; audiences often sing along to *Grease*'s lyrics, familiar from both play and movie performances. *The Rocky Horror Picture Show* (1979) has become a midnight cult film with participatory rituals which invite young people to consider (in a safe context) alternative sexualities.

Barry Levinson's *Diner* (1982) transports the George Lucas teen formula to older characters and a more serious mood. *Diner,* set in Baltimore in 1959, is about six young men in their early twenties who are still negotiating the transition from adolescence to adulthood. The film features ensemble acting, interwoven subplots, and a restricted time period—in this case, the week between Christmas and New Year's Eve. Popular music of the period fills the soundtrack, and the characters even debate the virtues of their favorite musicians. Much attention is paid to the customs and rituals of the social setting, in this case a middle-class, largely Jewish neighborhood. *Diner* does, however, dispense with the *American Graffiti* convention of end titles describing the future.

Writer-director Levinson has argued that the *American Graffiti* connection is more apparent than real. His film was perceived by MGM, its distributor, as a teen film, but when it was test-marketed to a teenage audience it failed. Levinson prefers to see *Diner* as a film in the line of Fellini's *I Vitelloni*—a comparison which reveals both the film's complex tone and Levinson's cinematic culture.[12] The Fellini film is an autobiographical meditation about the young men of Rimini. These "wastrels" in their early twenties are out of school, not fully involved in the world of work, not quite ready for marriage. The film presents a nostalgic but bittersweet view of late adolescence in a provincial town. *Diner* is similar to *I Vitelloni* not only in subject but in visual style and mood. *Diner*'s muted color (Baltimore in winter) is much closer to Fellini's subdued black and white than to the garish colors of *American Graffiti* or *Cooley High*. The teen film conventions are there, and they provide a narrative frame, but *Diner* is about a different, more somber moment of growing up. Vincent Canby describes the difference like this: "The characters in *American Graffiti* still had several years to go before experiencing the angst that hangs over the young men in *Diner* like not entirely unpleasant, greasy griddle smoke."[13]

Diner begins at a dance in a high school gym on Christmas night, but the main characters are far past their high school years. Shrevie (Daniel Stern) is already married to Beth (Ellen Barkin). Eddie (Steve Guttenberg) will marry Elise (Sharon Zinman) on New Year's Eve, but only if Elise passes a football quiz. The troubled Fenwick (Kevin Bacon) has "sold" his date Diane to another guy for five dollars. Boogie (Mickey Rourke), the womanizer in the group, smooths things over between Fenwick and Diane. Modell (Paul Reiser) is also hanging out at the dance. After the dance the women are dropped off, and the guys meet at the diner for coffee, food, and conversation. In the early morning, Shrevie, Boogie, and Fenwick go to the train station to pick up Billy (Timothy Daly), who is in grad school in New York and is coming in for his best friend Eddie's wedding. Then it's back to the diner for more conversation.

Barry Levinson comments that one of the keys to the movie is an "amazing naiveté" about women, "the guys' inability to understand them, their neglect of them." [14] Most of the incidents of *Diner* are about courtship but also about the estrangement of the protagonists from women. Shrevie cannot talk to his wife for five minutes, and yet he can chat for hours at the diner. Eddie admits to sexual inexperience, and to not knowing much about Elise. Boogie notes Fenwick's immaturity, yet he wants to place bets on his own ability to seduce a young woman. But the strongest and funniest variation on this theme in *Diner* is clearly the football quiz.

Eddie has required, as a condition of marriage, that Elise pass a detailed quiz (true and false, multiple choice, short answer) on the Baltimore Colts football team. Perhaps he is clinging to his boyhood, to his man-without-woman identity. Shrevie and Fenwick and Elise's father witness the quiz, in Elise's wood-paneled basement. Questions are asked and answered, judgments are made, fine points are discussed, all without on-screen recognition of the outrageousness of the situation. Further, Elise never appears in this scene; she is behind a wall somewhere, and we only hear her voice. The mise-en-scène underlines the barrier between future spouses that is the whole point of the scene. Will Elise really be welcome in the all-male world of the football quiz, or of the diner? Very doubtful.

An interesting question here is whether *Diner* repeats the sexual chauvinism of *American Graffiti* and *Animal House*, or whether it critiques the male-dominant position. I would support the second explanation. Levinson is sympathetic to his characters, yet he understands their weaknesses. The director's attitude is not at all equivalent to the characters' limited view. Thus, the quiz scene, a serious matter within the diegesis, is absurd and funny to the audience. Even more outrageously, the week covered by *Diner* includes a National Football League championship game played in Baltimore, and the characters attend—but Levinson never tells us who won! In retrospect, this football subtheme becomes even more memorable, because the Colts left Baltimore in 1984 and moved to Indianapolis. Thus *Diner*, like *American Graffiti*, becomes the tracing of a vanished world.

Many of the subplots of *Diner* are somber. For example, Billy discovers that Barbara, who slept with him once in November after several years of friendship, is now pregnant. Also, Boogie spends much of the film desperately trying to escape a large gambling debt. But the film is broken up by occasional moments of joy. In one extraordinary scene, Eddie and Billy visit a tawdry bar on Baltimore's Block (the adult entertainment district) and observe a tired stripper and a desultory saxophonist and drummer. After complaining about the music, Billy goes to the piano and lays down a strong boogie-woogie. The musicians pick up the beat, Eddie starts dancing with the stripper, and the bar's patrons cheer the spectacle. Billy has broken through the indifference of strangers and created a momentary community. This is underlined in the next scene, when Billy, Eddie, and the stripper go out for hamburgers and she says, "You guys are all right. You made my day."

The film ends with Eddie and Elise's wedding. All the guys are there, Shrevie with Beth, Fenwick with his date from the opening dance, Boogie with a gorgeous rich girl he saw riding a horse one morning. But the wedding is also a family and a generational affair, with people of all ages dancing, mingling, having fun. The narrow age group (a teen film convention) begins to dissolve into the wider social milieu. At one point, Modell grabs the mike and begins reminiscing about Eddie and the guys; his monologue is a synecdoche for the entire film. When Elise throws the bouquet, the unmarried girls bat it in the air a few times and it falls at the feet of the diner guys. The image then fades to sepia. This lovely moment concludes the film by making a common ritual both particularized and poignant. The young men confronted by the bouquet are delayed adolescents going nowhere. The bouquet challenges them to take the next step, to become adults, to understand and fully respond to women. On the other hand, the bouquet is just a bouquet.

Fast Times at Ridgemont High (1982) takes the *American Graffiti* teen-film conventions and places them firmly in the present. This film is about 1982, not some nostalgic past, and it features a familiar teenage landscape of shopping mall, video arcade, fast-food restaurant, and so on. The soundtrack is contemporary rock. As with other films in the cycle, parents are absent and the challenges and relationships of the film are within teenage society—although a few teachers do play minor roles. The suburban Los Angeles setting leads to occasional distinctive moments, for example scenes set around a backyard swimming pool. However, for the most part *Fast Times* is about generic teenagers—the mall and the high school could be almost anywhere.

Fast Times at Ridgemont High is based on a nonfiction book by Cameron Crowe—then a young journalist for *Rolling Stone,* now a screenwriter and film director.[15] Crowe actually attended Ridgemont High in Redondo Beach, California, for a few months, posing as a student. His book, like the film adapted from it, is thus based on current field work, not nostalgic memory. But this distinction is to some extent erased by the self-conscious approach of the film. Tom Doherty uses *Fast Times* as an example of "a new kind of calculated and consciously reflexive teenpix." Doherty sees a "double vision" in *Fast Times* and *Risky Business* (1983); both films have a teenage subject matter but also an irony and distance aimed at adults.[16] Consider this example. When Mark (Brian Backer), taking tickets at the local movie theater, says, "All the action's on the other side of the mall," his remark can be taken in two different ways. First, it's an unremarkable comment from an insecure teenager. Second, Mark's line has an irony addressed to the spectator, because we know that the other side of the mall must be very much like this side (malls are homogeneous). The double consciousness described by Doherty accomplishes approximately the same ends as the nostalgia of *American Graffiti*—it makes the film accessible to a broad range of spectators.

Much of the critical comment on *Fast Times* focuses on gender and sexuality. The female characters here are given equal weight to the men; indeed, if there is one primary character, it is Stacey (Jennifer Jason Leigh). Even more remarkable is the film's matter-of-fact treatment of teenage sexuality. High school freshman Stacey is eager to learn about sex. Her older friend Linda (Phoebe Cates) counsels her about male sexuality, pushes her to go out with an older guy, even gives a demonstration of fellatio—using a carrot. Stacey experiments with sex without losing her attractive, nice-girl qualities. After a couple of bad experiences, she decides that "Anybody can have sex, I'm looking for a relationship." At the end of the film, she is courting Mark, a nice guy who is not ready for adult sexuality. *Fast Times* might be considered a "post−sexual revolution" film—sex is considered a part of life, but not the be-all and end-all of teenage society. This is a quite different attitude from the male-centered sexual competition of *Cooley High, Animal House,* and *Diner* (*American Graffiti* might be a "pre−sexual revolution" film). Robin Wood attributes the change in attitudes to the presence of a woman, Amy Heckerling, as director of *Fast Times.*[17] However, the matter-of-fact treatment of sex, with equal attention to men and women, is already present in Cameron Crowe's book.

A fascinating departure from the *American Graffiti* model in *Fast Times* is the greater isolation of the characters. The four films discussed thus far in this chapter are about groups, and close friendships within groups. In *Fast Times,* there are a couple of friendships, each problematic in its own way, and no well-defined groups. Stacey and Linda are friends, but by the end of the film it is clear that the bond of sexual expert−sexual novice is based on a lie. Stacey understands that Linda's fiancé is imaginary; how this repeated lie will affect their friendship is an open question. Mark and Mike (Robert Romanus) are friends, but Mike's selfishness has attenuated if not ended the friendship by the final scene of the school dance. Brad, the character played by Judge Reinhold, has no close friends, just a former girlfriend; the fact that the actor is much too old for a high school film exacerbates the isolation of his character. Brad does comes through in a big way for Stacey, but this single act of kindness actually underlines the loneliness of all the characters. Finally, Spicoli (Sean Penn), the pothead, has a few pals but seems to live in a narcissistic world of his own.

The greater isolation in *Fast Times* vs. *American Graffiti* et al. might indicate an ideological shift−from the group-centered idealism of the 1960s and 1970s to a more self-centered narcissism of the 1980s, the yuppie period. But it might also be a function of Cameron Crowe's participant-observer reporting. Isolation and narcissism are familiar parts of the teenage experience, but they do not easily fit the social forms of drama and comedy. Crowe and his film adaptors have found a way to make teenage isolation a major part of a story that remains vivid, funny, and moving.

Affirming its connection to the *American Graffiti* subgenre of the teenpic, *Fast Times at Ridgemont High* ends with titles describing the futures of the characters. Brad becomes assistant manager at the Mi-T-Mart, Mike goes to work at 7-11, Mr. Vargas (the biology teacher) switches back from Sanka to coffee. Stacey and Mark are having a passionate affair but still haven't gone "all the way." These futures are remarkable because they indicate no change. Nobody grows up to be a writer, or even an insurance agent; nobody grows up at all. The teenfilm world is immanent and infinite.

However, let us not forget the "double vision" of *Fast Times*. On the one hand, the teenage world really will last forever; *Fast Times* is about good times, bad times, moments of experience that remain valid even if the film's characters and its audiences do grow up. On the other hand, a spectator can certainly see an irony in changes that equal no change. Brad and Mike have dead-end jobs, appropriate for teenagers but not for adults. Their "futures" represent the diminished horizon that is very much a part of contemporary American life. Mr. Vargas doesn't change, but he is already an adult. And Stacey and Mark get a true, though evanescent, teenage romance. *American Graffiti*'s idealized teenage culture here begins to seem bland and unsatisfying: "All the action's on the other side of the mall."

Chapter 7

Patton

General Patton and Colonel Kurtz

Apocalypse Now

Patton (1970) and *Apocalypse Now* [1] (1979) bookend the decade of the 1970s with two very different pictures of the American military at war. The first, a studio epic from Twentieth Century–Fox, gives a portrait of an eccentric general within a generally positive view of the U.S. Army in World War II. The second, made independently and at great expense by director Francis Coppola (though with financial backing—mainly loans—from United Artists), presents a complex and far more negative portrayal of the U.S. Army in Vietnam. Although the films explicitly address different wars, and this is important, they are also about contemporaneous issues of war and foreign policy. From this standpoint, both films could be seen as commenting on the Vietnam War. *Patton* is a film from the period when the Vietnam War could be addressed only indirectly in American cinema. (*The Green Berets*, made in 1968, is an interesting exception to the "rule.") Auster and Quart call this period "The War That Dared Not Speak Its Name." [2] *Apocalypse Now*, on the other hand, is one of the first films to directly confront the American experience in Vietnam. If *Apocalypse Now* is to some extent confused, this may be because it tries to fit into one film all that had been left out for more than a decade.

Francis Coppola had major creative roles in both films. He was co-screenwriter of *Patton,* with Edward North; both writers won Academy Awards for their efforts. He was co-screenwriter, director, and producer of *Apocalypse Now,* and therefore had a much broader influence on this later film. Although Coppola's creative personality certainly had an effect on the two films, my essay purposely does not treat him as an auteur. Instead, it will analyze the representation of the military, and the military hero, in relation to issues of history, of sources, and of collective authorship, for both films.

A key point to consider is the relation of fiction and nonfiction in both films. *Patton* is a Hollywood biography, a selective, scripted, acted retelling of a historical figure's life. *Apocalypse Now* is at first glance all fiction, a transposition of Conrad's *Heart of Darkness* to the Vietnam War. But *Apocalypse Now* is based on nonfiction sources as well, including Michael Herr's *Dispatches* and news reports on the case of Colonel Robert Rheault. Col. Rheault, commanding the U.S. Army Special Forces in Vietnam, was arrested in 1969 for the murder of a Vietnamese agent. The ensuing news coverage suggested that the Special Forces were involved in both espionage and guerilla warfare in Vietnam and neighboring countries, with very little centralized oversight or control. Colonel Rheault is one of the sources for the film's Colonel Kurtz. So, both *Patton* and *Apocalypse Now* are mixtures of the fictional and the real. *Patton* leans towards docudrama, whereas *Apocalypse Now* is more symbolic and allusive in its construction.

Patton has usually been discussed as a film with a dual meaning. It can be construed as patriotic, pro-Army, pro-war—presenting Patton as a hero. Or it can be interpreted as antipatriotic, antimilitary, antiwar—presenting Patton as a knave, fool, or psychotic. The film appealed to both pro-war and antiwar audiences in 1970, quite a trick given the polarization of the United States at that moment of the Vietnam War. My view is that the film is primarily a pro-war piece, a portrait of an unorthodox military hero. This is the perspective of the film's major source, Ladislas Farago's biography *Patton: Ordeal and Triumph.*[3] However, the points of view of the film's main collaborators are interestingly mixed. Also, in the charged atmosphere of 1970, the film's presentation of Patton's eccentricities could be interpreted as criticism of the military in general.

Vincent Canby, the influential critic of the *New York Times,* makes the point that *Patton* is primarily the creative product of its sponsoring studio, Twentieth Century – Fox. Canby notes that Darryl Zanuck, longtime production chief of Fox, "always has had a soft spot for the military . . . and Fox has often had military brass on its board of directors."[4] This orientation explains the presence of Frank McCarthy, producer of *Patton,* as an executive at Fox. McCarthy, a high-ranking staff officer in the U.S. Army during World War II, joined Fox as an administrator in 1949. He proposed *Patton,* with himself as producer, to Zanuck in 1951 but had to wait many years to make the film because of opposition from the Patton family. McCarthy, who knew Patton, told Mel Gussow that he wanted "a balanced script."[5] He added in a press release that Patton "was pious and profane, brutal and kind – and we show him with all his faults as well as his virtues."[6] But the film limits its criticism to individual eccentricities, singling out Patton and, to a lesser extent, the British General Montgomery. Unlike Farago's book, it never critiques the top U.S. commanders in Europe, Bradley and Eisenhower. Nor does it explicitly question the goals or means of the military enterprise in general – though hints of such a questioning might be teased out of the portrait of Patton.

If Zanuck and McCarthy are the pro-military hawks behind *Patton,* then Coppola and George C. Scott (who plays Patton) are the closest to being antimilitary doves. Coppola was at the very beginning of his career when he made *Patton;* he had worked on some Roger Corman pictures but had no reputation in big-budget Hollywood films. Patton was unfamiliar to him (he was too young), but he quickly figured out the parameters of what was required. In 1972, perhaps with the benefit of hindsight, Coppola had this to say about the *Patton* project: "Wait a minute, this guy was obviously nuts. If they want to make a film glorifying him as a great American hero, it will be laughed at. And if I write a film that condemns him, it won't be made at all."[7]

Coppola's solution was to write a script that allowed audiences to choose whether to empathize with Patton or to reject him. The film he imagined would be something like a Rorschach test, with audiences finding their own ideas within the pattern. Coppola notes that in the process of production his view of Patton's eccentricity was toned down: "They made it a more conventional war movie."[8]

When Francis Coppola wrote the script for *Patton* in 1965, he was a young writer with no defined political position. George C. Scott, on the other hand, when he acted the role of General Patton, was a major star used to speaking his mind on political issues. Scott's attitude on the Vietnam War had significantly changed from 1965, when he visited South Vietnam and wrote an *Esquire* article strongly backing the American war effort, to 1970, when he called the war an obscenity.[9] Speaking of *Patton*, however, he said that World War II was a war we had to fight, and that Patton was a complicated man who was respected by his troops.[10] Scott insisted that the producers go back to Coppola's script, with its ambivalent treatment of Patton, but his strong support and feeling for the American fighting man put him close to McCarthy and Zanuck. Scott saw the role of Patton as neither a caricature nor an ideological symbol. Scott summarizes the character as follows: "Patton was a mean sonofabitch, but he was also generous to his men . . . There are still things about him I hate and things I admire—which makes him a human being, I guess."[11] By understanding Patton as a flawed but in some ways admirable character, Scott established common ground with his producer, McCarthy. And by insisting on his prerogatives as star, Scott ensured that the film would focus on Patton's sometimes bizarre behavior rather than reverting to a Zanuck war movie.

Despite the auteur theory's emphasis on directors, Franklin Schaffner's contribution to *Patton* is difficult to "read." Schaffner, an up-and-coming director with *Planet of the Apes* (1968) his most recent work, did not have a clear and easily legible connection to General Patton (unlike producer McCarthy, for example). Schaffner seems to have been mainly interested in two things: Patton as a unique character, and the logistical challenges of making a war movie. Schaffner told interviewer Jack Hirschberg that "The intent here was simply to study the character of an enormously controversial, enormously anti-establishment, enormously provocative, enormously skillful professional." Schaffner added that Patton's particular profession, military officer, was "unimportant."[12] From what we see on screen, we can attribute to Schaffner a very good control of the large-scale war sequences and of more intimate moments. In many scenes, we view both the broad panorama of war (e.g., tanks advancing, planes strafing) and Patton's individual role of encouraging his men, planning a next move, etc. In controlling the mise-en-scène and moving along the action, Schaffner's direction is exemplary. Beyond this, he, like Scott, refrained from obvious editorializing.

It is important to remember that the starting point of *Patton* is Ladislas Farago's book, and not the overwhelming complexity of history itself. Farago's book has already created a narrative, eliminated inconvenient episodes and observations, and composed a portrait of Patton the man. The film does a remarkable job of condensing Farago's 800-page book into three hours of screen time (approximately 180 script pages), but two points must be stressed:

1. The book is by no means a complete, omniscient, or objective account of Patton's participation in World War II. It is one view of General Patton.
2. The film has no choice but to deviate from the book, for both negative and positive reasons. Negatively, the narrative *must* be shortened, and therefore characters disappear, incidents are combined, and complex motivations are simplified. Positively, the filmmakers have their own ideas on Patton, in at least one case (McCarthy) based on personal experience, and therefore do not slavishly reproduce Farago's attitudes.

Let us briefly look at both points. First of all, Farago himself has a position on Patton. He finds him to be flawed, sometimes childlike, a prima donna, and yet an exceptionally gifted commander. Farago can be ironic in talking about Patton; speaking of the general's emotional tendencies, he mentions at one point that Patton was "all aflutter." [13] Farago documents Patton's vanity, his willingness to ignore or flout orders, and the episodes (more than one) when he slapped shell-shocked soldiers. But Farago also finds Patton to be a wonderful tactician and strategist, an astute student of military history, a tough and charismatic leader. He suggests that Patton, though a flawed man, was crucial to the Allied war effort, and supports the efforts of his superiors (Bradley, Eisenhower, Marshall, Roosevelt) to utilize and control him.

The film's first choice in adapting Farago is to limit the time period to Patton's campaigns in World War II (1943–1945). The film begins with a scene of Patton addressing his troops at an unspecified time and place; the scene actually took place in France in 1944. Then the action moves to Patton landing in Tunisia in 1943, and from this point the story is strictly chronological. By skipping over General Patton's early life, though, the film

Patton TWENTIETH CENTURY−FOX.
General Patton (George C. Scott) and his orderly/valet Sergeant William
Meeks (James Edwards). Courtesy of Museum of Modern Art/Film Stills
Archive.

avoids comment on Patton's social class. He was born into a wealthy California family and married into an even wealthier family. He lived in luxury
in his various Army postings, renting big houses, keeping strings of polo
ponies, etc. He was therefore different in social class not only from the Army
enlisted men, but also from the officers (including his superiors). The film
suggests Patton's social class only via a few details—his taste for luxury, his
orderly/valet, his knowledge of French. But social class may be a key to
understanding Patton's position as "prima donna" within the U.S. Army—
for example, he had excellent access to politicians and the news media, but
not always the support of these same groups. Social class might also explain
Patton's sympathy in 1945 for the Germans rather than the Russians.

The film also necessarily omits the discussions of strategy and chain of command in the book. The Allied Command, for Farago, is a multilevel negotiation between American and British leaders. Patton's wartime career is contextualized in terms of both administrative structures and the attitudes of such Allied leaders as Bradley, Eisenhower, Marshall, Roosevelt, Montgomery, and Alexander. A Hollywood feature film simply cannot provide this depth of background information, and so the film *Patton* presents only Bradley (friend, then superior), Montgomery (rival within the Allied camp), Bedell Smith (aide to Eisenhower), and Eisenhower (the big boss, unseen) to give context to Patton's activities.

Despite these limitations, historian Paul Fussell comments that the film biography of General Patton "depicts his public behavior during those months [February 1943 to October 1945] with remarkable fidelity." [14] We see Patton's major campaigns, North Africa, Sicily and France; we observe him interacting with his staff, with Gen. Bradley, with soldiers in the field; we listen to his plans, hopes, and frustrations. We observe the man's erudition and his short fuse, his personal bravery and his intolerance for shell-shock, which he perceived as cowardice. History here becomes smoothed out, becomes dominated by narrative and character, but a good deal of Patton's war does make it to the screen.

The most striking and provocative scene in *Patton* is the first one, the long speech which Patton makes in front of an American flag. In the film's original release, this was set up as follows: first there is a two-minute overture with the flag filling the screen. Then Patton steps out, very small, in front of a corner of the huge flag. Then, in close up, he harangues an unseen audience which becomes simultaneously the troops under his command *and* the movie audience of 1970 and later years. This frontal approach to the audience asks us, in a very direct way, "What do you think of this general? What do you think of his profane but powerful oratory? How do you respond when he tells you not only to kill the enemy but to 'rip his guts out'?" Then the rest of the film allows us to test and refine our first impression, as we learn more about the character.

The mise-en-scène of this first scene is certainly powerful. An American flag filling the screen: in the America of 1970 this is an emotional but also controversial image. Is it an outsized appeal to patriotism? Or is it a piece of modern art, a deconstructed symbol? Vincent Canby says that the flag is

The first scene of **Patton** TWENTIETH CENTURY–FOX.
General Patton (George C. Scott) addresses his troops. Courtesy of Museum of Modern Art / Film Stills Archive.

"pure Rauschenberg" (perhaps Jasper Johns would be the better reference), and he compares it to Op art. He also writes, "The opening of the film . . . comes very close to being conscious Camp." [15] Stanley Kauffmann, on the other hand, reports on viewing *Patton* with an audience. To the filmgoers, the flag was an uncomplicated symbol of patriotism and traditional values: "The very first shot is an American flag in vivid color filling the wide, wide screen. . . . Then out steps General Patton, minute against the immense banner, and I felt the audience lunge toward him with relief. Everything was all right again, the old values were safe." [16] For Kauffmann, *Patton* is a well-made appeal to the group President Nixon labeled the "Silent Majority."

Given the two very different responses to the opening of *Patton*, and

Francis Coppola's description of deliberately seeking ambivalence in the screenplay, it may be imprudent to describe a univalent meaning to the film. However, I do think that this film favors one of the two directions. If *Patton* starts and ends in ambivalence, the body of the film stresses the narrative and physical movement of Patton's campaigns. Many factors—narrative, historical, symbolic, physiological—support our involvement with the momentum of the film. This momentum, which might also be called the film's narrative pleasure, can be stopped short by a distancing moment (e.g., Patton's slapping of the soldier), but it remains the dominant factor structuring the audience's attention. Therefore, unless the viewer comes into the movie with an unusual agenda (different from the entertainment-based agenda of Hollywood), most of *Patton* will be seen as a fairly conventional war movie. Though the choice and framing of the subject reflect to some degree the bitter controversies about Vietnam in 1970, the film *Patton* still maintains a close linkage with the consensus-building World War II movie.

Another strategy inflecting the movie toward Patton-as-hero is the development of a good-bad guy protagonist with no serious rivals. This is a familiar device of the 1960s and 1970s, which leads to identification with characters of doubtful morality. In *Bonnie and Clyde,* the spectator identifies with the title characters for multiple reasons: they are young and beautiful; they are robbing socially "bad" institutions; the chief lawman is a nasty character; they are played by movie stars; they are the on-camera centers of attraction. There is room to doubt the main characters (is Clyde really justified in shooting the bank employee?), but in general the film sympathizes with the good-bad guys. *Patton* employs strategies quite similar to those of *Bonnie and Clyde.* General Patton is the focus of identification because he is the *only* character available for audience sympathy. We experience what he experiences, we share his hopes and dreams, and we really have no alternatives for emotional investment. Montgomery is seen as foreign and strange, Bradley is bland and undeveloped, the Germans are on-screen just to show their respect for Patton. Occasionally, a distance develops in the spectator-Patton relationship, but overall the film narrative privileges Patton's subject position and encourages identification.

Paul Fussell, noting this tendency in the film, says that he would prefer a more complex, perhaps multiple-perspectived view of Patton. Such a view might show Patton as a dangerously out-of-control individual, instead of the eccentric-but-brilliant leader of myth. Fussell points to derogatory comments toward Eisenhower and King George VI, plus a disastrous plan to save his son-in-law from a Nazi prison camp, plus a battlefield affair with his niece as evidence of Patton's unreliable behavior. Fussell adds that "there are other real moments that the film wouldn't think of including, such as the sotto voce remark of one disgruntled junior officer to another after being forced to listen to a vainglorious Patton harangue: 'What an asshole!' That would constitute an interesting historic moment. I know it took place because I was the one who said it." [17] In this last passage, Fussell is advocating something like a postmodern history which allows for several conflicting interpretations of historical data.[18] His anecdote also suggests that the soldiers and officers under Patton's command were not passive vessels of the general's greatness; they were individuals with feelings and motivations of their own. A movie about General Patton could incorporate multiple perspectives, including, for example, a junior officer's point of view. This approach might demystify the figure of "the Great Man" Patton while enhancing our understanding of the U.S. war effort during World War II.

Apocalypse Now, which began filming in 1976, was planned as a large-scale, epic production which would break the Hollywood fiction film's silence on the war in Vietnam. Production assistance from the Defense Department was not forthcoming, so the film was made in the Philippines, with helicopters and other equipment borrowed from the U.S.-equipped Philippine armed forces. The Philippine setting and the production's logistical problems led to numerous delays; the troubled production is chronicled in Eleanor Coppola's book *Notes* and the feature-length documentary *Hearts of Darkness*. When *Apocalypse Now* was released in 1979 it was not the first of the postwar Hollywood films on Vietnam; *The Deer Hunter* and *Coming Home* had already received considerable praise. However, *Apocalypse Now* was the broadest and most ambitious Hollywood film on Vietnam made in the 1970s.

Apocalypse Now uses Joseph Conrad's *Heart of Darkness* as a way to understand the United States participation in Vietnam. The novella is clearly marked by British colonialism and has been criticized for this perspective. However, it comes quite late in the colonial period and is cynical about the motivations and morality of the colonists. Although it takes an ethnocentric point of view (as do American novels and films about Vietnam), the darkness it ultimately finds is in the hearts of the colonists. The experience of the African wilderness reveals something about the Europeans, who turn out to be at least as savage and primitive as the indigenous inhabitants of the Congo. This theme from the novella is taken up by the film, which shows from various standpoints the overwhelming carnage and irrationality of war. It concludes with the erratic and savage conduct of Special Forces Colonel Walter Kurtz (Marlon Brando), who has supposedly gone crazy in his Cambodian fort. As in *Heart of Darkness*, Kurtz in *Apocalypse Now* dies in conditions of squalid horror.

The basic narrative pattern of the film is also taken from *Heart of Darkness*. Captain Willard (Martin Sheen) travels upriver on a PT boat to confront and possibly assassinate Colonel Kurtz. The film begins in the "civilized" areas of Saigon and Nha Trang and then moves on a river journey through territory controlled (more or less) by American troops. As in *Heart of Darkness*, the trip upriver leads to progressively stranger and more dangerous experiences. The danger in *Apocalypse Now* comes first from the Viet Cong and North Vietnamese, but also from other sources. The Americans themselves behave with irrational violence, for example when the crew of the boat attacks a Vietnamese sampan. Nature becomes an unfathomable danger, notably when Willard and Chef (Frederick Forrest) go to pick mangoes and confront a tiger. Eventually, the boat arrives in a more primitive environment, where the inhabitants attack with arrows and spears. When Willard and the boat crew get to Kurtz's compound, a ruined temple complex decorated by severed Viet Cong heads, this primitive atavism is in full force. The river trip is a descent into a savage past, a loosening of all civilized restraints.

The journey into the interior, while tied to *Heart of Darkness*, also provides the opportunity for an original fresco of the Vietnam War. Here we see several important scenes. Colonel Kilgore (Robert Duvall) attacks a Vietnamese village so that a group of Californians can surf on "Charlie's point." *Playboy* bunnies descend from a helicopter to give a USO show, only to retreat hastily from a near-riot among the spectators. American soldiers fight Charlie every night at the Do Lung bridge, and Willard learns that (I paraphrase) "No one is in command." The crew of the PT boat boogie upriver to "I Can't Get No Satisfaction" and other rock and roll tunes. These and other scenes suggest that the Americans bring their culture with them, and they cannot escape that culture to interact in a meaningful way with Vietnam. Pierre Schoendorffer made the same point in his Vietnam War documentary *The Anderson Platoon* (1967), saying, "I went back to discover the Vietnam I had left thirteen years before, with the French Army. . . . I discovered, above all, America."

As an adaptation of *Heart of Darkness*, *Apocalypse Now* is a heavily symbolic film, lacking point-to-point correspondence with events of the Vietnam War. However, a second key intertext of the film, the so-called "Green Beret murder case" of 1969, offers a closer link between events and issues in the Vietnam War and the film narrative. In this murder investigation, much reported in the summer and fall of 1969 but now more or less forgotten,[19] seven Green Beret officers and one sergeant were accused of killing a Vietnamese agent, whom they suspected of being a double, or even a triple, agent. The accused included Col. Robert B. Rheault, head of the U.S. Army Special Forces in South Vietnam, and several officers specializing in intelligence. The case drew a great deal of attention in the American press, because it offered a window on aspects of the Vietnam War which were normally considered secret: unconventional warfare, espionage, the Phoenix Program, operations in Cambodia, links between the CIA and the military. The Green Berets contended that the elimination of enemy agents was standard procedure in this war, and that they were being railroaded by the commanding generals in Vietnam, as well as by the CIA.[20] The press speculated on a power struggle between the Special Forces, the Army top command, and the CIA, aimed at reducing the power and autonomy of the Special Forces.

The Special Forces ("Green Berets" is a nickname) had come to Vietnam in the early 1960s as advisors to the South Vietnamese. They organized large local forces (Civilian Irregular Defense Groups) in the mountains and frontier regions of South Vietnam, depending primarily on Montagnard troops. According to Shelby L. Stanton, "the Montagnards were fundamentally village-level aborigines scattered in more than a hundred different tribes that relied on hunting or slash-and-burn farming."[21] They had been driven from the most fertile areas of the country by the ethnic Vietnamese. The Montagnards hated the Vietnamese (of whatever political or ideological stripe) and therefore made alliances first with the French, then with the Americans. The Special Forces–led Montagnard troops had considerable success in gathering information, disrupting North Vietnamese supply lines, and even contesting territory that would otherwise have been ceded to the enemy.

Apocalypse Now has been criticized for inventing its picture of primitive tribesmen and Americans reverting to primitivism, but a good deal of this material comes from the actual experiences of the Special Forces organizing Montagnard soldiers. Stanton comments on the Special Forces–Montagnard relationship as follows: "The Special Forces found the Montagnard aborigines incredibly simplistic and superstitious. To gain their allegiance, the Special Forces soldiers carefully learned tribal customs and studied the local dialects, ate the tribal food, endured the cold, mixed indigenous garb with their uniforms, and participated in rituals and ceremonies. . . . Montagnards accepted only those who shared their lifestyles and dangers." [22] The savagery of the Cambodian camp is wildly exaggerated, drawing on *Heart of Darkness* plus the imaginations of the filmmakers, but it does have some basis in the encounter between Special Forces and Montagnards. For example, the sacrifice of the water buffalo, filmed with the Ifugao people of the Philippines, is not an arbitrary invention. It is analogous to an important ritual of the Montagnards. [23]

The imprint of the Green Beret murder case on *Apocalypse Now* is strongly visible in an early draft of the screenplay by John Milius. [24] In this draft, Captain Willard is summoned to meet with three unnamed Army officers at an Intelligence headquarters near Nha Trang. Here he is given the assignment to find and kill Captain (not Colonel) Kurtz. Unlike the way this scene plays in the finished film, much of the discussion revolves around Colonel Rheult (the name is misspelled) and the Green Beret case. Willard's interlocutors say things like "This Green Beret thing has gotten out of hand" (16) and "We are discrediting Special Forces. That's the nature of the case against Rheult" (18). The scene ends, in the script draft as in the film, with Willard being instructed to "Terminate with extreme prejudice." This evocative phrase first came to public attention during the Green Beret murder case. [25]

In the Milius script draft, Willard next goes to visit Col. Rheult in the Long Binh Jail. Willard justifies his visit in a voice-over: "He was an impressive officer, Rheult. He was different from the others. I would have to kill a man just like him" (25). Rheult says that Kurtz is "a great officer—an exceptional officer." He asks if Willard is "trying to frame Kurtz, too?" (27). The parallelism is clear: Kurtz is like Rheult [*sic*], Rheult is like Kurtz, both are rebels from the military establishment. The link is made one more time in the Milius draft when a letter from Mrs. Kurtz to Kurtz makes prominent mention of "Bob" (Rheult) (82–83).

Milius began writing the script for *Apocalypse Now* in 1969.[26] He probably took material about the Special Forces and the murder case directly from the headlines of the day. He started from the press's somewhat romantic view of a very independent Special Forces role in Vietnam and embroidered it into the story of a renegade officer and his loyal, even reverential, Montagnards. In addition to the broad story outline, some very specific details of *Apocalypse Now* may stem from press coverage of the Green Beret case. For example, the packet of biographical information about Kurtz, including a variety of photos, may be based on the photo essay in *Life* about Col. Rheault.[27]

In the finished film, all references to Col. Rheult or Rheault have been dropped, but parallels to the Green Beret case remain. In the Nha Trang office where Willard is summoned, an unnamed general tells him that Walt Kurtz was a brilliant officer, but when he joined the Special Forces "his ideas . . . methods . . . became . . . unsound." The general mentions that Kurtz was about to be tried for the murder of Vietnamese agents when he disappeared into Cambodia with his worshipful Montagnards. The general continues: "He's out there operating without any decent restraint, totally beyond the pale of any acceptable human conduct." The Kurtz of *Heart of Darkness*, who is tempted by greed and power to behave without restraint, has been conflated with the circumstances of the Green Beret murder case. The meeting in Nha Trang, which now involves two army officers and one civilian (presumably CIA), is still a representation of the Army-CIA-Special Forces tension. And the scene still ends with the phrase "Terminate with extreme prejudice." It is now uttered melodramatically by the CIA man, who says nothing else in the meeting.

Aside from the conflict between regular army and unconventional warfare, a second influence of the Green Beret murder case on the film concerns the morality of murder in wartime. Is it moral to kill Kurtz without a trial? Does his conduct in the field forfeit a right to fair treatment? How does one judge the barbarous behavior of Kurtz in a war marked by many kinds

Apocalypse Now UNITED ARTISTS.
Colonel Kurtz (Marlon Brando) welcomes Captain Willard (Martin Sheen), the man sent to "terminate" him. Courtesy of Museum of Modern Art/Film Stills Archive.

of barbarism? All of these questions were anticipated by the Green Beret murder case, where attorneys for the accused officers tried to document thousands of killings ordered by the CIA, by the Phoenix Program, and by others. In this context, how could officers be prosecuted for doing what they perceived to be absolutely consistent with the war effort?

Apocalypse Now gives complicated and sometimes contradictory answers to these questions. Its sympathies are split between Willard, Kurtz, the crew of the boat, and the Vietnamese peasants. Parts of the film seem to be Hawkish and pro-war; other parts seem to be strongly antiwar. To get at the roots of this complexity, let us examine the film's two primary authors.

We begin with John Milius, one of the more eccentric members of the film school–trained "movie brat" generation in Hollywood. In view of what *Apocalypse Now* eventually became, it is interesting that Milius can be characterized as a romantic lover-of-war with extreme-Right politics. As a filmmaker, he is the screenwriter of *The Man Who Would Be King* and the writer-director of *Conan the Barbarian* and *Red Dawn*. The original plan for *Apocalypse Now* was to film a low-budget action-adventure movie on location in Vietnam,[28] with Milius as writer and George Lucas (several years before *Star Wars*) as director. The film would take a pro-war, action-oriented approach while at the same time supporting and clarifying the "unconventional warfare" methods of the U.S. Army Special Forces. Script drafts for *Apocalypse Now* include a disdainful reference to John Wayne's *The Green Berets* (a film which treats the Special Forces within a very conventional war movie formula): "I've seen the movie."[29]

What Milius and Lucas were thinking about is suggested by the first scene in Milius's previously cited script draft for *Apocalypse Now*. An American soldier rises slowly out of a swamp. The first thing we see is his helmet, inscribed "Gook Killer" in psychedelic writing. This is the beginning of an ambush scene in which bizarrely dressed Special Forces troops successfully attack a group of North Vietnamese regulars. The idea is that American troops will have fun and win the war by adopting Green Beret–style, guerrilla methods. Milius later noted that he and Lucas were "great connoisseurs of the Vietnam War";[30] one imagines young boys with an enthusiasm for all things military.

However, the Milius script draft also contains, in almost exactly the form in which it was eventually released, the long sequence in which Colonel Kilgore ("Kharnage" in the script draft) attacks the village at the surfing point.[31] This sequence, too, suggests that war is fun, but in its gleeful exaggeration of the "Americanization" of the war effort, it becomes a powerful satire of the Vietnam War. If an airborne attack is mounted so that surfers can surf, then the conduct of the war becomes arbitrary, selfish, and out of control. The scene suggests that the Vietnam War has been so taken over by American wealth, technology, and popular culture that all underlying issues and motivations have been muddied. A passage of narration written (by Michael Herr) long after Milius's draft pulls another key theme from the scene: If Colonel Kilgore's bizarre behavior is accepted, why is the army worried about Kurtz?[32] The satire here seems to be sharply critical of the war effort, even though in other sections of the script Milius is pro-war. There is certainly an irreverent edge to Milius's script.

Scriptwriter Milius's attitude to his material might be described as an odd

Apocalypse Now UNITED ARTISTS.
Robert Duvall as the aptly named Colonel Kilgore. Courtesy of Museum of Modern Art/Film Stills Archive.

mixture of enthusiasm, sympathy, and revulsion. Milius clearly relishes the excitement of the opening ambush, the helicopter attack, the exchange of fire at the bridge. Milius even has Willard say, at one point, "I usually liked war" (12). Milius has considerable sympathy for the Special Forces and their unconventional methods—guerrilla warfare, sabotage, incursions into Cambodia. This recapitulates a theme of some Right-wing critics of the Vietnam War, who advocated few or no restraints in the U.S. conduct of the war.[33] It also recalls the generally positive press treatment of the Special Forces during the murder case. However, the use of *Heart of Darkness* as the primary source suggests that Milius also is repulsed by the embrace of barbarism—by executions, severed heads, and so forth. This barbarism may have been largely in Milius's head (he had no first-hand experience with the Vietnam War), but he does seem to be advocating limits in the conduct of war. The contradiction between love and revulsion for the Vietnam War is left unresolved by the Milius script.

Francis Coppola became involved with *Apocalypse Now* as Milius was writing the script in 1969. He originally intended to produce the film for Lucas and Milius, as part of a contract between American Zoetrope (Coppola's production company) and Warner Brothers. However, when Warner Brothers backed out of the contract, Coppola bought back the rights to the *Apocalypse Now* script and eventually decided to direct it himself. Coppola's script draft of December 3, 1975, is similar in narrative design to Milius's earlier draft.[34] Coppola's changes lie mainly in character development and in building a more philosophical context for the trip upriver. However, as Coppola continued to rework the film during production and postproduction, some of the more outlandish scenes were removed: the "gook killer" opening, the crew having sex with the *Playboy* bunnies, more sex at an embattled French rubber plantation. Under Coppola's supervision, *Apocalypse Now* became less a wild adventure in the Vietnam War and more a tragic descent into bestiality and madness.

Coppola's vision of the war is even more evident in the images and sounds than in the narrative. From the opening images, the film becomes an environment of fire, water, and darkness. It presents the imagery of a man-made hell, with napalm, rockets, bombs, and bullets producing almost constant fire and noise, and Kilgore (a version of Mephistopheles?) proclaiming, "I love the smell of napalm in the morning." The film is also crammed with images of limited vision: smoke, water, fog, jungle, and darkness. These elements suggest a lack of awareness, even blindness, characteristic of America's intervention in Vietnam. Willard does not know where he's going or why, the crew knows even less, the officers behind the lines know least of all. Only Kurtz sees more or less clearly, and his awareness has driven him mad. This countercultural view of the follies of war is reinforced by the rock and roll soundtrack, prominently featuring the Doors singing "This Is the End." Mysterious, tragic, satanic, the song provides the proper tone for a film with "Apocalypse" in the title.

Leslie Fiedler has argued that *Apocalypse Now* owes its contradictory, unresolved quality to the collaboration between John Milius the Hawk and Francis Coppola the Dove.[35] His observation is useful, but too simple. Milius is pro-war but also a satirist of war, as discussed above. Coppola, for his part, is critical of the war, especially in the mise-en-scène, but also caught up with the excitement of war. The helicopter attack on the village is an over-the-top satire *and* one of the most exciting, heart-pounding war sequences ever filmed. Adding Wagner's music to the attack (already indicated in the Milius draft, but beautifully realized by Coppola) increases both the visceral effect and the critical distance inherent in this scene. It's a hair-raising moment, but it also recalls European myths of battle and Wagner's link to Nazi ideology. Coppola the Dove can coexist with Milius the Hawk because each shares some of the values of the other.

I would agree with Fiedler that this kind of contradiction does not need to be resolved.[36] *Apocalypse Now* embodies some of the contradictions of the Vietnam War without finding a solution. It does a much better job than *Patton* of balancing two distinct attitudes toward its subject. I do not, however, agree with Coppola's famous statement at the 1979 Cannes Film Festival that his film became identical with the Vietnam War ("We were in the jungle. There were too many of us. We had access to too much money, too much equipment. And little by little, we went insane").[37] This statement, though provocative, masks the fact that *Apocalypse Now* is much better when it provides a critical representation of the Vietnam War, instead of trying to *be* that war.

Patton and *Apocalypse Now* are not polar opposites; they might better be conceptualized as two points on a scale. Both are historical films, with *Patton* taking the conventional approach of dramatized biography and *Apocalypse Now* the less conventional route of combining *Heart of Darkness* and the Green Beret murder case into a synecdochic journey through the Vietnam War. Both films manifest a certain skepticism toward the military enterprise, a skepticism undoubtedly linked to the social context of an unpopular war (the Vietnam War was current news when *Patton* was released in 1970, and a bitter recent memory when *Apocalypse Now* came out in 1979). *Patton*'s skepticism involves showing the eccentricities and weaknesses of its protagonist, but this film still promotes the value and the necessity of "fighting the good fight." *Apocalypse Now*'s skepticism is far more all-encompassing: it presents the experience of the Vietnam War as fragmented, incoherent, and out of control.

The two films' differing positions on the value of war and the purpose of the war movie can be clearly grasped via the portraits of Patton and Kurtz.

We are asked to *believe* in General Patton, the charismatic leader gone only slightly awry. We *cannot believe* in Colonel Kurtz, the charismatic leader gone mad, and this throws us back to the incoherent experience of the ordinary soldier. With the affirmation of the commander as hero, *Patton* builds a case for supporting the U.S. military both historically and in the present. The complexity of its psychological portrait of Patton adds a touch of realism (and may even provide the possibility of reading "against the grain"). With the denial of the commander as hero, *Apocalypse Now* becomes an ironic war movie, deeply questioning the value of military action. The bald, grossly overweight, muttering Kurtz, surrounded by severed heads, becomes emblematic of war's corrosive effect on the individual psyche. However, *Apocalypse Now* is not unequivocally an antiwar piece; it retains a sense of the excitement of war.

General Patton is eccentric but brilliant; Colonel Kurtz is brilliant but mad. Both *Patton* and *Apocalypse Now* participate in a questioning of the American military during, and directly after, the Vietnam War. But *Patton* is ultimately a recuperative film, reconstructing the military hero, whereas *Apocalypse Now* trails off into savagery.

Chapter 8

Shaft

Superfly

Claudine

From Blaxploitation to African American Film

Leadbelly

Killer of Sheep

Films made by and for the African American community have a long history. In the silent film period, Oscar Micheaux and others were already making feature films with black casts for black audiences. In the 1930s, with the advent of sound films, this approach to film was formularized as "race movies," low-budget films for the African American audience which often repeated the most popular white genres: mystery, Western, and so on. Black people appeared in Hollywood films only in stereotyped roles (e.g., the maid played by Hattie McDaniel in *Gone With the Wind*). In the 1950s and 1960s, this began to change as Sidney Poitier and Harry Belafonte became black Hollywood stars. However, Poitier was heavily criticized within the black community for his nonaggressive, nonsexual persona.[1]

The presentation of African Americans in Hollywood film changed dramatically in the years around 1970. In response to the social changes of the time, a series of films starred proud, aggressive African American heroes. Many of these were fairly standard action films featuring black athletes such as Jim Brown, O.J. Simpson, and Fred Williamson. However, more original views of fiercely independent black heroes came from *Sweet Sweetback's Badasssss Song* (Melvin Van Peebles, 1969), *Shaft* (Gordon Parks, 1971), and *Superfly* (Gordon Parks Jr., 1972). These three films used slang, music, fashion, and attitude to define current trends and concerns within the African American community. *Sweetback*, an independently produced film, actually presents violent resistance to the white-dominated status quo. *Shaft* and *Superfly*, both produced within the Hollywood system, show independent characters (one a detective, one a drug pusher) functioning within current social reality. All three films were commercially successful, indicating the black audience's hunger for a new self-image.

The success of the new black action film was soon codified into a genre, popularly called "blaxploitation." The formula was simple: lots of action, lots of sex, and a black hero (or heroine) who is, in Thomas Doherty's words, "invariably dangerous and individualistic."[2] The films were made cheaply and often financed by white producers. The label blaxploitation (black + exploitation) suggests that a degree of cynicism was involved. Nevertheless, this genre was surprisingly popular in the early 1970s. According to Ed Guerrero, approximately sixty blaxploitation films were made.[3] Darius James, in the quirky interview book *That's Blaxploitation*, presents at length the oral history of blaxploitation (as delivered by filmmakers of the era).[4]

The history of African American film in the 1970s can be considered a two-part process: first, the rise and fall of the blaxploitation genre; second, the elaboration of alternatives to blaxploitation. The black action hits of the early 1970s showed that there was an African American audience eager to see more positive treatment of the black community on film. The success of blaxploitation provided opportunities for a whole generation of African American actors, directors, and writers. But the repetition of blaxploitation ultimately proved unsatisfactory to both the creative talent and the audience. Therefore, by the mid-1970s the African American film was moving in other directions, including comedy, big-budget musical, and social drama. So much had changed so rapidly that critic James Monaco speaks of "the Black revolution in film."[5] This chapter cannot provide a full history of the African American film of the 1970s, but it will suggest the line of development by discussing two of the founding films of blaxploitation, *Shaft* and *Superfly*, plus three films which depart from blaxploitation.

Shaft (1971) is a reworking of the hard-boiled detective story popularized

Shaft M G M .
Private detective John Shaft (Richard Roundtree) meets with the New York City Police Department. Courtesy of Museum of Modern Art/Film Stills Archive.

by novelists Dashiell Hammett and Raymond Chandler and brought to the
screen in such classic films as *The Maltese Falcon* (1941), *Murder My Sweet*
(1944), and *The Big Sleep* (1946). Private detective John Shaft (Richard
Roundtree) is hired by Bumpy Jonas (Moses Gunn), head of the Harlem
rackets, to find Bumpy's kidnapped daughter Marcie. Bumpy suggests that
radical leader Ben Buford (Christopher St. John), head of the Lumumbas,
may be involved. Police lieutenant Vic Anderozzi (Charles Cioffi) also wants
Shaft to look into a possible "war" in Harlem. After some violent misadventures, Shaft discovers that the Mafia has kidnapped Marcie in a dispute over
the Harlem drug trade. Shaft, Buford, and Buford's men attack the Mafia
in a Greenwich Village hotel. Marcie is freed, and Shaft calls Vic to say that
the case has busted wide open—Vic should now close it himself.

What is immediately striking about *Shaft* is the look and sound of the
film. Gordon Parks was, in 1971, a world-renowned still photographer. He

Shaft MGM.
John Shaft (Richard Roundtree) on the streets of Manhattan. Courtesy of Museum of Modern Art/Film Stills Archive.

had been, for example, a top photojournalist at *Life* magazine. *Shaft* does a good job of showing the variety and vitality of New York in winter: the busy streets of midtown, the stoops and alleys of Harlem, a hip Greenwich Village coffeehouse. Parks's hero, played by Richard Roundtree, looks like a confident, independent man with his own sense of style. He's tall, athletic, well dressed in leather coat, sport jacket, and turtleneck. He acts like the king of New York, striding through a variety of neighborhoods with equal authority. When Roundtree is moving and Isaac Hayes's score is playing, *Shaft* is an exceptional movie. Roundtree is good in dialogue scenes involving jive talking or conflict, but less impressive in moments of exposition.

Isaac Hayes won a well-deserved Academy Award for his music for *Shaft*. The opening theme over the credits, percussive and bluesy with a stuttering electric guitar, suggests that this will not be just another Hollywood movie. Eventually, the theme adds a vocal track, with male and female voices providing background on John Shaft. At one point the vocal becomes call and response and we hear:

That Shaft is a mean mother . . .
Watch your mouth!
Talking about Shaft.

This exchange suggests first, a sense of fun, and second, that the film will push the limits of polite discourse, but not too far.[6] Isaac Hayes also provides, early in the film, a wonderful song introducing the community of Harlem. After this, the music becomes less obtrusive, underlining the action scenes but not becoming an important, contrapuntal line. However, the music of the opening third of the film suggests how crucial music can be in defining a black attitude and milieu.

Shaft is an adaptation of a novel by Ernest Tidyman, with a script by Tidyman and John D. F. Black. Tidyman, a white man, had a background as a newspaper reporter and a writer of action scripts (including *The French Connection*). His novel and script for *Shaft* raise the issue of black revolution, via Ben Buford and the Lumumbas, but only to scare and titillate the audience. A black militant "army" exists in *Shaft* (though Buford's men are less skilled at fighting than Shaft), but the threat of race war is a false lead. The conflict feared by Lieutenant Anderozzi turns out to be a conflict between criminal gangs. Providing the Mafia as Shaft's main antagonists means that the black audience can cheer for black over white without making an emotional commitment to Buford's political group. It also means that a white audience can enjoy *Shaft* without being threatened by armed revolt. Gordon Parks described *Shaft* as an entertainment, "a Saturday night fun picture which people go to see because they want to see the black guy winning."[7]

A further social/political message lies in the behavior of the main character, in Shaft as role model. John Shaft is a proud black man. He is not a separatist like Buford; he functions in both the black and white communities. Bumpy's bodyguard actually calls him "Snow White," but Shaft does remain in touch with his roots. At one point he says: "I got two problems, baby, I was born black and I was born poor." Shaft is comfortable and at home on the streets of Harlem and in a bar in Greenwich Village. An early shot even shows him striding through a host of taxis in Midtown, against the light—no mean feat. Shaft is also aggressively sexual. He has a middle-class black girlfriend, who lives with her child in a nice apartment. This arrangement does not keep him from spending the night with a pretty white woman (when asked if he's interested, Shaft replies, "I'm alive."). In its sexual attitudes, *Shaft* is a somewhat more realistic version of a James Bond film, with women presented mainly as bed partners. This macho attitude became a central element of blaxploitation.

Superfly, directed by Gordon Parks Jr., is clearly derivative of *Shaft*. *Superfly* begins with shots of the New York streets accompanied by a percussive rhythm and blues tune, this time by Curtis Mayfield. The main character, Priest (Ron O'Neal), has sex with both a black woman and a white woman. Black militants appear in *Superfly*, as in *Shaft*, but in both films they are seen as more or less irrelevant to the everyday problems of the hero. Most importantly, Priest, like John Shaft, is an aggressive, confident black man who achieves considerable autonomy in the dangerous world of New York City.

The major difference between *Superfly* and *Shaft* lies in the protagonist's profession. *Shaft* is a private detective, a man licensed by society to carry a gun, to investigate crime, even to commit violent acts on occasion (or so the conventions of detective fiction would suggest). The detective character combines a great deal of individual freedom with at least some degree of social responsibility. Priest, on the other hand, is a cocaine dealer and a social outlaw. Priest wears the elaborate, expensive costumes of the dealer or the pimp—long fur coat, broad-brimmed hat, double breasted suit. His hair is very long at the sides, and he has a huge moustache.[8] Priest is a user as well as a pusher, and in the most flamboyant touch of all he typically snorts cocaine from a crucifix/coke spoon he wears around his neck.

The less than exceptional plot of *Superfly* involves Priest's attempt to earn a quick half-million dollars and "get out of the life." He becomes a middleman for a group of "dirty" policemen, all of them white, and finds that his new bosses won't let him quit. In a final confrontation, Priest meets the big boss, deputy police commissioner Riordan. Riordan threatens Priest's life, but Priest responds that he has a murder contract out on Riordan and his family. If Priest dies, so do they. Having vanquished whitey, Priest walks off into the sunset.

Unlike *Easy Rider,* which glossed over the heroes' drug dealing to stress their liberty, *Superfly* presents the life of the drug dealer in meticulous detail. Curtis Mayfield's fine song "Pusher Man," heard on several occasions, suggests the excitement of cocaine but also the tragedy of addiction ("I've gotta Jones / Runnin' through my bones"). At one point, Gordon Parks Jr. presents a long, multiscreen montage of still images on the preparation, distribution, and consumption of cocaine. The montage shows, among other things, that many kinds of people, white as well as black, use cocaine. Parks Jr.'s focus on cocaine allows for realistic observation of a distinctive subculture, but it runs the risk of glorifying the drug and the dealers. If Priest is a hero (and he clearly is), then in the terms of the film cocaine must be all right.

Superfly's only strategy for eluding an endorsement of cocaine is to blame everything on the white man. Early in the film, Priest's partner Eddie (Carl Lee) says about dealing: "I know it's a rotten game. It's the only one the Man left us to play." The Man here is the white power structure, the same power structure which, as we eventually find out, controls large-scale cocaine dealing in Harlem. So, the only way to be free is to be a dealer, but a big dealer is led back inexorably to the Man. The crooked cops kill two of Priest's associates in the film, including his mentor Scatter (Julius Harris), but Priest himself takes great glee in outwitting them. As in *Shaft,* the point of *Superfly* is "to see the black guy winning." But the implicit question posed by Gordon Parks Jr.'s film is whether the audience can accept a hero from the drug trade.

A very different picture of the African American community is provided by *Claudine* (1974). Claudine (Diahann Carroll) is a thirty-six-year-old twice-divorced mother of six, who lives with her children in a New York City apartment. She is on welfare *and* she has a job as housecleaner for a wealthy couple in the suburbs. In other words, Claudine is a welfare cheat. She is also quietly heroic as she keeps her family together, confronts a number of crises, and embarks on a relationship with a man.

Claudine is a refreshing movie made from ordinary lives, a mixture of neorealism and romantic/family comedy. All the main characters are black, except for the nosy social worker. We are far from blaxploitation here; *Claudine* includes no guns and no killing. It could be a movie made for television, except for two things. First, the film is sexually frank beyond the limits of

Claudine TWENTIETH CENTURY − FOX.
Diahann Carroll as Claudine, a twice-divorced woman on welfare. Courtesy of Museum of Modern Art / Film Stills Archive.

1970s television, though not beyond the PG rating. Second, the film presents
a moral and ideological position rarely seen on American television.

The impetus for the story involves Claudine accepting a dinner invitation
from Roop (James Earl Jones), a garbage collector of about her age. Despite
an inauspicious first evening and resistance from her children, they are soon
a couple. Claudine is pushed and pulled between the problems of her family
and the relationship with Roop. Roop is caught between a developing love
for Claudine and the child support he must pay for his own children. Both
members of the couple have little freedom of action because of past mis-
takes. Also, Claudine's relationship with a man brings with it further hazards
from the Welfare Department. If Roop gives her anything, it's supposed to
be deducted from her welfare stipend. If she marries, she loses her welfare

money, though the children will continue to receive their stipends. Strange as this may seem, the system is set up to encourage single female heads of household.

Claudine and Roop survive these conditions with surprising grace, though Roop does go through an episode of drunkenness and despair. In a reversal of cliché, the children are more bitter than the adults about life in the inner city. Francis (Eric Jones), one of Claudine's little boys, tells Roop his ambition is to be invisible when he grows up; Francis often writes or draws instead of speaking. Charles (Lawrence Hilton-Jacobs), Claudine's oldest boy, joins a militant Black Power group. Unfortunately, this group seems to be both dangerous to its members and ineffective. He also has a vasectomy at age eighteen, so he will not bring more children into the world. Charlene (Tamu), the oldest girl, becomes pregnant at sixteen, thus repeating the cycle of poverty and dependence. She talks about living with her boyfriend and finding a job, but she knows her prospects are dim. When she discovers the pregnancy, Claudine beats Charlene with a hairbrush, then hugs her fiercely.

As opposed to current ideas about welfare and the perpetuation of poverty, this film sees welfare as essential to maintaining dignity and family stability. Claudine has had some bad breaks in life; welfare is her family's safety net. The fathers of her kids are presumably not available or not able to pay child support, and welfare is the support of last resort. Claudine's struggle to raise a family with welfare and the illegal housekeeping job requires intelligence, determination, devotion, and stamina. This welfare mother is a role model.

The production history of the film adds an interesting twist to the view of welfare as a necessary and positive part of the black community. *Claudine* was the first film produced by Third World Cinema Corporation, a New York−based company founded by actor-director Ossie Davis in collaboration with a number of other show-business figures: Rita Moreno, James Earl Jones, Brock Peters, Diana Sands, Godfrey Cambridge, Piri Thomas, John O. Killens, and Hannah Weinstein.[9] Third World Cinema had two objectives: (1) to train blacks and other minorities for work in the film industry, and (2) to make feature films from a minority perspective. Much of the funding for the organization came from federal grants, including $200,000 from the U.S. Manpower Career and Development Administration, and $400,000 from the Model Cities program.[10] This is a remarkable way to launch a film company, though the goal of training minorities for high-paying crew positions is laudable. Despite Third World Cinema's partial dependence on the federal government (I do not know whether any production funds for *Claudine* came from a government source), the film is highly critical of the welfare system. The film suggests that welfare is a right and that federal caseworkers should not be monitoring their welfare clients.

Claudine certainly gets beyond the genre limitations of blaxploitation set by *Shaft* and *Superfly*. It is a well-told story about people and emotions which happens to be set in the black ghetto. The two stars are wonderful American actors who happen to be black. Diahann Carroll as Claudine speaks out to her children and to Roop with a moral force. She refuses to apologize for having six children, and she objects to the stereotype of welfare mother as morally lax. James Earl Jones as Roop is handsome and emotionally powerful; it is good to see him play a role outside of genre stereotypes. Roop has four children of his own. He never sees them, but his wages are garnisheed for their support. Though Roop is generally a happy and outgoing man, even he is troubled by the prospect of finding a way to support his children, plus Claudine's family.

Claudine's strength is also its weakness. The two stars seem to be "larger than life," too beautiful and perfect for their modest social positions. Diahann Carroll, who established a national reputation as star of the TV sitcom "Julia" (1968–1971), has the figure and posture of a fashion model. James Earl Jones, already in 1974 a stage, film, and TV star, has the presence and emotional range of a Shakespearian actor. We often see powerful actors in modest social roles in the theater, and to some extent in Hollywood films. But in a film of neorealist ambitions, this kind of "larger than life" acting can be a problem. Imagine Cary Grant playing the lead role in *The Bicycle Thief*, a casting choice which director Vittorio de Sica refused. With a Hollywood star, *The Bicycle Thief* would move closer to melodrama and farther from a socially rooted "slice of life." Something similar happens in *Claudine*. With Diahann Carroll and James Earl Jones, the film becomes more accessible to an audience but less successful in conveying the mood and texture of the community. It threatens at times to become a conventional romantic comedy.

Still, writer-director John Berry, a veteran of the Hollywood blacklist who happens to be white, has done a creditable job of portraying the working/welfaring poor in an African American community. Though not ignoring topical references (e.g., the Black Power group), he focuses on social class rather than race in defining Claudine and her circle. This cuts through many stereotypes and provides a fresh look at families who depend on welfare. The film suggests that economic dependence is not inevitably linked to moral decline. Instead, people on welfare are complex human beings and valuable citizens.

Leadbelly (1976), directed by Gordon Parks Sr., is an interesting response to the blaxploitation film and to white packaging of black culture. It tells the story of Huddie Ledbetter, nicknamed "Leadbelly," a historical figure who was a crucial part of the popularization of the Blues music of the rural South. The film begins in Angola State Prison in Louisiana in the 1930s, where John Lomax and his son Alex, representing the Library of Congress, have come to record the convict Ledbetter. These recordings sparked a great deal of interest in Leadbelly, the Blues, and folk music generally. According to Michael Paris, most of the interest came from the white middle class, and John Lomax presented Leadbelly's music as "folkloric" to fit the needs of this cultured audience.[11] Gordon Parks's film recognizes the importance of Leadbelly's "discovery" but also critiques the Lomaxes' motivations and reclaims Leadbelly as an exemplary figure for the black community.

The bulk of the film occurs as a flashback from the Lomax-Leadbelly recording session. We see Huddie Ledbetter as a hot-tempered young musician fleeing his home after a drunken fight. He moves first to Shreveport, where he plays in a black whorehouse; then he travels to Texas, where he meets the legendary Blues musician Blind Lemon Jefferson. Ledbetter is repeatedly in trouble with the law. At one point he starts a brawl at a white dance because his employer (a racist drunk) insists that he play several hours extra for no pay. He is in and out of jail and eventually finds himself working on a prison chain gang. He is pardoned by Texas governor Roy Neff because of his musical talent. Returning home to Louisiana, he defends himself against some white toughs and immediately lands back in prison, where the Lomaxes find him.

Leadbelly asks what John Lomax will do with his music and objects to Lomax's notion of collecting songs "like they's butterflies." Leadbelly announces that he will sing his own songs in Washington, Chicago, Memphis, and New York. Six months later, when he is released from prison, Leadbelly proclaims, "They ain't broke my body, they ain't broke my mind, they ain't broke my spirit." An end title confirms that after his release, Leadbelly "sang his way across America, all the way to Carnegie Hall."

As presented by Gordon Parks, Huddie Ledbetter is far from a saint. He is headstrong, quick to pull a knife or gun, not a planner or a thinker. He is more faithful to his music than to the women in his life, though he does have a long-term relationship with Martha, a woman he meets in the cotton fields of Texas. Yet Huddie does have one admirable quality: he refuses to be objectified and mistreated by the white men who rule the segregated South. Even in prison, he insists on the dignity of fighting back when he is beaten and abused. Huddie has to learn by bitter experience that physical violence is not the only way of fighting; in the words of an inmate friend, "when they wants to kill you, just living is winning."

Huddie's newfound patience is expressed in the almost surreal scene where he is called to play before Governor Neff. The scene begins with a young white boy, impeccably dressed in a white suit, walking behind a black chain gang at work. The camera pulls back and we see that a formal garden party, with everyone in white, has come to the prison grounds to hear Leadbelly play. Leadbelly becomes a grateful, shuffling Negro in this scene, and he sings a song asking Governor Neff for a pardon. The governor, laughing and lording it over the scene, promises that pardoning Leadbelly will be the last thing he does in office. Some years later, Leadbelly is released, because Governor Neff kept his word. This scene is both an expression of white privilege and an indication of the large role chance plays in individual lives.

The retelling of Ledbetter's life makes him not a revolutionary, not a political figure of any kind, but still an embodiment of black resistance. He fights back, he perseveres, and ultimately he wins his freedom. Unlike John Shaft, whose heroism is mainly a matter of style, Ledbetter's struggle involves key historical issues. Shaft goes out to rescue Marcie Jonas for a variety of reasons (professionalism, money, perhaps even fun), but no social, political, or ethical principle is invoked. In general, blaxploitation is about action, not ideas. *Leadbelly* has its share of sex and violence, but it is also about black-white relations, the suppression of black men by the prison system, destructive behavior within the black community, the economics and culture of the black South, the role of music in black culture. In other words, Gordon Parks has moved from a poetics of style to more fundamental matters.

As a musical film, *Leadbelly* takes Huddie Ledbetter out of the historicist framework of "collector" John Lomax and restores his music to the black community. Most of the music in the film is diegetic and attached to a specific cultural setting. We hear, for example, the music of the whorehouses and bars on Fannin Street in Shreveport; music of black and also white dances; music of the cotton fields; music of the chain gang. At one point we see a train and hear Ledbetter singing "Rock Island Line"; this appears to be nondiegetic music, but then the film cuts to Ledbetter playing in a black passenger car to an appreciative audience. *Leadbelly* also recapitulates the old adage that the emotion of the Blues can come only from lived experience. In Shreveport, Leadbelly is a young, naïve guitar virtuoso. His employer and lover Miss Eula (Madge Sinclair) tells him, "You got to feel the Blues." After a life of violent incidents and prison terms, this is not a problem; Leadbelly has learned to feel the Blues.

Though *Leadbelly* was an artistic advance over *Shaft*, it did not repeat the commercial success of the earlier film. According to Gordon Parks himself, *Leadbelly* suffered from a change of administrations at Paramount. When Barry Diller took over, he had no interest in supporting and promoting *Leadbelly*.[12] James Monaco reports that the film "was dumped with an inefficient ad campaign and quick, perfunctory bookings."[13] Parks responded by leaving Hollywood and recommitting his attention to photography and other interests.

Killer of Sheep (1977) is a low-budget, black-and-white film written and directed by Charles Burnett that demonstrates the possibility of making African American films differently—out of the Hollywood mainstream—in the 1970s. The film presents the story of Stan, a slaughterhouse worker (thus "killer of sheep"), and his family in a poor, black neighborhood of Los Angeles. Stan is beaten down by work, poverty, and the chaotic lives of those around him, yet he manages to hold a job and maintain strong relationships with his wife and daughter. His son, perhaps twelve years old, seems to be wandering off into the purposeless, violent life of the ghetto, but this may be only a temporary stage. At the end of the film, for all his troubles, Stan can actually smile.

Ntongela Masilela describes Charles Burnett as a member of the first

wave of the "Los Angeles School" of African American and African independent filmmakers.[14] Other members of this group, who studied at UCLA in
the 1970s, are Haile Gerima, Ben Caldwell, Larry Clark, Jamaa Fanaka, Billy
Mayberry, and the critic/historian Teshome Gabriel. The importance of the
university setting was twofold: (1) it provided an opportunity for screening,
discussion, and practice of non-Hollywood approaches to narrative film;
and (2) the members of the group inspired each other and helped each other
to make feature films. Given the generally low percentage of film students
who become successful filmmakers, it is remarkable that this group produced two major talents (Burnett and Gerima), in addition to others who
made promising films in both commercial and noncommercial styles.

Charles Burnett acknowledges the influence of the British documentary
school of the 1930s and the Italian neorealist movement on his films. He
studied at UCLA with Basil Wright, perhaps the most visually eloquent of
the Grierson group of documentarists. Burnett describes Wright's approach
to teaching documentary as follows: "In the films he discussed, every shot
contained a human element or touch. The subjects in front of the camera
were treated like *people,* not just props and objects and things to be manipulated."[15] *Killer of Sheep* does have strong documentary qualities. It was shot
on location, with hand-held camera and inexperienced actors. The photography shows, without editorializing, the grim surroundings and the sometimes cruel, sometimes compassionate interactions between people in the
neighborhood.

Since *Killer of Sheep* is a scripted, fiction film using documentary techniques, a strong link can be made to Italian neorealism. *Killer of Sheep* is a
portrait of a poor family in desperate trouble, and like *Claudine,* it bears
some resemblance to Vittorio de Sica's *The Bicycle Thief.* However, in *The
Bicycle Thief* the trouble facing the poor family is specific: the hero needs a
bicycle to keep a job, and the bicycle is stolen. Aside from this problem, both
the family and the surrounding cultural milieu are generally supportive. In
Killer of Sheep, the trouble is diffuse: crime is endemic, violence is endemic,
jobs are low-paying and spirit-sapping, people in the neighborhood have
stopped trying to build a life.

What distinguishes *Killer of Sheep* from neorealism, and previous African
American films, is a unique, fragmented audiovisual style. Story is minimized in favor of observation, and the spectator is left to make his or her

own inferences and conclusions. Many scenes have little or no dialogue but contain images verging on the symbolic. We see the harsh working conditions at the slaughterhouse, Stan's son at violent play, mother and daughter putting on makeup, daughter playing with a white doll, and so on. Continuity is often dispensed with, and the sense of a totalized situation comes via juxtaposition and accretion. The dialogue sequences present some of the temptations of the black ghetto—two men proposing that Stan join them in committing a crime, a visit to a "friend" who explains that he just doesn't care if someone kicks his injured nephew. Stan suffers from the surrounding conditions; he has problems with both insomnia and impotence. Yet he stubbornly persists, with the effort and the patience of Sisyphus, in building a life.[16] In the film's system, a simple scene of dancing with one's wife can become life affirming.

Killer of Sheep might be described as a non-Hollywood film at the boundary of narrative, documentary, and experimental. It requires that the spectator actively work at creating a meaning for the film. In this particular instance, at least, the formal experimentation leads to a new content, because *Killer of Sheep* presents the ebb and flow of ghetto life in a way unavailable to more conventional narrative. Every scene has a certain amount of autonomy, and yet it links to other scenes and to a sense of the whole. The effect is somewhat akin to Jim Jarmusch's isolated tableaux in *Stranger than Paradise* (1984), but *Killer of Sheep* avoids the blackouts punctuating Jarmusch's film. Charles Burnett manages to balance fragmentation and connection in a precarious yet stimulating way.

Despite its ultra-low budget, *Killer of Sheep* is sometimes described as a masterpiece—and I would concur with this assessment.[17] Unfortunately, it is probably too experimental for a mainstream movie audience. Making films differently and finding an audience is a very knotty problem. Burnett and his UCLA contemporary Haile Gerima succeeded in reaching broader audiences only in the 1990s: Burnett with *To Sleep with Anger* (1990), and Gerima with *Sankofa* (1993).

Chapter 9

Hester Street

An Unmarried Woman

Girlfriends

Starting Over

Head over Heels/Chilly Scenes of Winter

Coming Home

The China Syndrome

Feminisms

One of the most controversial ideas of the 1970s was feminism: the idea that women were discriminated against in both Western and non-Western societies and that gender roles needed to be first analyzed and then reshaped by social and political processes. Feminism was an important force in the arts, in the universities, in the workplace, in the political arena. Feminist writers such as Betty Friedan, Kate Millett, and Gloria Steinem became household names, as did such antifeminist figures as Phyllis Schlafly and Anita Bryant. A very public debate swirled around women's rights, women's roles, and women's psychology.

Surprisingly little of this debate found its way to the Hollywood film industry. The key films of the early 1970s, whether radical or conservative, are overwhelmingly about the problems of men (consider *Easy Rider, Midnight Cowboy, The Godfather, The French Connection, Dirty Harry, Jaws*).

Only a few films seriously examine women's psychology (e.g., *Klute*, from 1971). By mid-decade, romantic comedies, always sensitive to fashion, had begun to sort out some features of the new battle of the sexes. And at the end of the decade, we see both strongly feminist and strongly antifeminist films. But there is no great feminist director, and no great feminist master-piece, in the American film industry of the 1970s. Hollywood seems to have resisted this strand of social change more than it resisted the youth culture or the antiwar movement or the Black Pride movement. Any changes in the sexual politics of American film have been gradual, incremental.

To illustrate the slow progress of feminism in 1970s American film I have chosen to look at a mix of independent and Hollywood films. Discussion of these films is organized thematically, rather than via strict chronology, to suggest the range of responses to feminism. As a secondary emphasis of this chapter, I explore the influence of directors (Joan Micklin Silver, Claudia Weill) and actresses (Jill Clayburgh, Jane Fonda) on the content and style of their films.

ETHNICITY AND THE AMERICAN PAST

Joan Micklin Silver's first film, *Hester Street* (1975), is a low-budget, black-and-white production based on the novel *Yekl* by Abraham Cahan. Its subject, broadly construed, is ethnic consciousness. What constitutes an American? What is the relationship between our cultures of origin and the common American culture we (to a greater or lesser extent) embrace? Within the film industry, *Hester Street* is part of the breakdown of a white, Anglo-Saxon–oriented Hollywood in favor of a far more diverse ethnic stew. Italian American, Jewish American, and African American films are the most prominent non-WASP groupings in the new, ethnically conscious American film of the 1970s.

Hester Street is a story of assimilation set in 1896 on the Lower East Side of Manhattan. Jake (Steven Keats) is a Russian Jewish immigrant who has been in America for three years. He works as a sweatshop tailor and social-izes with a group of young, single immigrants. The group is aggressively secular and Americanized, with men and women going to a dancing school run by the attractive Mamie (Dorrie Kavanaugh). Jake is pulled away from this group by the arrival of his wife, Gitl (Carol Kane), and his son, Yossele

(Paul Freedman), at Ellis Island. He is overjoyed to see his son, whom he immediately names Joey, but much cooler to Gitl, who wears the traditional wig of a married Jewish woman. Jake is more interested in Mamie than in his wife.

Left alone much of the time, Gitl develops friendships with her landlady and with Jake's subtenant Bernstein (Mel Howard). Bernstein is a former Yeshiva student who works in the sweatshop by day but still studies Torah at night. He thus maintains the traditional Jewish values of Eastern Europe. Jake eventually sends an intermediary to ask Gitl for a divorce (a "get," in Yiddish). She agrees, and when the divorce is completed Jake and Mamie go off to City Hall to be married. Gitl and Bernstein are also planning a marriage.

Though Jake is the active, aggressive character, and he has the greatest amount of screen time, the film's sympathy is with Gitl. We see scenes of her bewilderment in New York, knowing nobody and totally dependent on a husband who avoids her. Wide-eyed, timid, and lonely, she struggles with a new environment. Gradually Gitl learns a bit of English and develops a support network of sympathetic women. Silver and actress Carol Kane do a wonderful job of developing Gitl's character nonverbally, through facial expressions, posture, changes of dress. For example, at one point she bravely abandons the wig and greets Jake with her own, very curly hair peeking out of a kerchief. He is so angry that he pulls her hair, because she still does not correspond to American ideas of beauty. Gitl is crushed.

Gitl is ultimately not, however, a victim. In the scene of negotiating the get, she silently forces Jake's intermediary to raise the price. The scene fades out at one hundred dollars, but we later learn that the agreed amount was three hundred dollars! This is almost the entire fortune which Mamie has laboriously saved—so one of the attractions of Jake's Americanized girl-friend has been removed. Additionally, though the announced purpose of the get is to free Jake to marry Mamie, it is clear that Gitl will end up with the more compatible Bernstein. At one point, Gitl tells Bernstein she will buy a grocery store with the three hundred dollars. Gitl eventually emerges as a very practical woman, and Jake as a man manipulated by the women in his life. Gitl is also becoming assimilated, though at her own pace. In the scene where the rabbi officiates at the get, she declares emphatically that her son's name is "Joey."

Hester Street MIDWEST FILMS.
The bewildered Gitl (Carol Kane), a Jewish immigrant to late-nineteenth-century New York. Courtesy of Museum of Modern Art / Film Stills Archive.

Sonya Michel points out that the film's portrait of male-female relations is entirely consistent with the stressful experiences of Jewish immigrants arriving one hundred years ago in America. In East European shtetl life, the most prestigious role for men was Talmudic scholar. Women were expected to work, to aid their men, sometimes to be the sole support of the family. Thus, Gitl's practical business abilities would have been culturally acquired.

But in the American society, men were expected to work and to support a family, whereas women were supposed to be beautiful and "ladylike." Some immigrants, like Jake, plunged into this new set of social values, while others, like Gitl and Bernstein, found them distressing.[1] Audiences of 1975 may have found the clash of values analogous to the contemporary uproar about gender and social change.

However, Jake, too, may be conflicted about the new values. The film hints that Jake and Gitl's split has to do with guilt as well as assimilation. An early scene fades out with Jake and Mamie on a couch in Mamie's rented room, with other boarders sleeping close by. A sexual relationship is suggested, though not confirmed. When Gitl comes to New York, Jake specifically avoids her in bed. Then in a later scene, Mamie rejects Jake's advances (she has learned about his wife), and he goes to visit a prostitute—not for the first time. These brief scenes lay the basis for another explanation of the divorce. Jake may be ashamed of his conduct; he is divorcing Gitl because he has not lived up to her (and his) high standards. The nonverbal cues in the get scene suggest a swirl of emotion around Jake and Gitl—attraction, guilt, anger.

Though the 1970s was known for nostalgic films, the Lower East Side in the 1890s is an extraordinary subject, to say the least. Joan Micklin Silver deserves much credit for getting audiences involved with a slow-moving, black-and-white film which is partly in a foreign language (Yiddish). Visually, the film is quietly competent, paying detailed attention to the clothes and furniture and street scenes of its setting. There is little action, but a depth of character and ideas carries this example of "chamber cinema." *Hester Street* was self-distributed by Raphael Silver (Joan's husband), because no major studio would support it, and was surprisingly successful on the art film circuit.

INDEPENDENT WOMEN

An Unmarried Woman (1978), directed by Paul Mazursky, is the first star vehicle for Jill Clayburgh. It is also one of the first Hollywood films to represent feminist-influenced attitudes toward love, sex, marriage, work, women's friendships, and so on. Clayburgh plays Erica Benton, an upper-middle-class wife and mother living in Manhattan, whose husband, Martin

(Michael Murphy), confesses he is in love with a younger woman. Martin moves out, so Erica and her fifteen-year-old daughter, Pattie, are on their own. After a great deal of pain and stress, Erica begins to find her way as an "unmarried woman." She meets Saul (Alan Bates), a painter, at the gallery where she works and starts an affair with him. Saul is a wonderful man, yet Erica refuses to spend the summer in Vermont with him. She clings to her independence.

The above outline is very simple because *An Unmarried Woman* is a film stressing performances and visuals, not plot. For example, Erica is always doing something. She jogs, ice skates, mimics a ballerina; she walks, takes a cab, goes to lunch, to dinner, to parties; she works, sees a therapist, spends time with friends, spends time with her kid. Even in the rockiest times, she keeps active and accomplishes a lot. So, by the accretion of small details, we get a positive sense of this character. Martin, on the other hand, is morose and not very functional outside of his Wall Street job. Martin can barely jog; Erica goes by him on a couple of occasions. But Saul is competent and comfortable not only in his work but in the bedroom, at a party, even in the tricky scene where he meets Pattie. When we see Martin in his spacious office, he's doing nothing; Saul, on the other hand, is a very physical, self-assured painter.

Another key to Erica's character is that she's never entirely isolated. She has a group of women friends who meet once a week for dinner or just to talk. Erica is the third of the four women to seek a divorce. This group is described once as a "club" and once, in a self-deprecating way, as "consciousness raising." The two labels are very apt, because this group falls somewhere between a traditional and unthreatening women's club and a more self-consciously feminist women's support group. Writer-director Mazursky here shows how a feminist idea can enter into and be softened by middle-class customs. When things get particularly rough, Erica seeks the help of a blunt female therapist, who tells her it's all right to feel loneliness and pain. Erica also benefits from the social contacts she has made in the art world. When she hesitantly ventures into a Soho bar on her own, she almost immediately meets artists she knows.

Clayburgh's Erica Benton is a previously sheltered woman who responds to changed circumstances with surprising strength. Slender, energetic, articulate, she is deeply hurt but not destroyed by her husband's infidelity. In the scene of greatest tension, she comes home from a disastrous blind date and finds Pattie necking with her boyfriend in the apartment. She kicks the boy out of the house, screams hysterically at Pattie, and then calms down and apologizes. This scene is needed to show how close Erica is to cracking. When Erica herself is ready to be with men again, she is direct yet uninvolved. After sex with Saul, she jumps up and says "I'm experimenting." She doesn't know what she feels, she's not ready to feel, and she tells him this right away. Erica is a very sexual person, yet she is not sexy or provocative in a conventional way. We see her in partial undress, but the camera does not linger on her body. She is undressed because this is what an energetic, sexual woman would do.

The film overall is not as impressive as Clayburgh's star turn. The upscale milieu is nicely observed, and the major roles are fine, but Mazursky's script is sometimes too cute. What is the point, for example, of contrasting Martin and Saul's reactions after they step in dog shit? There are other cute, repeated situations involving kippered herring (supposedly Saul's inspiration for abstract painting) and whether the man or the woman will decline to spend the night. Also, the script verges on fairy tale or simplistic romance when Erica quickly meets an almost perfect man. Saul, as it happens, is bright, talented, wealthy, kind, and sexy.[2] Mazursky draws back from a fairy-tale conclusion, however, when Erica refuses a full-summer vacation with Saul.

Saul responds rather devilishly by leaving Erica on a New York street corner with a large and presumably valuable painting. The painting is almost impossible to carry, it sometimes acts as a sail in the wind, and yet it is also a token of Saul's esteem. Erica bravely takes off down the street, and her physical predicament oddly summarizes the whole film. The charm of this and other moments in *An Unmarried Woman* suggests that Mazursky's gift lies in the details of observation and character, not in the well-constructed plot.

Paul Mazursky describes the qualities he was looking for from Jill Clayburgh as "intelligence, vulnerability, and a sexuality that wasn't brazen."[3] Other interviews and articles from the late 1970s affirm that these qualities are key aspects of her star image. In a "male gaze" movie, female intelligence can be threatening; thus the title of a 1976 *New York Times* article on Clayburgh reads "Too Intelligent to be a Movie Star?"[4] Vulnerability balances the singularity of intelligence, making Clayburgh understandable and accessible to a wide range of spectators. Clayburgh's vulnerability is brought out both through her movie roles and in press reports of her long-term relationships with actor Al Pacino and writer David Rabe. Clayburgh is a sensual, physical woman even though she lacks the hourglass figure of the Hollywood (or *Playboy*) pinup. Again, her sexuality emerges from the gossip columns (live-in relationships without marriage) as well as the movies.

With the three qualities mentioned by Mazursky, Clayburgh's star image sketches out some of the attributes, and conflicts, of a 1970s feminist (or feminist-influenced) woman. Her characters are intelligent and therefore freethinking and potentially independent. They are also vulnerable, unsure of themselves in the new environment brought on by feminism. Finally, Clayburgh's characters experiment, sometimes cautiously, sometimes not so cautiously, with the new sexual freedoms of 1970s America. The suddenly "unmarried" Erica needs to figure out how she feels about dating, the bar scene, a new romantic partner, and her daughter's sexuality in the absence of moral absolutes.

Claudia Weill's *Girlfriends* (1978) makes an interesting companion piece to *An Unmarried Woman*—indeed, the two films came out at about the same time and were frequently compared as examples of a new feminist sensibility in film. *Girlfriends* is a low-budget, independently made narrative film with an informal, almost-documentary look and pace. Like *Hester Street*, it is one of the few American films of the 1970s directed by a woman. Claudia Weill, who had previously worked in documentary, cobbled together financing from grants and private investors. Then, after editing was complete, Warner Brothers agreed to distribute her film. So despite its independent origins, *Girlfriends* had a fairly broad release.

The film has three intertwined narrative lines, all centered on Susan Weinblatt (Melanie Mayron), a young, would-be photographer living in New York. First, it is about the friendship between Susan and Anne (Anita Skinner), a would-be writer who is Susan's roommate before she gets married to Martin (Bob Balaban). Second, it presents Susan's slow progress in making a career as a photographer; she begins with bar mitzvahs and ends with a two-woman show at a gallery. Third, the film is about Susan's romantic adventures or misadventures, ending with an unresolved decision about whether to move in with Eric (Christopher Guest), a young university teacher.

Like *An Unmarried Woman, Girlfriends* is episodic, perhaps because the central characters in both films are in such uncertain situations. But unlike Erica in *An Unmarried Woman,* who remains active and extroverted even in her most confused moments, Susan often seems aimless and vulnerable after Anne moves out. *Girlfriends* is a film about befuddlement, and it has a slow, befuddled pace. A few scenes show Susan alone in her apartment, developing pictures, talking to herself, shouting "I hate it" when the electricity goes out (she is behind on the electric bill). Other scenes show desperate attempts to hook up with men: kisses and promises from the fiftyish Rabbi Gold (Eli Wallach) who gets her bar mitzvah work, a one-night stand with Eric after a party. Some weeks later, Eric knocks on Susan's door, perhaps because he and she are equally lonely and insecure.

Critics have disagreed on the relative importance of the three narrative strands in *Girlfriends*—work, same-sex friendship, opposite-sex relationship. According to Barbara Koenig Quart, the film is about work; Susan is "defined above all through her work, as a woman with a camera."[5] For Karen Hollinger, on the other hand, *Girlfriends* moves beyond the traditional duality of career or marriage as women's life choices to show "the crucial importance of female friendship in women's lives." Female friendship, Hollinger adds, "is just as important as . . . heterosexual relationships" in the film.[6] My own attitude is closer to Hollinger's: all three strands are important, but the film is first and foremost about friendships between women. Susan in *Girlfriends* is certainly more engaged in her work than Erica in *An Unmarried Woman.* But living alone and working is not enough for Susan, and her heterosexual encounters are not particularly romantic. The infatuation with Rabbi Gold is a dead end, and the relationship with Eric is marked by fear and hesitancy on both sides.

As the film's title suggests, the originality of *Girlfriends* lies in its subtle representation of female friendships. In the film's first few minutes, Susan and Anne provide support for each other, as people and artists. When Anne leaves, neither she nor Susan acknowledges the depth or importance of their bond. They see each other occasionally after the marriage, but seem to have less and less in common. Anne is a wife and soon a mother; Susan is pursuing success as an artist. Meanwhile, two other women provide at least some companionship for Susan. Ceil, a dancer whom Susan picks up as a hitchhiker in Vermont, becomes a non-rent-paying roommate for a while. At one point

Ceil makes a sexual pass at Susan but is rejected. Julie, a photographer, is Susan's rival, then employer, then coequal in a two-woman show. Julie, too, becomes an occasional roommate (she stays with Susan when in New York) but not a replacement for Anne.

The last few scenes of *Girlfriends* present the most complete picture of this theme of friendship. At the opening night of the photography show, we see many of the important people in Susan's life. Her parents are there, the rabbi (who is clearly of the parents' generation), Eric, Julie. Martin shows up, but not Anne—she has left for the couple's house in the country. Susan drives to the country house to celebrate the opening with her friend and finds that Anne has had an abortion. Martin doesn't know, because Anne didn't want to be talked out of it. Susan and Anne get drunk on tequila, confess their fears, renew their friendship. Then a car's lights appear outside the window, and Anne says "Uh oh, I think that's Martin." The two women laugh. But Anne quickly gets up to greet Martin, and the camera stays on a close-up of Susan's face. The close-up reveals, without words, that Susan realizes, and accepts, and regrets, that Anne is to some extent lost to her. The film ends.

The documentary-influenced *Girlfriends* lacks the high production values and overall polish of *An Unmarried Woman* or *The China Syndrome* (discussed later in this chapter). The pace is slow, the photography simple, the acting adequate. Melanie Mayron is a kind of everywoman figure, with frizzy hair and an "attractively clumsy gait,"[7] not a glamorous movie star. But paradoxically, this lack of Hollywood polish may be an advantage. In *An Unmarried Woman*, the need to please a large audience results in some unfortunate stereotypes—e.g., the "bad husband" versus the "kind lover." *Girlfriends* makes less concessions to narrative conflict and narrative drive and therefore can be more subtle. For example, Martin is a "good husband," as far as we know: he is kind, gentle, funny. Anne nevertheless feels frustrated and to some extent trapped. Her frustration, not directly expressed, comes shockingly to light via the abortion. The film offers no easy solutions.

Girlfriends is, in the context of the 1970s, an original look at the options facing young women. It carefully suggests that some possibilities are lost when women marry, have children, take on domestic responsibilities. It also suggests the very real difficulties involved with refusing the roles of wife and mother. Though not militantly feminist, *Girlfriends* does present some of the complexities of being female at a moment when gender expectations are slowly changing.

MEN AND WOMEN IN A NEW SOCIAL WORLD

Starting Over (1978), directed by Alan J. Pakula, is a bleak romantic comedy about divorce and the changed landscape of male-female relationships. This is a male "backlash" film about the difficulties caused by feminism. Like *Kramer vs. Kramer, Author!, Author!, Mr. Mom,* and even *Tootsie,* it shows that males can be caring people, can "emerge from their masculine carapaces and learn to love."[8] However, instead of replacing a recalcitrant woman with an empathetic man (e.g., *Kramer vs. Kramer*), *Starting Over* shows a male protagonist learning to live in a feminist-influenced world.

Based on the novel by Dan Wakefield, *Starting Over* is set in a gloomy New England winter. The images are dark, enclosed, often empty of life— a wonderful evocation of a time of year and a lonely mood. Sven Nykvist, known for his long collaboration with Ingmar Bergman, was the cinematographer. The story centers on Phil Potter (Burt Reynolds), a recently divorced man who has moved from New York to start a new life in Boston. With the help of his brother Michael (Charles Durning) and sister-in-law Marva (Frances Sternhagen), he is introduced to Marilyn (Jill Clayburgh), a single woman of about his age who works as a nursery school teacher. The body of the film is about their slow-to-blossom romance, counterpointed by Phil's continuing attraction to his ex-wife Jessie (Candice Bergen). At the end of the film, Phil proposes to Marilyn, and we are back to a more or less conventional romantic comedy.

However, before the ending *Starting Over* offers a detailed and sympathetic portrait of the divorced man. Phil Potter's experiences include saying goodbye to Jessie, whom he still loves; putting up with well-intentioned relatives; moving to a new apartment in a new town; joining a divorced men's support group; starting to date after years of marriage; and responding to Jessie's attempts to regenerate their marriage. His most important experience, clearly, is meeting Marilyn, a woman who is every bit as cautious and complicated as he is. Burt Reynolds plays Phil with admirable restraint—he is sometimes angry, sometimes depressed, but he usually maintains a wry sense of humor.

The two main characters meet in a scene that nicely expresses the post-feminist tensions of the late 1970s. Phil and Marilyn both get off a bus in the Boston suburbs on their way to Michael and Marva's home. The camera favors Marilyn as Phil walks behind her, following so closely that we, the spectators, get nervous. There are certain "rules" of personal space (how close one individual can get to another) that operate in any society. These rules can become a matter of safety in certain circumstances—e.g., at night, in a lonely place, when a woman is alone. Potter ignores all this, and Marilyn responds by confronting him and screaming "Get the fuck away from me, I've got a knife, I'll cut your fucking balls off." Then she runs to Michael and Marva's house. When Marilyn and Phil are introduced, a few minutes later, Phil repeats exactly what she said, and Marilyn complains that a gentleman would not repeat such a story. This scene demonstrates the aura of fear attending male-female relationships in the late 1970s. One component of feminism was (and is) self-defense training.

Clayburgh's character in this film is an independent—but not too inde-pendent—woman. Marilyn has worked very hard to establish herself as a single woman, and now Potter appears and she might want to depend on him. Marilyn is cautious, sometimes defiant, usually confused. On two oc-casions she firmly tells Potter to go away, but she nevertheless allows him to come back. This character has a knack for embarrassing situations (e.g., the "meet-cute" scene), but she usually manages to right herself. At times Clay-burgh demonstrates a gift for physical comedy. For example, when Marilyn is moving back from Potter's apartment to her own, she grabs a huge load of her belongings from Potter's car to show that she doesn't need his help. She drops most of the load in the middle of the street but strides on, angry and a bit ridiculous. Her embarrassing moments might have something to do with a male point of view, and with Potter's lingering anger toward all women. But they could also be an indication that we are all vulnerable and sometimes ridiculous. Potter himself has a number of awkward, embarrass-ing moments.

Though *Starting Over* is largely about male loss and male anger, it is not inconsistent with feminism. If feminism is about changing roles and atti-tudes, it must include men as well as women. The film's Phil Potter is a decent guy struggling with a new emotional landscape. Marilyn, the woman to whom he eventually proposes, is herself a scared veteran of the new sexual mores. At the end of the film, it's still winter, still bleak, but some progress has been made in building a relationship.

Head over Heels/Chilly Scenes of Winter (1979, 1982) is Joan Micklin Silver's adaptation of Ann Beattie's first novel. The compound title of the film is necessary because it was released in two different versions. In 1979, *Head Over Heels* concludes with an improbably happy ending, whereas in the retitled 1982 version the lovers go their separate ways. I will be commenting primarily on *Chilly Scenes of Winter* (1982), which is the version available on videotape.

Like *Starting Over*, the book and film of *Chilly Scenes of Winter* center on a sensitive and lonely male. Beattie's novel is the story of Charles, a young man whose present life is depressing and who dreams of the two-month affair he had with Laura. The story takes place in an unnamed city in midwinter, and as in *Starting Over*, winter takes on metaphoric and emotional meanings. Charles has a dull government job, a mother who is in and out of a mental hospital, and only one friend, Sam. His escape is the memory of Laura, a young married woman who briefly lived with him, then moved back to her husband's A-frame. The novel flits back and forth between the "chilly" details of the present and Charles's obsessive thoughts of Laura— not only memories, but stratagems to see her, to talk to her, to get her back. Charles sometimes has an ironic sense of how foolish and out of control he is; he plunges on just the same. At the end of the book, Laura has left her husband once again and has moved in with a female friend. She is willing to see Charles but remains cool to his declarations of love.

Silver's adaptation is also an extension of the Harry-Abbie subplot in *Between the Lines* (see chapter 4). John Heard plays the lovesick and possessive Charles as an elaboration of his earlier Harry character. We frequently experience the film from his point of view. The viewer identifies with Charles but also observes his obsessive, even disturbed side. On a few occasions, Charles creates a distance between himself and the spectator by threatening violence (which is never carried out). Charles is so caught up in his romantic fantasy that he loses touch with those around him. As to Laura, she rightly points out that she is not so special, but she lacks the strength to definitively break with Charles. She is unlike *Between the Lines*'s Abbie, who is comfortable with herself and her career and thus does not need to define herself via one big romance.

Much of the interest in Beattie's novel lies in the way it slides between the narrative present and a stream of thoughts and memories. Beattie creates a balance between a truly unpleasant present and a mental life bordering on delusion. In a feature film of ninety-some minutes,[9] Silver has less time to work between exterior and interior lives, so she concentrates on the relationship between Charles and Laura. The "chilly scenes of winter," filmed in a snowy Salt Lake City, are progressively crowded out by thoughts and dreams of the loved one. The necessity of translating Beatty's stream-of-consciousness into film leads Silver into some adventuresome techniques—voice-over narration, flashbacks, even direct address to the audience. Some of this material stems from the book, but Silver adds new scenes as well. The most notable addition is a set of scenes in which Charles builds a miniature A-frame, complete with dolls representing Laura and Jim (nicknamed "Ox").

At the end of the 1982 film, it is Charles, not Laura, who finds his way out of the labyrinth of their relationship. After an unsatisfactory visit, he asks Laura if she will come back to him. She says nothing, and he walks away. Then, in a brief scene at work, he tells us in voice-over: "It's not that it doesn't still hurt, it's that you get used to it." This remarkable statement on surviving an obsessive love is original to the film. Robin Wood comments: "It (*Chilly Scenes*) is perhaps the first Hollywood film where the happy ending consists, not in the lovers' union, but in their relinquishing its possibility." [10]

The 1979 version of the film is identical to the 1982 re-release, except that the film goes on for a few minutes after Charles thinks he has given up on Laura. In the added minutes, Charles comes home one day to find Laura cooking his favorite, obsessively loved dessert in the kitchen. She has kept his key for over a year and has decided to surprise him at home with a declaration of love.[11] This feels like an imposed "studio ending" (similar to the ending of Welles's *The Magnificent Ambersons*), but it was in fact Silver's choice in 1979. Perhaps she had internalized the pressure to come up with a happy ending; *Head Over Heels/Chilly Scenes of Winter*, financed by United Artists, was her first studio film. At any rate, by simply snipping off the last few minutes in 1982, Silver arrived at a more powerful and provocative film.[12]

Head Over Heels/Chilly Scenes of Winter is both a variation and a critique of the "male backlash/sensitive man" cycle of the late 1970s and early 1980s. Like *Starting Over* and *Kramer vs. Kramer*, it suggests that males can be sensitive, caring human beings. But Joan Micklin Silver (working from Ann Beattie's novel) puts a deft twist on this cycle of films by showing that men can be obsessive, men can be lovesick, men can be emotionally out of control. In other words, gender roles are sufficiently flexible so that men can take on not only female strengths but also traditional female weaknesses.

FEMINISM AND POLITICS

Hester Street, An Unmarried Woman, Girlfriends, Starting Over, and *Chilly Scenes of Winter* are feminist works in the sense that they examine the changing status of women and men in American social life. All of these films are quite cautious in their modeling of behavior. For example, *An Unmarried Woman* is somewhere between feminist fable and conventional romantic comedy, and even *Girlfriends* presents a modest and contingent case for getting beyond the traditional definition of woman as wife and mother. Claudia Weill describes *Girlfriends* as "a very slight shift in consciousness on the part of one girl."[13]

The late 1970s films of actress-producer Jane Fonda, on the other hand, present a more self-conscious and explicitly political variant of feminism. They model changes of behavior and link feminism to a broader political agenda. Fonda's films do not, however, completely break with the aesthetic and business structures of Hollywood. *Coming Home* (1978) and *The China Syndrome* (1979), Fonda's most important films of the period, aim to combine a new content with the familiar and repeated conventions of melodrama.

After a series of rapid professional transformations, from serious young actress to international sex symbol to political radical,[14] Jane Fonda solidified her status as a commercially viable Hollywood star with *Fun with Dick and Jane* (1977) and *Julia* (1977). The first was a romantic comedy with modest social overtones (a satire of consumerism), and the second was a high-prestige historical drama directed by Hollywood veteran Fred Zinnemann (*High Noon, A Man for All Seasons*). *Julia,* in particular, established Fonda as someone who could carry a major Hollywood production. Based on a story from Lillian Hellman's memoir *Pentimento,* it describes a friendship between Lilly (Fonda) and Julia (Vanessa Redgrave) in the context of anti-Nazi resistance in Europe before World War II. The self-absorbed Lilly, a budding American playwright, is inspired by her friend Julia to a single act of political commitment—she smuggles money to the Resistance inside Germany. Critics noted that a film about female friendship was in itself note-worthy in Hollywood (other examples from the period were *The Turning Point* and *Girlfriends*), but in other respects *Julia* is a quite conventional movie. The anti-Nazi theme is uncontroversial, and the film's careful, sym-metrical mise-en-scène recalls American films of the 1930s and 1940s.

Following the great success of *Julia*, Fonda moved to take greater control of her career by becoming the producer as well as star of her next film, *Coming Home*. She had founded a production company named IPC Films, for Indochina Peace Campaign, with fellow activist Bruce Gilbert in 1973.[15] IPC Films spent five years developing a script by Nancy Dowd (originally titled "Buffalo Ghosts") about the relationship between two women whose men go off to the Vietnam War. Fonda and Gilbert wanted to change the film into a more conventional love triangle, Fonda between two men, and Dowd left the project rather than make that change.[16] The screenplay of *Coming Home*, based on this new premise, was written by Waldo Salt (*Midnight Cow-boy, Serpico, Day of the Locust*) and Robert Jones. Nancy Dowd retained story credit. The director was Hal Ashby, a former editor who had become a much-in-demand director (*The Last Detail, Shampoo*). The central theme of *Coming Home* is, as in *Julia*, the transformation of a young woman played by Fonda. However, in contrast to *Julia*'s classicism, *Coming Home* shows the nervous rhythms and rebellious spirit of the late 1960s.

The film is set in 1968 (like *Shampoo*), after the Tet offensive and before the U.S. election. Marine captain Bob Hyde (Bruce Dern) has been ordered to Vietnam and is leaving his prim and proper wife Sally (Fonda) behind in California. After Bob leaves, Sally becomes friendly with Vi (Penelope Mit-ford), who has a boyfriend in Vietnam and an emotionally disturbed brother in the local VA hospital. Sally volunteers at the hospital and meets Luke Martin (Jon Voight), a high school acquaintance who is now a veteran with a disability. They become friends and eventually lovers. The angry Luke at one point chains himself and his wheelchair to the door of a Marine recruit-ing office and attracts the attention of the FBI. When Bob returns from the war, after a self-inflicted wound, the FBI tells him of his wife's affair. Bob confronts Sally and Luke with a rifle and then drives to the beach and walks into the ocean, presumably to drown.

This story can be reduced to melodrama. Sally is torn between two men, one distant and confused (Bob), the other warm, passionate, articulate (Luke). She at least provisionally chooses the charismatic, "forbidden" lover over the absent and inadequate husband. The film departs from romance novels, though, in that Luke is paralyzed from the waist down. *Coming Home* is an R-rated film which courageously shows that people with disabilities can be sexually active.[17] In one much-noticed scene, Luke orally brings Sally to an orgasm. But this returns us to a simplistic contrast between men, because an earlier scene has shown that Sally is not sexually satisfied by Bob. The contrast combines melodrama with a message that is "politically correct" in a double sense: (1) it demonstrates that the disabled can be loving, feeling, sexual beings; and (2) it suggests that sexual potency is somehow an aspect of the antiwar movement and the Left.[18]

At the beginning of the film, Fonda's character is a conservatively dressed, heavily made up, small-town girl. She defers to her husband and socializes only with other officers' wives. Under the influence of Vi, and also because of her volunteer work at the hospital, Sally quickly loosens up. She starts wearing jeans, she buys a sports car, she even curls her previously straight hair into a wild mop. This last change recalls Maria Schneider's changed hairstyle in *Last Tango in Paris*, with both transformations implying a new, more aggressive approach to sexuality. Indeed, *Coming Home* can be considered at least partially a remake of *Last Tango*. The major differences are the explicitly political elements explored by *Coming Home*, including feminism, the antiwar movement, and the social/political cause of people with disabilities. Perhaps one should speak of "women's liberation" instead of "feminism," because Sally liberates herself from a thoroughly repressive system. Sally is expected by her husband and by her peers (the officers' wives) to ignore injustice, to do nothing useful, to wait passively for her man. Her refusal to do so catapults her into new personal relationships and a new political awareness.

The strangest aspect of *Coming Home* is a disjunction between message and style. On the one hand, this is a didactic film with a certain number of political points to make. The political message is couched in personal, sometimes sentimental terms to attract an audience. But stylistically, *Coming Home* has an indirect, process-oriented, multidimensional quality that can probably be attributed to the director, Hal Ashby. The film is full of odd, complicated juxtapositions that make some sense but also trail off into ambiguity. Consider, for example, the film's opening. In the credit sequence, a montage juxtaposes Bob jogging in a sweatsuit with shots of men in wheelchairs at the VA hospital, as Mick Jagger sings "You're out of touch, my baby."[19] The sequence is nicely cut to the beat of the song. But who is "out of touch," "out of time," "out of place"? And why is Jagger singing to a woman, when the subjects on screen are obviously men? I think that both Bob and the veterans are in different ways "out of touch." Further, Bob is feminized by the lyrics and by shots of his lower body, because, as the song suggests, he doesn't know what is going on around him.

The opening scenes also include conversations between disabled veterans playing pool and talking about the war. One veteran says that the Vietnam War was about freedom and that he would do it again. Another veteran says it was all for nothing, and there's no way to justify the ruined bodies at the hospital. This dialogue is documentary footage shot by Ashby and cinematographer Haskell Wexler at a hospital near Los Angeles. The documentary material gives us an authoritative view of the disabled veterans' bitterness and further underlines that Bob Hyde (Dern) is "out of touch." Bob's legs are working, but he doesn't know what he's doing or why. These contrasts begin to explain the opening scenes, but at first viewing they seem confusing—why juxtapose documentary, fiction, and the Rolling Stones?

The ending moments of the film are equally complex and allusive. Bob drives to the beach in winter, strips, and runs out into the water. This is a conventional rendering of suicide, and it concludes one of the less impressive aspects of *Coming Home*—the presenting of the "politically incorrect" character as a weakling. But there is one more image in the film—a shot of Sally and Vi in the supermarket, ending as they approach a door labeled "Lucky out." "Lucky" is a supermarket chain in California, so the shot has a realistic referent. It is an informal, unobtrusive image of two women in a market. But, of course, "Lucky out" has a symbolic meaning as well. Bob had earlier talked about "going out a hero"; this is not quite the same thing. The "lucky out" could also refer to Sally, who is now out of a troubled marriage. "Lucky out" could even be Ashby's comment on a plot too melo-dramatic for his offhand, observational style. The film does not explain or resolve; it just ends.

In producing *Coming Home*, Fonda and her IPC partner, Bruce Gilbert, put together an impressive package of Hollywood talent: Fonda herself, Voight, Dern, Salt, Ashby, and so on. However, the theme of a woman gain-ing consciousness and becoming a social activist does not always mesh with Ashby's informal direction. The result is fascinating though not entirely co-herent. *Coming Home* is ultimately two good but incompatible movies stuck in the same 116 minutes.

The China Syndrome (1979) is another film produced by Fonda and Gil-bert's IPC Films, in association this time with actor/producer (and costar) Michael Douglas. The film is based on a script critical of the nuclear power industry by filmmaker James Bridges. Fonda and Gilbert convinced Bridges to write a part for Fonda (the journalist was originally a man) and offered him a chance to direct the film.[20] A well-made blend of politics and enter-tainment, *The China Syndrome* combines Fonda's characteristic theme of a woman's sociopolitical awakening with broader political issues. *The China Syndrome* is probably the most important American film dealing with nu-clear power and related issues (radioactive waste, public safety, regulatory control). This film also has an interesting perspective on the essentially con-servative, ratings-driven world of television news.

Kimberly Wells (Fonda) is a new on-air reporter at a Los Angeles tele-vision station. She aspires to hard news stories but at the moment is stuck in very soft features, for example a birthday party at the zoo. While shooting a fairly routine energy special, Kimberly and her freelance crew, camera-man Richard Adams (Michael Douglas) and soundman Hector Salas (Daniel Valdez) visit a (fictional) nuclear power plant at Ventana. Here they witness the control room crew responding to an evidently serious "accident" or "event." The station general manager, Mr. Jacovich (Peter Donat), refuses to put their footage on the air, but Kimberly and Richard investigate fur-ther. With the aid of Ventana control room supervisor Jack Godel (Jack Lemmon), they discover a quality control problem in construction that threatens the safety of the plant. Godel eventually takes over the control room with a gun, and he asks Kimberly to do an on-air interview with him. Godel is killed by a SWAT team before he can get his message across, but

Kimberly and Ted Spindler (Wilford Brimley), another control room employee, raise the necessary questions about safety at the plant. In the film's final lines, Mr. Jacovich, who has treated Kimberly as a decorative airhead throughout, says he's not surprised by her excellent work.

The China Syndrome is, among other things, a film about the changing world of television journalism. In the 1970s, women and minorities were welcomed in front of the camera as never before, but what did this mean? Was it merely a ploy for ratings and community relations? Early in the film, Kimberly is complimented on her hairstyle and her ratings and told, "Don't you worry your pretty little head" about other things. Unlike her freelancer friend Richard, she is unwilling to defy the station over the Ventana footage, but she does not drop it, either. She makes a trip to Ventana on her own, meets Jack Godel, finds out his concerns about the plant. At the end of the film, in an extremely emotional and pressure-filled situation, she manages to get the key points across on-air. Kimberly has grown up professionally. The plot highlights both her personal development and the need for women to be full partners (not decorative bimbos) in the news-gathering business. Note, however, that the change described in the film is only incremental. Kimberly has gained respect, but one cannot expect a conservative and paternalistic station to transform itself overnight.

The key sociopolitical issues here are (1) the regulation of the nuclear power industry and (2) the tension between profit and social responsibility in big business in general. Regarding nuclear power, we are shown that the plants are well designed, the crews well trained, but there is always a margin for error. A control room crew can make a mistake, and (more troubling) construction specifications can be fudged. In *The China Syndrome* the crucial error discovered by Godel is that certain welds were not properly checked. A more general problem is that business is so driven by profit that it may ignore other matters, including public safety. The plant manager and the chairman of the board are so focused on the licensing of a second nuclear plant that they insist on covering up any problems at Ventana. The possible loss of hundreds of millions of dollars outweighs any other concerns.

In a curious way, *The China Syndrome* is a film in the line of *Airport*, *The Poseidon Adventure*, and *Jaws*. Here, as in the earlier films, an American community is threatened by a disaster. As in *Airport* and *Poseidon*, the disaster is technological. But whereas the earlier films used technology as a somewhat arbitrary start for a suspense film, *The China Syndrome* investigates technological and organizational problems in detail. Whereas *Airport* lauds the prowess of American industry, *The China Syndrome* questions that prowess. It seems almost inevitable, in retrospect, that *The China Syndrome* was released during the Presidency of Jimmy Carter, a period in which the limits of social, political, and technological power were much discussed.

Beyond this overall congruence between film and era, in a strange coincidence *The China Syndrome* was released just a few weeks before a serious and highly publicized accident at the Three Mile Island nuclear plant near Harrisburg, Pennsylvania. Kai Erickson describes the Three Mile Island accident as follows: "On the morning of March 29, 1979, one of two generating units at a little-known place called Three Mile Island experienced an odd sequence of equipment failures and human errors, resulting in the escape of several puffs of radioactive steam. It was a moment of considerable potential danger, as we all were soon to learn." [21] At least in superficial terms, the fictional scenario and the real-life accident were a close match. The Three Mile Island incident showed that considerable safety risks did indeed exist at American nuclear power plants. Thus validated by breaking news, *The China Syndrome* went on to a successful commercial run.

The China Syndrome can be compared to *Jaws* with regard to the group which protects and saves society. In *Jaws*, as previously mentioned, it is an all-male group which saves the day. The older generation, represented by Quint, dies in the process, and the younger generation of Brody and Hooper (perhaps representing a working-class–middle-class alliance) returns to society. The enemy is entirely separate from human society, so that killing the shark does not imply major changes in how human institutions work. In *The China Syndrome*, the group which saves society consists of three young people—Kimberly, Richard, and Hector—plus the whistle-blowing, middle-aged Jack Godel. Women (Kimberly) and minorities (Hector) are prominently represented. Also, whereas Brody, Quint, and Hooper set out with the full support of the "city fathers," the heroes in *The China Syndrome* succeed by disobeying the management of the TV station and the power plant. Their victory suggests that changes are needed in the way America does business. Paradoxically, though, *The China Syndrome*'s challenge to

The China Syndrome COLUMBIA PICTURES.
Hector (Daniel Valdez), Kimberly (Jane Fonda), and Richard (Michael Douglas) visit the Ventana nuclear power plant. Courtesy of Museum of Modern Art / Film Stills Archive.

authority is based on a traditional American value—the First Amendment right to a free press.

As a producer and a major star, Jane Fonda had substantial influence over her projects in the late 1970s, including subject, script, and casting. Therefore, it is not surprising to see a consistency of character and theme in such Fonda vehicles as *Julia, Coming Home,* and *The China Syndrome.* In each film Fonda plays a naïve woman who is transformed into a politically active and self-aware character by her experiences. She becomes attuned to feminist issues in all three films, but the specific critique and reshaping of women's roles is quite different from film to film. Also, each film links feminism to other political issues—the fight against Nazism in *Julia,* the anti–Vietnam War movement and the rights of people with disabilities in *Coming Home,* the dangers of nuclear power in *The China Syndrome.*

Although Jane Fonda is certainly more consistent in her thematic interests than a Joan Micklin Silver or a Jill Clayburgh,[22] her films are not simply cookie-cutter versions of one another. The contributions of other creative participants, notably Dowd, Salt, and Ashby on *Coming Home*, and Bridges and Douglas on *The China Syndrome*, inflect the films in other directions. This is actually a good thing, because Fonda's characteristic themes risk being both too didactic and too melodramatic. With her collaborators adding other interests—e.g., the theme of the disabled veteran in *Coming Home*—the films become more complex and more involving as realistic fictions.

Both *Coming Home* and *The China Syndrome* portray the beginnings of a feminist and political transformation. Jane Fonda has explained that she wanted to reach a broad audience by starting from "a pro-war or apolitical woman existing in a situation most average people live in, helping to clarify the situation for other women."[23] This strategy may be necessary in order to work within the Hollywood system. But Fonda's chosen strategy of political melodrama carries with it some significant choices. To begin with, *Coming Home* and *The China Syndrome* both feature naïve heroines tutored by more politically aware men—Luke Martin (Jon Voight) in the first film, Richard Adams (Michael Douglas) in the second.[24] This is an aspect of melodramatic structure, since the politics of *Coming Home* is intertwined with the romantic triangle, and the politics of *The China Syndrome* is intertwined with the heroic group (and Richard clearly is the leader of the group). But male tutelage is probably not the best plot device for feminist films; note that in *Girlfriends*, like *The China Syndrome* a film about professional coming-of-age, Susan is helped primarily by women.

A second implication of Fonda's broad-based melodramas is that there will be no films about confident, competent women who are guided in some way by feminist ideals. Fonda is probably correct in her calculation that a film about the beginnings of feminist consciousness will attract a larger audience than a film about a woman who has already established competence and autonomy. Still, it would be exciting to see a Jane Fonda film which went beyond beginnings to show women successfully balancing personal, professional, and political lives.

Chapter 10

Star Wars

Alien

Whose Future?

Blade Runner

The science fiction film, as a construction removed from everyday reality, is a privileged vehicle for the presentation of ideology. Because it is less concerned than other genres with the surface structure of social reality, science fiction can pay more attention to the deep structure of what is and what ought to be. In practice, this means that science fiction films vividly embody ideological positions and that comparing science fiction films of the same era becomes an analysis of conflicting social visions. Such visions cannot, however, be reduced to a simple, discursive message. Instead, the total semiotic output of a film — images, sounds, textures, relationships — is a carrier of ideology.

As a test of this hypothesis, consider three popular films from the years around 1980: *Star Wars* (1977), *Alien* (1979), and *Blade Runner* (1982).[1] These films have much in common. All three are key moments in the renaissance of science fiction film, which stretches from the late 1970s to the present. And all three films are renowned for the quality of their visual design and special effects. However, *Star Wars* creates an ideologically conservative future, whereas *Alien* and *Blade Runner* create futures linked to liberal and socially critical ideas.

What factors account for *Star Wars*'s overwhelming success with the public? Certainly the film's narrative provides a partial answer. *Star Wars* is a modern quest narrative, blending such sources as Arthurian legend, *Paradise Lost*, *Lord of the Rings*, the Western, *The Wizard of Oz*, and the metadiscourse of Joseph Campbell's *The Hero with a Thousand Faces*.[2] Young, naïve Luke Skywalker sets out on an adventure both physical and spiritual, which involves saving the princess, defeating the Evil Empire, and establishing a more just government. The story has a mythic or fairy-tale dimension, but also a lightness of tone; Luke (Mark Hamill), Princess Leia (Carrie Fisher), and Han Solo (Harrison Ford) wisecrack their way through difficult situations. There are some weak points to the narrative. One is a problem with character development, particularly apparent in the minor roles—e.g., Uncle Owen and Aunt Beru. Another is the lack of emotional response to destruction of an *entire inhabited planet!*[3] However, the quest narrative of *Star Wars* has proved sufficiently compelling and resilient to support three film sequels (with more in process), numerous authorized novels, and a great deal of fan activity.

A second explanation is that *Star Wars* owes much of its popularity to a richness of audiovisual invention that is rare in science fiction or any other genre. From spaceships and space wars to planetary ecology and alien beings (not one species of intelligent aliens, but perhaps a dozen), George Lucas and his collaborators deserve much credit for creating such a sweeping and detailed science fiction universe. John J. Pierce calls this level of invention "world creation" and notes that it is a prized aspect of science fiction novels but hard to find in science fiction films. Such world building requires a sweeping imagination that is also disciplined and thorough.[4] An example from *Star Wars* would be the distinctively realized look, sound, and behavior of the two droids, R2-D2 and C-3PO. These two robots are original, detailed, and consistent; they may be the most interesting characters in the film. The created world in *Star Wars* is both packed with audiovisual information and given an imperfect, lived-in quality. For example, the sound effects generally start from complex natural sounds (e.g., a movie projector as the basis for the hum of the light sabers) rather than simpler, cleaner synthetic audio. Ben Burtt, the film's sound designer, explains that "The sounds of the real world are complicated and kind of dirty. They simply cannot be duplicated on a synthesizer."[5]

John Seabrook, writing in the *New Yorker*, gives a more technical explanation of *Star Wars*'s success. According to Seabrook, the film's "secret" is its control of the kinetic aspects of moviemaking: "The first *Star Wars* movie is like a two hour image of raw speed." Lucas is not a particularly gifted director of actors, but his control of "editing and pace" creates a feeling of "pure kinetic energy which has become a part of the world's visual imagination." "Every time a studio executive tells a writer that his piercing and true story needs an 'action beat' every ten minutes, the writer has George Lucas to thank."[6] This explanation seems to me far too simplistic. It leaves out *Star Wars*'s most original use of kinetic filmmaking, which is genre based: science fiction film can use the whole film frame to invent new kinds of motion. Lucas is very good at doing this, and he is a fine editor, but he does not deserve credit for singlehandedly changing the emphasis of American cinema. To take just one example from among Lucas's contemporaries, William Friedkin in *The French Connection* (1971) and *The Exorcist* (1973) is every bit as visual and kinetic as George Lucas in *Star Wars*. Yet no one would posit Friedkin as the sole inventor of contemporary film style. The increased emphasis on action and pace is undoubtedly a group creation, influenced as much by television (including commercials) as by film.

Star Wars is conservative in its ideological underpinnings. Men are active heroes, Princess Leia is a damsel in distress, good and evil are clearly separated, and Luke is guided by the benevolent father figure Obi-Wan Kenobi. The film is very consciously a break from the antiheroes and antigenres of many films of the early 1970s. According to Dale Pollock's biography of Lucas, the film's return to family entertainment and traditional morality was a conscious decision by its writer-director: "Lucas wanted to present positive values to the audience. In the 1970s traditional religion was out of fashion and the family structure was disintegrating. There was no moral anchor. Lucas remembered how protected he had felt growing up in the cocoonlike culture of the 1950s, a feeling he wanted to communicate in *Star Wars*."[7] Pollock lists the values of the film as "Hard work, self-sacrifice, friendship, loyalty, and a commitment to a higher purpose." Lucas himself comments, "I mean, there's a reason this film is so popular. It's not that I'm giving out propaganda nobody wants to hear."[8]

Star Wars has often been discussed as a harbinger of the renewed American conservatism of the Reagan presidency. It is certainly part of the move toward simple, optimistic genre films in the late 1970s. The clean-cut, well-spoken white youths of the film seem to come out of an idealized version of the 1950s, and the clear division between good and evil governments suggests the Cold War. Indeed, some phrases borrowed from the film became key ideological points of the Reagan years: "Star Wars" (meaning a futuristic missile defense system), "the Evil Empire" (meaning the Soviet Union). More recently, the name "Jedi Knights" was used by a U.S. Army group planning the Gulf War.[9] Lucas is not responsible for the uses politicians and governments make of his film. But the ease with which his ideas were put to political and military ends shows something about the Manichaean quality of the story.

Though *Star Wars* is part of a shift in film entertainment, away from socially critical work and toward optimistic genre films, that shift was neither simple nor complete. An alternate science fiction vision of the period can be analyzed in two films directed by Ridley Scott, *Alien* and *Blade Runner*. Both films are developments on George Lucas's combination of mythic storytelling and detailed "world creation" of the future in *Star Wars*. Ridley Scott is excellently suited for this type of science fiction filmmaking, because he is both a gifted director and a world-class art director.[10] In *Alien*, Scott takes on one part of the *Star Wars* legacy by creating an intricate and haunting portrait of a starship—the ancient *Nostromo*. He also develops a stunning variant on a 1950s science fiction cliché, the malevolent alien creature. In *Blade Runner*, Scott puts together a more complex version of *Star Wars*'s world-building project by creating a physically and emotionally convincing Los Angeles of the year 2019. *Blade Runner*, like *Alien*, draws on other influences as well, such as the look of 1940s film noir and the odd science fiction novels of Philip K. Dick.

The narrative premise of *Alien* is eminently simple: the monster attacks. Robbie Robertson has shown that the alien being with its savage survival logic has antecedents in science fiction literature, for example in the work of A. E. Van Vogt.[11] Other antecedents would be science fiction films of the 1950s, including the Japanese *Godzilla*. Looking to mythology, the story relates to myths of the dragon, of the sea monster, of Jonah and the whale. In each case, human heroes are threatened by powerful, mysterious creatures

which exaggerate the traits of known animals. In *Alien*, the monster designed by surrealist artist H. R. Giger is reptilian and thus related to fear of
snakes, dinosaurs, and sea creatures.

Though simple, the premise of *Alien* is also transgeneric, a blend of science fiction and horror. One borrowing from the traditional horror film is
a stretched-out anticipation of the monster's attack. Several scenes use silence and false cues to play with the moment of attack; this might be called
the "haunted house" motif of horror film. As Scott Bukatman notes, *Alien*
also presents a more contemporary (perhaps postmodern) horror motif: the
link between the monster and the human body. The alien creature in *Alien*
does not merely kill humans; it uses them as hosts for a process of reproduction. This is terrifyingly shown in the scene in which a small alien bursts
from an astronaut's chest, killing him as a by-product of "birth." Like the
vampire, the werewolf, the zombie, the alien is thus a threat to the integrity
of the human body. It could be seen as a disguised version of "monstrous"
processes that are normally hidden, such as birth and sexuality.[12]

Alien is unlike *Star Wars* and *Blade Runner* in that it deals with a restricted space. The main set is the human spaceship, with a few minutes
spent on the planet and in the alien ship. In the limited environment of the
Nostromo, Ridley Scott and his collaborators present in a matter-of-fact way
the organization and technology which make the ship work. Hibernation
coffins, hospital room, airlock, galley, control room, escape module, ship-
controlling computer: all are presented simply and effectively. The ship also
has a variety of hidden or "waste" spaces—vents, crawlways, corridors—
and this becomes important in fighting a creature which exists apart from
human spatial and conceptual logic. A particularly useful future technology
invented by Scott and crew is a motion sensor that can indicate the distance
of a moving object but not the direction or location.

In *Star Wars* the future is clean (though not shiny and new), wholesome,
and morally clear. *Alien* reverses all three points. The starship in *Alien* is
dank, dark, and messy. It is an old freighter owned by a large corporation
and therefore is maintained for utility rather than pride (compare the Millennium Falcon, *Star Wars*'s version of a beloved hotrod). The unknown
planet is a fiercely inhospitable environment, with strong winds and swirling
gas clouds. The alien ship's scariest feature is an uncanny mixture of organic
and inorganic forms. The walls and corridors of the ship seem also to be the

Alien TWENTIETH CENTURY – FOX.
Entering the alien ship. An uncanny mixture of organic and inorganic forms.
Courtesy of Museum of Modern Art / Film Stills Archive.

skeleton of an organic creature, with spines and ribs and dripping mucous.
Threat-as-body is thus part of the film's visual design in ways that go beyond
the blatant threat of the monster itself.

Discussion of the ideological differences between *Star Wars* and *Alien*
requires that we return for a moment to George Lucas's film. I have labeled
Star Wars conservative, but it does present itself as a rebellious act. The

rebels of the story have risen up against an oppressive Empire. Further, the main representative of the Empire is Darth Vader, a lightly disguised version of "Dark Father." So, *Star Wars* is a revolt against the father. However, the Rebel Alliance itself seems to be hierarchical and perhaps even authoritarian; it celebrates victory with an ending scene weirdly quoted from Leni Riefenstahl.[13] One should also remember that *Star Wars*'s rebellion in no way challenges gender, race, or class relations. White male humans are "naturally" in positions of authority. The boy Luke grows up and takes his place as a responsible male leader. As Robin Wood says, the film's dominant tone is reassurance; things change so that they can return to a comfortable norm.[14]

Alien presents a more significant challenge to authority. In this film the "Company," boss and organizer of the crew, turns out to be an evil force, the malevolent twin of the monster. The Company is represented on board

Alien TWENTIETH CENTURY–FOX.
The outsiders on the crew. Ripley (Sigourney Weaver) and engine mechanics Parker (Yaphet Kotto) and Brett (Harry Dean Stanton). Courtesy of Museum of Modern Art/Film Stills Archive.

by "Mother," the controlling computer; the nickname indicates the crew's dependence on the Company-programmed machine. The Company is also represented by Ash (Ian Holm), the science officer, who (unknown to other crew members) is an android. Ash's secret orders are to capture and bring back the alien; the crew is expendable. These orders are based on the commercial and military potentials of the alien creature. The Company responds to profit and puts little value on human life. Superficially, the theme is reminiscent of *The Poseidon Adventure* (1972), where the ship owners have neglected needed repairs and put passengers and crew at risk. But in *The Poseidon Adventure* this theme seems perfunctory, a way to start the action; the film concludes with a powerful defense of patriarchal authority. In *Alien*, on the other hand, the Company's action is part of a pervasive pattern of oppression and paranoia. The film sympathizes with the outsiders on the crew, the proletarian engine mechanics and the independent-minded Ripley (Sigourney Weaver).

Blade Runner is designed around two intersecting myths. First, there is the film noir detective fighting crime and corruption in the decaying city. The detective is a version of the medieval knight, someone who embodies right values in the struggle between good and evil.[15] A complication of film noir is that good and evil may be hard to ascertain in the modern city. Further, the damsel in distress may not want to be saved. A second mythic plot in *Blade Runner* involves four "replicants," androids of superior strength and intelligence who have illegally made their way to earth. At one level, these replicants are the villains of the narrative. Deckard (Harrison Ford), the hero, is a "blade runner"—a specialized assassin hired to find and terminate replicants. But the replicants are also angels fallen to Earth, humanlike beings with their own histories, needs, emotions, and morality. The link to angels is made explicit by a near-quote from William Blake uttered by Roy Batty (Rutger Hauer), leader of the replicants: "Fiery the Angels fell, while thunder roared around their shores, burning with the fires of Orc."[16]

As the conflict between the two myths suggests, Deckard's job as a blade runner is brought into question. Is he killing "skin jobs," nonhuman criminals? Or is he killing angels, humanlike or more-than-human beings whose differences are to be respected? The film suggests that the replicants, despite differences of genesis and history, are emotionally and morally human. This point is made by the character of Rachael (Sean Young), a replicant who

Blade Runner WARNER BROTHERS.
Roy Batty (Rutger Hauer), leader of the replicants. Courtesy of Museum of Modern Art/Film
Stills Archive.

does not know her origins and is therefore completely human in behavior.
It is reinforced when Roy Batty, who seems to be *Blade Runner*'s arch-
villain, ultimately saves Deckard's life in a Christ-like gesture of compassion.
The theme of android and human mixing and merging in unforeseen ways
has its roots in the source novel for *Blade Runner,* Philip K. Dick's *Do Androids Dream of Electric Sheep?*

In visual design, *Blade Runner* catapults us not into an idealized environment of the 1950s, but rather into the darkness of 1940s film noir. Fashions
are part retro-1940s and part futuristic. The chiaroscuro lighting of film
noir mixes with enormous electronic billboards of the future. The film is set
in an overpopulated, highly polluted Los Angeles in the year 2019. The cli-
mate has changed drastically, so that it rains all the time (convenient for
film noir). Smoke and smog mask the city, and many residents wear gas
masks outdoors. Asians, Hispanics, blacks, and Eastern Europeans crowd the
streets; most Caucasian Americans seem to have departed for off-world colo-

nies. A paramilitary police force maintains order, and enormous corporate headquarters dominate the skyline. Clearly, this is not the best of all possible worlds.

Although *Star Wars* presents a dozen alien races, it assumes the pre-eminence of humans. Both the Empire and the rebels are led by humans; most of the aliens are relegated to the "freak show" of the spacefarers' bar. Even Chewbacca, the one alien among the small group of heroes, is shown as Han Solo's sidekick. In this film, man is the measure of all things. *Blade Runner*, on the other hand, entertains ideas of "not-quite-human," "different-than-human," even "more-than-human." The elusive border between machine and human is shown visually in the scene where the replicant Pris (Daryl Hannah) hides among a bunch of animated toy figures maintained by the lonely J. R. Sebastian (William Sanderson). Sebastian's toys talk and move and seem to be emotionally attached to their owner. Though Pris can hide among the toys, she is different from them because of superior intelligence and strength plus an independent spirit, a will to live. In some ways replicants are superior to humans, not just to toys. But they are limited by a built-in four-year lifespan. Because of their short lifespan, replicants can be childlike at one moment, adult and philosophical the next.[17] The film ultimately affirms the validity of replicants as thinking, feeling beings, notably via the love affair between Deckard and Rachael. It thus makes an eloquent statement for acceptance of the Other.

Both *Alien* and *Blade Runner* project a future of oppressive institutions and therefore continue the socially critical American cinema of *Chinatown* (1974), *Nashville* (1975), and *One Flew Over the Cuckoo's Nest* (1976). They are far different in ideological hue from the optimistic, Norman Rockwellish vision of the future in *Star Wars*.[18] The first part of this essay has presented an overview of the films' conflicting approaches. The second part turns from this general exposition to discuss one aspect of the science fiction film: sex.

Vivian Sobchack, in her fine essay "On the Virginity of Astronauts," suggests that the American science fiction film is characterized by an absence of women and sexuality. Astronauts are primarily male, they wear unisex coveralls and spacesuits, their environment is technological and asexual. But, says Sobchack, if the signifiers of women and sex have been omitted from the science fiction film on the surface level, they return in the deep (subconscious) layer. Space travel is often presented as a penetration; both spaceship and space itself are wombs; alien threats are often sexual, and female.[19]

Before applying Sobchack's model to the three film examples, I would like to consider an exception to Sobchack which proves the rule. The prize-winning science fiction writer C. J. Cherryh (Carolyn J. Cherryh) has paid considerable attention to how sex and reproduction could be handled in starship-based cultures. For example, in a culture of family-operated merchant spaceships, where everyone on board is likely to be blood kin, both sex and the reproduction of the culture are made possible by "dockside sleepovers." Cherryh sketches out a pattern of sexual exchange between spaceships which allows for both individual self-expression and conventions protecting the greater social good. One example of the controlling social conventions is that children take the mother's name and stay with the mother's ship. The remarkable thing about Cherryh's approach to a space-faring culture is that almost no one, in science fiction novels or films, has considered similar questions.[20]

Let us return to our film examples. In *Star Wars* there simply is no sex. The society of the film is primarily male, or technologically neuter (the droids). The one prominent female character, Princess Leia, does not appear in sexual terms. According to Sobchack, Leia is "simultaneously protected and desexed by her social position (princesses are to fight for, not to sleep with) and by her acerbic and pragmatically critical attitude."[21] Dale Pollock quotes Marcia Lucas (ex-wife of George Lucas) as saying that *Star Wars* was conceptualized as a movie that would appeal to ten-year-old boys.[22] *Star Wars* is a movie coming out of the latency period, a movie which elides the adult problem of sexuality. This is curiously confirmed by the eventual revelation in the *Star Wars* trilogy that Leia is Luke's sister.

Star Wars does not, however, strongly support Sobchack's observation that sexuality repressed on the conscious level will return in subconscious symbolism. The film is not haunted by womb imagery or female monsters. Perhaps the preadolescent tone is so strong that it mutes such condensed or displaced signifiers. And, of course, audiences of all ages welcomed this tone, using it to escape current malaise and to return to a simpler, more conservative time. Only two scenes in *Star Wars* suggest to me the displaced sexuality described by Sobchack. First, there is an odd scene, peripheral to the main action, in which several characters are caught in a disposal chute/compactor, and they are attacked by a tentacled creature. This scene, played for laughs in *Star Wars*, nevertheless presents the threat of bodily functions and unknown organic antagonists. It thus anticipates *Alien*. Second, in the final attack on the Death Star, the one-man fighters penetrating the sphere could certainly be a representation of human reproduction, with the combination of sexual and mechanical imagery recalling *Dr. Strangelove*.

Unlike *Star Wars*, *Alien* is very specifically about a female, sexual threat. The alien creature is associated with darkness, rounded spaces, eggs, slime. Its temple-like ship has doors in the shape of vaginas. The alien's offspring may be male and phallic (e.g., the thing which springs into life from a male astronaut's chest), but the original threat is female. This is made even more explicit in *Aliens* (1986), the sequel to *Alien*, where the human expedition confronts an enormous, egg-laying alien Queen.

In a reversal of the common practice of science fiction films, the protagonist in *Alien* is a female. Ripley, one of two female astronauts, is the toughest, most suspicious, most resourceful of the *Nostromo*'s crew. She, and not the captain or the male crew members, becomes the focus of audience hopes for human survival. Is this reversal incidental, or does it have important ideological consequences for the film? Sobchack notes that Ripley was originally scripted as a male, and that for most of the film she "is not marked as either a woman or sexual."[23] In other words, Ripley is an asexual astronaut among asexual astronauts. However, at the end of the film she strips down to her underwear (preparing for a mechanically aided hibernation), and becomes clearly and challengingly a human female. Sobchack comments as follows: "Ripley no longer represents a rational and asexual functioning subject, but an irrational, potent, sexual object—a woman, the truly threatening alien generally repressed by the male-conceived and dominated genre."[24] Here I partially disagree with Sobchack. I agree that this scene reveals the irrational and sexual side of the main character, but not that it suggests an equivalence with the alien monster. Rather, the revelation is that the primary conflict of *Alien* is not technological vs. primitive, or any variation on that theme, but rather species vs. species, irrational vs. irrational. The irrational side of Ripley's character is further brought out by her determination to save the cat—not a rational calculation, but perhaps a motherly instinct. The cat represents Ripley's animal nature as well as her instinct for self-preservation and the preservation of those she loves.[25] In this film, such instincts are positive, whereas the rational calculations of the Company are shown as thoroughly negative. Ripley in her underwear is affirmed as a complex human individual, not presented as "the true threatening alien."

In *Blade Runner*, the representations of femaleness run all through the mise-en-scène. Los Angeles, 2019, is a dank, dark place, with smoke swirling and rain constantly falling. The *Nostromo* and the alien ship, both ancient and womblike, have as their equivalent an entire city. Only the occasional corporate headquarters (e.g., Tyrell Corporation) have the clean, clear lines of technological masculinity.

As noted earlier, *Blade Runner* combines elements of two male-oriented genres, science fiction and film noir. The combination is important to our current thread of discussion, because film noir commonly includes rather direct, though threatening, images of female sexuality, whereas science fiction represses such images. *Blade Runner* generally follows the film noir paradigm in presenting the three female replicants, Pris, Zhora (Joanna Cassidy), and Rachael. Zhora the snake-charmer has a threatening sexuality, and Pris, despite her childlike side, is threatening as well. Rachael, though she looks like the raven-haired fatal woman of film noir, is a little different. Raised in ignorance of her replicant status, she is a mediating character between the decaying human society and the new, artificially constructed superhumans. The human hero Deckard's continuing love affair with Rachael is, despite her mediating status, a break with film noir and science fiction convention and a major statement about acceptance of diversity. *Blade Runner* is film noir/science fiction with the woman as alien *not repressed*.

The theme of acceptance of diversity receives an added twist via the Director's Cut of *Blade Runner*, released in 1992 and now the most readily available version of the film. In this reedited version, Ridley Scott provides a clue that points to Deckard himself being a replicant. In an added scene Deckard, seated at the piano in his apartment, has a brief vision of a unicorn moving through a natural landscape. This links up with a moment late in the film when Gaff (Edward James Olmos), another blade runner, leaves an origami of a unicorn in front of Deckard's door. The suggestion is that Gaff knows Deckard's visions because Deckard is programmed, Deckard is a replicant. From one point of view, the message of humanness being de-

Blade Runner WARNER BROTHERS.
Replicant Pris (Daryl Hannah) among the robotic toys. Courtesy of Museum of Modern Art/
Film Stills Archive.

fined by behavior rather than by external categories gets lost here, because
Deckard is now no different than Rachael. But another point of view would
be that the audience's identification with Deckard in itself proves that
humanness is not a matter of categories such as natural/synthetic birth (or
racial, sexual, national, or political identity).

Blade Runner's theme of replicant as more-than-human brings with it
some other sexual/ideological possibilities. One, unfortunately, is the possible connection between large, blond Roy Batty, played by Rutger Hauer,
and the Nazi theory of an Aryan master race.[26] Another, far more positive
line of speculation, is that a more-than-human character can break sexual
boundaries. Roy, stronger and smarter than a human, is a fiercely burning
Blakean angel with a maximum four-year life span. He overrides human
cultural limits in a variety of ways, one of which seems to be bisexuality. He
kisses his creator, Tyrell, fully on the lips, and his final duel with Deckard
has strong sexual as well as violent content. Significantly, after Roy saves

Deckard and dies himself, the original release version of *Blade Runner* concludes with a voice-over of affirmation: "They just wanted what everyone else wanted. Answers to the basic questions: Who am I? Where did I come from? Where am I going?" A violent-sexual combat here melds into understanding and empathy.

Alien and *Blade Runner* are clearly descendants of *Star Wars*, works which build on the revelation that audiences would support mythic, world-creating science fiction films. But the two Ridley Scott films do not follow George Lucas's political line. Whereas *Star Wars* advocates a return to heroism and traditional morality, the Ridley Scott films show a distrust of authority and an openness to characters outside traditional definitions of heroism (e.g., Ripley and the replicants). When looked at together, these three films present a kind of debate about the (imagined) future. George Lucas sees the future as a revision of the past, as a chance to get basic moral precepts right this time. The legend of King Arthur can be replayed in a possible future. For Ridley Scott and his collaborators, on the other hand, the future provides a way to look at other issues: the place of women in society, the threat of an unexamined rationalism, the acceptance of the Other, the merging of humanity and technology. In simple terms, George Lucas is backward looking and traditional—in other words, a conservative. Ridley Scott is forward looking and accepting of diversity—in other words, a liberal. Audiences drawn to these films are thus, among other things, experiencing an ongoing political dialogue.

Conclusion

Fredric Jameson suggests that the 1970s were characterized by a "peculiar aimlessness" which followed the "strongly generational self-consciousness" of the 1960s. Nostalgia seems to have been the dominant mode of the period: "the recombination of various stereotypes of the past." As we noted in the discussion of *American Graffiti* (Chapter 6), nostalgia can be interpreted as a representation of social forces in the present. However, Jameson concludes the chapter on "Film" in his book *Postmodernism* by saying that this recombination of stereotypes ultimately has no identity, and that the specificity of the seventies "seemed most of the time to consist in having no specificity." Instead of a historically grounded identity coming out of the 1970s and 1980s, Jameson sees the development of postmodernism, an aesthetic style of pastiche and surface.[1]

Periodization is one area in which my view of American film in the 1970s does not agree with Jameson's broad generalization of recent cultural history. If "The Sixties," the period of social and cultural contestation, has a general congruence with the decade 1960–1970, with particular emphasis on the period after November 1963 (the assassination of President John F. Kennedy), this congruence does not extend to the American feature film industry. In the expensive and usually conservative medium of film, the ideological and aesthetic questioning of established norms characteristic of "The Sixties" does not get underway until about 1967 (*Bonnie and Clyde*).[2] The socially critical cycle of films peaks in 1969–1970, with *Easy Rider*, *Midnight Cowboy*, *Alice's Restaurant*, and *Woodstock*; but then it continues in various guises through the entire decade of the 1970s. Even the seeming exhaustion of political themes at mid-decade (*Chinatown*, *Nashville*) does not end this cycle of films; see, for example, *Coming Home* (1978) and *Apocalypse Now* (1979). To use Jameson's terminology, the "strongly generational self-consciousness" of the 1960s persists, not necessarily as the dominant culture, long after the decade is over.

As to the developing style of nostalgia and postmodernism which Jameson posits as a response to the political/aesthetic experimentation of the sixties, this style is certainly a part of the film history of the 1970s. It is represented in my discussion by *American Graffiti* and *Star Wars*; one could add many other titles. However, in my view the film history of the period cannot be limited to a dialectical contrast between "The Sixties" and "nostalgia." This is not just a matter of defining periods, though overlaps and contradictions (e.g., *Chinatown* as nostalgia) do make any periodization hazardous. There are too many other things going on—the right-wing cop films of the early 1970s, the great diversity of films by and about the African American community, the debate on technology exemplified by *Airport* and *The China Syndrome*. If the 1970s lacks an identity, it is not because of a withdrawal into pastiche, but because the ideological and aesthetic currents are complex.

Social historian Peter N. Carroll views the United States in the 1970s somewhat differently than theorist and aesthetician Fredric Jameson. In *It Seemed Like Nothing Happened*, Carroll presents the early part of the decade as a period of contention—a continuation of the 1960s, with a clumsy government, an unpopular war, and numerous constituencies clamoring for rights. This is followed by a pause during which the failure of liberal government causes a conservative reaction: tax cuts, deregulation of business, and the New Right's promise "to restore a world of simple virtues, an old America based on family, church, and the work ethic."[3] This vision of a backward-looking America might correspond to the traditional morality of *American Graffiti* and *Star Wars* and to the restoration of patriarchal authority in *Airport* and *Jaws*. It also evokes Jameson's "recombination of various stereotypes of the past," especially the use of the 1950s as a simpler, less anxious time.

However, despite his pessimism about politics and government in the late 1970s, Carroll asserts that important social changes continued under the surface. Liberal issues such as women's rights and the curtailment of nuclear power faced opposition in Washington but had strong support at the local level. According to Carroll, people were disillusioned with government but still striving to solve many problems raised by the dissent of the 1960s. "As conventional answers failed to resolve the problems of the age, Americans looked increasingly toward alternative values and institutions to create a new sense of community."[4]

Carroll's social history suggests a continuing dialogue in American society on how to solve the "problems of the age." The dialogue may encounter a period of exhaustion (represented in politics by Watergate), it may change venues and methods, but it does not disappear. In the 1970s, a great deal of this social dialogue took place via the medium of film. The "counterculture" was represented by *Easy Rider, Alice's Restaurant,* and *Five Easy Pieces;* the Right-wing reaction by *Joe, The French Connection,* and *Dirty Harry.* The exhaustion of the Watergate period was examined in *Chinatown, The Parallax View,* and *Nashville.* The end of the sixties was interpreted, in various ways, by *Shampoo, Star Wars, The Return of the Secaucus Seven,* and *The Big Chill.* The explosion of Black Pride and African American culture was presented by *Shaft, Claudine, Leadbelly,* and *Killer of Sheep,* among many other titles. A new awareness of women's roles and women's rights appeared in *Hester Street, An Unmarried Woman, Julia, Coming Home,* and *Alien.*[5] It is worth noting that this profusion of socially rooted, quality filmmaking was not limited to the first few years of the decade. Indeed, director Martin Scorsese told the *New York Times* in 1997 that "The end of the 70s was the last golden period of cinema in America."[6]

Most observers agree that as the millennium approaches we are no longer in a golden age of American film. Instead of commenting on the problems of the age in a profusion of conflicting visions, the big-budget films of today are about excitement, about thrills and chills, perhaps even about special effects and marketing. The metaphors of thrill ride and amusement park are often used to talk about Hollywood film, and indeed some of the studios are in the amusement park business (MGM, Universal, and Disney). The rather bleak condition of contemporary American film might be modified if one looks to independent directors—to John Sayles, Victor Nunez, Haile Gerima, Allison Anders, Charles Burnett, Jim Jarmusch, Nancy Savoca, Kevin Smith, Gus Van Sant, and others. A critic from 2020 might choose their films rather than *Independence Day* or *Titanic* as representative of the age. Still, those of us watching films in the United States today are not getting much sustenance from the moving image.

What happened? A detailed response would go beyond the limits of this book, but there does seem to be a cluster of explanations relating to the film business. First of all, as Peter Biskind reports in his best-seller *Easy Riders, Raging Bulls*, in the late 1970s a Hollywood culture dominated by directors (i.e., creative people) was supplanted by a culture dominated by executives, agents, and lawyers (i.e., business people). A key moment of this change, per Biskind, was Barry Diller's installation as the top film executive at Paramount, replacing Frank Yablans.[7] Not coincidentally, it was this same management change which caused Gordon Parks's departure from Hollywood.

A second change that took place in the late 1970s and early 1980s was a new reliance on advertising and marketing. Films were judged on the quality of their ad campaign, which was often prepared *before* production. The idea of "high concept" took hold, meaning that commercially successful films were supposed to be summarizable in one sentence, or one visual print ad. Though *Jaws* was brilliantly summarized in a print ad, many of the important films of the 1970s were irreducible to such simple terms. But high concept films could be test-marketed with a fair degree of success, and in a business marked by continuing uncertainties and escalating costs, even some degree of predictability was a welcome change.

A third significant change in the film industry of the late 1970s involved exhibition patterns. Instead of releasing films slowly and waiting for attention to build, studios started releasing films in one thousand to two thousand theaters with a concentrated burst of advertising, especially TV ads. This approach aimed at a quick profit rather than gradual returns, and it relied heavily on high-concept ads. If a film was badly advertised or mishandled in the first few weeks, it might never find an audience. This happened notably with *Blade Runner*, which was mislabeled as a "kid's movie" and did badly in first run, only to be rescued by second-run and art theater releases.

A fourth change involved several new ways of viewing films: via cable, pay-per-view, videocassette, and laserdisc. These new income streams were at one level a great aid to the film business, and for a while they stimulated an increase in independent production. However, the new home-viewing technologies also altered the very concept of a film "audience." Whereas filmgoing was once a collective ritual, with at least a possible concomitant feeling of social solidarity, video viewing was by and large an isolating experience.

One should not overly romanticize the films of the 1970s. In a period of uncertainty and change, many mediocre films were made. Though aiming at diversity, my selection has left out the sleazy sex movies, the superficiality of disco, the well-publicized failures of auteurism (e.g., Dennis Hopper's *The Last Movie*).[8] A 1980 account, "Why Are Movies So Bad?" by Pauline Kael, focuses on how the business of film distorts the creative content of film, and comments (prophetically) that "in all probability it will get worse, not better." Kael adds that a lack of values and structure in film production can lead to directorial "megalomania."[9] A recent "Personal History" by actor/writer Fiona Lewis describes the cynicism and sexual exploitation of such movies as *Lisztomania* (1975), *Drum* (1976), and *The Fury* (1978) — all films in which she appeared. Lewis summarizes the period as follows: "In the seventies in Los Angeles, there was an ambience of adventure in the movie business — a kind of Barnum & Bailey, have-a-go spirit which has long since disappeared. . . . This led to some truly terrible movies."[10]

Putting the failures aside, the decade of the 1970s in American film was remarkable for its pluralism, its heterogeneity. In this anarchic period a number of compelling visions competed for the audience's attention. I have organized these visions primarily by theme, and not by director, to show that the aesthetic trends of the period corresponded rather directly to conflicting ideological currents. If the 1970s were "the last golden period of cinema in America,"[11] it is because of the excitement of a dialogue between filmmakers. *Easy Rider, Dirty Harry, Jaws, Chinatown, Leadbelly, Star Wars, The China Syndrome:* all are key moments of a debate on what America is and what America should be. In the more settled Hollywood of the late 1990s, we have lost the passion of that debate.

Appendix 1

AMERICAN

HISTORY, **Time Line, 1968–1983**

AMERICAN

FILM

This listing of important moments in the social and political history of the United States, 1968–1983, is intended to briefly sketch a context for the film history of the period. The time line should be of particular use to students and others who did not experience the era as adults. Bear in mind, however, that it may take years for a film to progress from first draft script to finished print. Therefore, apparently significant connections between historical event and filmic representation may be more serendipitous than planned.

The time line was assembled from about fifteen sources, including history texts, reference books, internet sources, and an amazingly thorough volume entitled *Chronicle of the 20th Century* (Mount Kisco, NY: Chronicle Publications, 1987). Thanks to David Harley, Martin H. McKibbin, and George Vázquez for their assistance.

As part of the time line, release dates are given for all of the movies discussed at length in this book. Other movies, no matter what their merits, are not listed.

1968

Tet Offensive by Viet Cong and North Vietnamese troops.

North Korea captures the U.S. intelligence ship Pueblo, holds eighty-three crew members as spies.

President Johnson wins the New Hampshire Democratic primary. Eugene McCarthy, running on an antiwar platform, wins 40 percent of the vote.

Kerner Commission condemns racism in the United States and calls for aid to black communities.

President Johnson announces that he will not run for reelection.

Five hundred sixty-seven South Vietnamese peasants are killed by U.S. Army platoon in the village of My Lai.

Dr. Martin Luther King Jr. assassinated. Rioting by African Americans follows in several American cities.

United States breaks the seventy-six-day siege of Khe Sanh.

Columbia University students occupy five buildings to protest the university's expansion into the Morningside Heights neighborhood and its links to the Institute for Defense Analysis.

National Airlines DC-8 is hijacked to Cuba.

Gay men riot after police raid on the Stonewall Inn in Greenwich Village.

Robert Kennedy assassinated.

First direct commercial airline flights begin between New York City and Moscow.

Antiwar protests at the Democratic National Convention in Chicago result in violent confrontations between police and demonstrators. Much of the violence is televised live.

Motion Picture Production Code replaced by Ratings System.

Richard Nixon elected President.

Pueblo Crew released after eleven months in North Korea.

Inflation (Consumer Price Index) is 4.2 percent. Unemployment (annual average of monthly figures) is 3.6 percent.

1969

Neil Armstrong and Buzz Aldrin walk on the moon.

Paris peace talks begin, aimed at a peaceful resolution of the Vietnam War.

Mary Jo Kopechne drowns on Chappaquiddick Island in Massachusetts. Senator Edward Kennedy pleads guilty to leaving the scene of the accident.

American soldiers dead in Vietnam now number 33,641. This number is higher than that of American deaths during the entire Korean War.

Actress Sharon Tate and four others are brutally killed in Los Angeles.

Earl Warren retires as Chief Justice of the Supreme Court. Warren Burger replaces him.

Murder charges brought against Col. Robert Rheault, Special Forces commander in Vietnam, and seven of his men, for the killing of a Vietnamese said to be a double agent. Charges are later withdrawn.

President Nixon makes his "Silent Majority" speech.

On Veterans Day, demonstrations support U.S. policy in Vietnam.

Broad coalition of antiwar protesters demonstrates across the country in the Vietnam Moratorium.

Boeing 747 put into service.

Charles Manson and four members of his commune are indicted in the murders of Sharon Tate and others.

Oh Calcutta opens in New York.

Supreme Court orders immediate desegregation of thirty-three school districts in Mississippi.

Troops now serving in Vietnam number 540,000. President Nixon announces plan to withdraw about 110,000.

Rock concert at Woodstock.

Inflation is 5.5 percent. Unemployment is 3.5 percent.

Release of *Alice's Restaurant, Easy Rider.*

1970

President Nixon sends several thousand American troops into Cambodia.

Millions of Americans march in celebration of the first Earth Day.

Student demonstrators protesting the Vietnam War are shot and killed at Kent State and Jackson State.

Students at many campuses in the United States go on strike to protest the killings at Kent State and Jackson State and the invasion of Cambodia.

Construction workers in lower Manhattan demonstrate in favor of the Vietnam War. Crowds on Wall Street applaud.

FBI agents capture fugitive priest the Reverend Daniel J. Berrigan. Berrigan and eight other Roman Catholics had been convicted of burning draft records in Catonsville, Maryland.

Gay rights demonstration in New York protests laws that make homosexual acts illegal.

Janis Joplin and Jimi Hendrix die in drug-related incidents.

President Nixon proposes a five-point peace plan for Indochina, including an immediate cease-fire and the release of prisoners of war. The North Vietnamese reject this proposal.

President Nixon announces a planned reduction of 150,000 U.S. personnel in Vietnam by early 1971.

Black militant Angela Davis is captured in New York City after a two-month nationwide search. She is accused of involvement in a courtroom shootout in San Rafael, California.

Environmental Protection Agency is established.

National Air Quality Control Act is passed.

Inflation is 5.7 percent. Unemployment is 4.9 percent.

Release of *Airport, Five Easy Pieces, Joe, Patton.*

1971

Charles Manson and three others found guilty of murder after 121-day trial.

Twenty-sixth Amendment lowers voting age to eighteen.

United States lifts trade embargo on China.

National Institute of Mental Health survey finds that 31 percent of college students have tried marijuana, and 14 percent are regular users.

Amtrak, also known as the National Railroad Passenger Corporation, begins operation.

Governor Reagan of California urges large reduction of welfare rolls.

A bomb planted by the radical group Weather Underground goes off in a restroom of the U.S. Capitol. No one is injured.

Supreme Court rules that busing children outside their neighborhoods to desegregate schools is constitutional.

Lieutenant William Calley is convicted of killing twenty people at My Lai in South Vietnam in 1968.

United States marshals remove fifteen Indians from Alcatraz Island and end a nineteen-month occupation of the island.

New York Times publishes the "Pentagon Papers," articles based on a secret Defense Department study of the Vietnam War.

Congress passes a bill providing a $250 million loan guarantee to Lockheed Aircraft.

U.S. Army announces it will test servicemen in Vietnam for heroin use.

President Nixon announces wage and price controls in an attempt to combat inflation and strengthen the dollar.

A prison riot at Attica State Correctional Facility in New York results in forty-three deaths.

Lewis Powell and William Rehnquist are confirmed by the Senate as Supreme Court Justices.

U.S. troops in Vietnam number 230,000. The total number of American servicemen who have died in Indochina is 45,384.

Congressional Black Caucus is organized.

The People's Republic of China becomes a member of the United Nations, with support from the United States.

Inflation is 4.4 percent. Unemployment is 5.9 percent.

Release of *Dirty Harry, The French Connection, Shaft.*

1972

President Nixon proposes eight-point peace plan for Indochina.

Thousands of North Vietnamese troops invade South Vietnam. President Nixon orders bombing raids of North Vietnam.

President Nixon visits China.

Equal Rights Amendment passed by Congress with strong support from feminist groups. By the end of the year, twenty-two of the required thirty-eight states have ratified it.

President Nixon becomes the first American President to visit Moscow. Nixon and Soviet Communist Party Secretary Leonid Brezhnev sign the SALT arms limitation agreement.

Angela Davis is found not guilty of charges of murder, kidnapping, and criminal conspiracy stemming from a 1970 shooting in a San Rafael, California, courtroom.

Watergate break-in. Agents working for the Nixon campaign break into Democratic National Committee office.

Jane Fonda visits Hanoi at the invitation of the North Vietnamese government. She returns to the United States and makes public statements against the U.S. bombing of North Vietnam.

George McGovern is nominated as candidate for President at the Democratic National Convention. Senator Thomas Eagleton, the nominee for Vice President, withdraws after revealing he has in the past undergone electroshock treatments for depression.

The last U.S. ground troops are withdrawn from Vietnam. The United States continues to support and supply South Vietnamese forces.

To prevent hijacking, screening of passengers and luggage becomes mandatory for all foreign and domestic flights by U.S. airlines.

Alabama Governor George Wallace is shot while campaigning in the Maryland presidential primary. He is paralyzed from the waist down.

Federal Trade Commission charges Xerox with monopoly on office copiers.

Water Pollution Control Act is passed over President Nixon's veto.

Gloria Steinem starts *Ms.* magazine.

President Nixon is reelected by a wide margin.

President Nixon orders an end to bombing raids of North Vietnam and agrees to resume the peace talks in Paris.

Inflation is 3.2 percent. Unemployment is 5.6 percent.

Release of *The Poseidon Adventure, Superfly.*

1973

Supreme Court decision *Roe v. Wade* finds that state laws prohibiting abortion during the first trimester of pregnancy are unconstitutional.

President Nixon ends mandatory wage and price controls except in the food, health, and building sectors.

United States agrees to a cease-fire in Vietnam. Since 1961, 45,997 Americans have been killed in combat in Vietnam; 10,928 Americans have died from noncombat causes; and 303,640 have been wounded.

G. Gordon Liddy and James W. McCord are found guilty of spying on the Democrats in the Watergate case.

Members of the American Indian Movement occupy the town of Wounded Knee, South Dakota.

The U.S. Senate hears testimony that the CIA and ITT (International Telephone and Telegraph) attempted to block the election of Salvador Allende in Chile.

Watergate scandal develops. Special prosecutor named, congressional hearings begin. White House tapes are subpoenaed as evidence.

North and South Vietnam sign a peace agreement.

Socialist President Salvador Allende is killed in military coup in Chile. General Augusto Pinochet takes power.

Egypt and Syria attack Israel in Yom Kippur War. Israel successfully counterattacks, aided by resupply from the United States.

Vice President Spiro Agnew is forced to resign because of bribery charges.

Gerald Ford becomes Vice President.

Arab nations place oil embargo on the United States in protest of U.S. support for Israel during the Yom Kippur War.

American Psychiatric Association changes its view on homosexuality, no longer classifying it as a mental illness.

Inflation is 6.2 percent. Unemployment is 4.9 percent.

Release of *American Graffiti, Last Tango in Paris.*

1974

Price of oil quadruples because of Arab oil embargo. Gasoline shortages lead to long lines at gas stations.

Presidential impeachment hearings begin.

Patricia Hearst, daughter of wealthy publisher Randolph Hearst, is kidnapped by the Symbionese Liberation Army.

Arab oil embargo ends, but prices remain high.

Patricia Hearst joins her captors in helping to rob a San Francisco bank.

To avoid being impeached, President Nixon resigns.

Gerald Ford becomes President. Nelson Rockefeller becomes Vice President.

President Ford grants Richard Nixon a full and unconditional pardon for Watergate-related activities.

President Ford proclaims amnesty for Vietnam War draft resisters.

United States files antitrust suit aimed at breaking the telephone service monopoly of AT&T.

Congress passes the Freedom of Information Act, providing expanded public access to federal government files, over President Ford's veto.

The retail price of sugar more than triples in a year.

Inflation is 11.0 percent (due in part to the cost of oil). Unemployment is 5.6 percent.

Release of *Chinatown, Claudine, Death Wish, The Parallax View, Shampoo.*

1975

John Mitchell, H. R. Haldeman, and John Ehrlichman sentenced to prison terms because of their roles in the Watergate coverup.

North Vietnam attacks the northern part of South Vietnam, takes the major cities of Hue and Da Nang.

Fall of Saigon. South Vietnam surrenders to North Vietnam. Helicopters evacuate 1,400 U.S. citizens and 5,500 South Vietnamese and third-country nationals from the U.S. Embassy and Tan Son Nhut Airfield.

Communists take Phnom Penh, win the civil war in Cambodia.

Federal judge orders Boston to bus 21,000 children to implement an integration plan.

U.S.-registered merchant vessel *Mayaguez* is captured by Cambodian forces. It is retaken three days later by American Marines. Sixteen U.S. servicemen are killed.

Suez Canal reopens after eight years. (It had been closed in the 1967 Arab-Israeli War.)

Congress extends the Voting Rights Act for seven years and includes Hispanics as a protected group under this Act.

Oil price controls end.

United States, Soviet Union, and thirty-three other nations sign the Helsinki Accords, which reject the use of force and call for protection of human rights.

Two separate attempts, both by women, are made to assassinate President Ford.

Teamsters leader Jimmy Hoffa disappears.

The last of 130,000 Indochinese refugees settling in the United States leave the processing center at Fort Chafee, Arkansas.

FCC drops television's equal time ruling.

New York City threatened by bankruptcy.

Inflation is 9.1 percent. Unemployment is 8.5 percent.

Release of *Cooley High, Hester Street, Jaws, Nashville.*

1976

United States Bicentennial celebrated.

Supreme Court upholds busing of school children in Boston to integrate schools.

Widespread cheating is reported at the United States Military Academy (generally known as West Point). Seven hundred cadets are implicated in violations of the honor code.

Five Croatian terrorists hijack an airplane at La Guardia Airport in New York and fly to Paris, where they surrender.

U.S. Census Bureau reports dramatic population growth in the South and Southwest. Eleven of the thirteen fastest-growing metropolitan areas are in Florida, Texas, and Arizona.

A New York court disbars Richard Nixon for his role in Watergate.

Discovery of Lyme disease, a virus carried by ticks.

Jimmy Carter elected President.

United States vetoes Vietnam's application for membership in the United Nations.

Roots, by Alex Haley, is published.

Steve Jobs and Steve Wozniak design the Apple I personal computer.

President-elect Carter promises to prevent bankruptcy of New York City.

Inflation is 5.8 percent. Unemployment is 7.7 percent.

1977

Roots becomes a television miniseries, drawing a record audience of 80 million viewers.

President Carter pardons Vietnam draft evaders.

Larry Flynt, publisher of *Hustler* magazine, is convicted of obscenity in Cincinnati.

President Carter warns the United States of dwindling energy supplies. He calls for conservation, higher prices, and higher taxes.

Production of B-1 bomber halted.

Department of Energy created.

Trans-Alaska Pipeline begins operation.

Space shuttle Enterprise passes first test in Mojave Desert.

Elvis Presley dies.

Panama Canal Treaties signed by the governments of United States and Panama. The treaties give control of the canal to Panama at the end of 1999.

President Carter says United States will support United Nations arms embargo on South Africa.

Clean Air Bill passed.

Reader's Digest settles sex discrimination case, agrees to pay 2,600 (past and present) female employees a total of $1.5 million.

Inflation is 6.5 percent. Unemployment is 7.1 percent.

Release of *Between the Lines, Killer of Sheep, Star Wars*.

1978

U.S. oil tanker *Amoco Cadiz* causes huge oil spill off the Brittany coast of France.

California passes tax cut referendum Proposition 13.

Air Transport Deregulation Act passed.

Supreme Court decision *Bakke v. California* limits affirmative action in college admissions.

Families begin to leave the heavily polluted Love Canal area of Niagara Falls, New York. Hooker Chemical will help pay for a cleanup of the area.

Prime Minister Begin of Israel and President Sadat of Egypt sign the Camp David Accords, creating a framework for peace between their nations. President Carter of the United States is given credit for keeping the negotiations on track.

Reverend Jim Jones and more than nine hundred of his cult members die in Guyana. Most of them voluntarily participate in a mass suicide ordered by Jones. Some resist and are shot or poisoned. A few cult members escape.

Mayor George Moscone and Supervisor Harvey Milk of San Francisco are killed by former Supervisor Dan White. Harvey Milk was the first openly gay Supervisor in San Francisco; Dan White was anti-gay.

City of Cleveland, Ohio, defaults on short-term loans, becoming the first major city to default since the mid-1930s.

Millions of protesters, organized by Shiite Muslim leaders, march against the U.S.–supported Shah of Iran.

Inflation is 7.6 percent. Unemployment is 6.1 percent.

Release of *Animal House, Coming Home, Girlfriends, Starting Over, An Unmarried Woman.*

1979

The Shah of Iran flees Iran. Opposition leader Ayatollah Khomeini is welcomed back from exile.

Egypt-Israel Peace Treaty, brokered by President Carter.

Three Mile Island nuclear accident in Pennsylvania.

United States says that eight nuclear reactors made by Babcock and Wilson (makers of the Three Mile Island reactor) may continue to operate.

President Carter and Soviet leader Leonid Brezhnev sign SALT II arms control agreement.

General Anastasio Somoza resigns as President of Nicaragua and flees the country. The Sandinista rebels take power.

Shah of Iran is admitted to United States for medical treatment.

Iranian students seize the American embassy and take fifty-one U.S. citizens as hostages.

Federal government bails out Chrysler Corporation.

Soviet troops invade Afghanistan.

Inflation is 11.3 percent. Unemployment is 5.8 percent.

Release of *Alien, Apocalypse Now, Head Over Heels, The China Syndrome, The Return of the Secaucus Seven.*

1980

President Carter suspends grain and high-technology sales to the Soviet Union in protest of the Soviet invasion of Afghanistan.

Mission to rescue Iranian hostages fails. Eight U.S. soldiers die in a helicopter crash.

John Lennon killed outside his apartment building in New York City.

EPA finds evidence of chromosome damage in residents of Love Canal area.

Mount St. Helens erupts.

Olympic Games open in Moscow. The United States and many of its allies are not competing because of the Soviet invasion of Afghanistan.

Ford and General Motors report substantial operating losses. U.S. automakers are losing sales to more fuel-efficient Japanese imports.

Ronald Reagan elected President.

Inflation and recession in the United States. Consumer prices rise 13 percent. Unemployment is 7.1 percent.

1981

Iranian hostages released as President Reagan takes office.

Owners of Three Mile Island nuclear plant settle with local residents for $25 million.

United States cuts off economic aid to Nicaragua, begins training Nicaraguan contras (anti-Sandinista forces) in Florida.

President Reagan is shot and wounded after addressing a labor convention in Washington. He slowly recovers.

Space shuttle *Columbia* successfully completes its first orbital flight.

Federal air traffic controllers go on strike. President Reagan fires the 12,000 strikers.

National debt rises to one trillion dollars. Reagan administration predicts 1982 debt of $109 million.

U.S. Senate confirms the appointment of Sandra Day O'Connor as the first female Associate Justice of the Supreme Court.

Reagan supply-side economics plan passed by Congress. It includes a reduction in federal income taxes.

Doctors identify a previously unknown disease, AIDS, with no known cure. First case of AIDS in the United States may have been in 1969.

Inflation is 10.3 percent. Unemployment is 7.6 percent.

1982

Gasoline prices fall because of a world oil glut.

John Belushi dies of a drug overdose in Los Angeles.

United States bans travel to Cuba.

Eight hundred thousand people march in New York against nuclear proliferation.

Voting Rights Act is strengthened and extended for twenty-five years.

Reagan Administration announces economic sanctions against Libya, which is accused of supporting international terrorism.

Equal Rights Amendment is not ratified by a sufficient number of states to become part of the Constitution.

Census bureau says the poverty rate is 14 percent, the highest rate in fifteen years.

United States sends a peacekeeping unit to Beirut, Lebanon.

Vietnam War Memorial is dedicated in Washington, D.C.

First successful artificial heart transplant is completed.

United States offers multibillion-dollar aid plan to help Mexico out of financial emergency.

Inflation slows to 6.2 percent. Unemployment is 9.7 percent.

Release of *Blade Runner, Chilly Scenes of Winter, Diner, Fast Times at Ridgemont High.*

1983

President Reagan calls the Soviet Union "the focus of evil in the modern world."

President Reagan introduces the Strategic Defense Initiative (popularly known as "Star Wars").

U.S. embassy in Beirut is bombed. Sixty-three people are killed, including seventeen Americans.

President Reagan defends U.S. aid to the Nicaraguan contras.

Sally K. Ride becomes the first woman astronaut.

Terrorist truck bomb explodes at U.S. Marine barracks in Beirut, killing 237.

United States troops invade Grenada.

President Reagan signs bill making Martin Luther King Jr.'s birthday a national holiday.

Inflation is 3.2 percent. Unemployment remains high at 9.6 percent.

Release of *The Big Chill.*

Appendix 2

Filmography

Airport UNIVERSAL, 1970. Screenplay: George Seaton, based on the novel by Arthur Hailey. Director: George Seaton. Cinematography: Ernest Laszlo. Cast: Burt Lancaster (Mel Bakersfield); Dean Martin (Vernon Demerest); Jean Seberg (Tanya Livingston); Jacqueline Bisset (Gwen Meighen); George Kennedy (Joe Patroni); Van Heflin (D. O. Guerrero).

Alice's Restaurant UNITED ARTISTS, 1969. Screenplay: Venable Herndon and Arthur Penn, based on the song by Arlo Guthrie. Director: Arthur Penn. Cinematography: Michael Nebbia. Cast: Arlo Guthrie (Arlo); Patricia Quinn (Alice Brock); James Broderick (Ray Brock); Michael McClanathan (Shelly); Geoff Outlaw (Roger); Tina Chen (Mari-chan); William Obanheim (Officer Obie).

Alien TWENTIETH CENTURY – FOX, 1979. Screenplay: Dan O'Bannon, based on a story by Dan O'Bannon and Ronald Shusett. Director: Ridley Scott. Cinematography: Derek Vanlint. Cast: Sigourney Weaver (Ripley); Tom Skerritt (Dallas); John Hurt (Kane); Ian Holm (Ash); Harry Dean Stanton (Brett); Yaphet Kotto (Parker); Veronica Cartwright (Lambert).

American Graffiti UNIVERSAL, 1973. Screenplay: Willard Huyck, Gloria Katz, George Lucas. Director: George Lucas. Cinematography: Haskell Wexler. Cast: Richard Dreyfuss (Curt Henderson); Ron Howard (Steve Bolander); Paul Le Mat (John Milner); Charles Martin Smith (Terry Fields); Cindy Williams (Laurie Henderson); Candy Clark (Debbie); Mackenzie Phillips (Carol); Harrison Ford (Bob Falfa); Wolfman Jack (himself).

Animal House UNIVERSAL, 1978. Screenplay: Douglas Kenney, Chris Miller, Harold Ramis, based on short stories by Chris Miller. Director: John Landis. Cinematography: Charles Correll. Cast: Tom Hulce (Larry "Pinto" Kroger); Stephen Furst (Kent "Flounder" Dorfman); John Belushi (Bluto); James Widdoes (Hoover); Karen Allen (Katy); Tim Matheson (Otter); Peter Riegert (Boon); John Vernon (Dean Vernon Wormser).

Apocalypse Now UNITED ARTISTS, 1979. Screenplay: John Milius, Francis Coppola, loosely based on the novel *Heart of Darkness* by Joseph Conrad. Director: Francis Coppola. Cinematography: Vittorio Storaro. Cast: Martin Sheen (Capt. Willard); Marlon Brando (Col. Kurtz); Robert Duvall (Col. Kilgore); Sam Bottoms (Lance); Dennis Hopper (journalist).

Between the Lines MIDWEST FILMS, 1977. Screenplay: Fred Barron, based on a story by Fred Barron and David Helpern. Director: Joan Micklin Silver. Cinematography: Kenneth Van Sickle. Cast: John Heard (Harry); Lindsay Crouse (Abbie); Jeff Goldblum (Max); Jill Eikenberry (Lynn); Bruno Kirby (David); Gwen Welles (Laura); Stephen Collins (Michael).

The Big Chill COLUMBIA, 1983. Screenplay: Barbara Benedek, Lawrence Kasdan. Director: Lawrence Kasdan. Cinematography: John Bailey. Cast: Tom Berenger (Sam); Glenn Close (Sarah); Jeff Goldblum (Michael); William Hurt (Nick); Kevin Kline (Harold); Mary Kay Place (Meg); Meg Tilly (Chloe); JoBeth Williams (Karen).

Blade Runner WARNER BROTHERS, 1982. Screenplay: Hampton Fancher and David Peoples, based on the novel *Do Androids Dream of Electric Sheep?* by Philip K. Dick. Director: Ridley Scott. Cinematography: Jordan Cronenweth. Cast: Harrison Ford (Deckard); Rutger Hauer (Roy Batty); Sean Young (Rachael); Edward James Olmos (Gaff); M. Emmet Walsh (Bryant); Daryl Hannah (Pris); William Sanderson (J. F. Sebastian); Brion James (Leon); Joe Turkel (Tyrell); Joanna Cassidy (Zhora).

Chilly Scenes of Winter UNITED ARTISTS, RELEASED 1982, ORIGINALLY TITLED *Head over Heels*, RELEASED 1979. Screenplay: Joan Micklin Silver, based on the novel by Ann Beattie. Director: Joan Micklin Silver. Cinematography: Bobby Byrne. Cast: John Heard (Charles); Mary Beth Hurt (Laura);

Peter Riegert (Sam); Kenneth McMillan (Pete); Gloria Grahame (Clara); Nora Heflin (Betty).

The China Syndrome COLUMBIA, 1979. Screenplay by Mike Gray, T. S. Cook, and James Bridges. Direction: James Bridges. Cinematography: James Crabe. Cast: Jane Fonda (Kimberly Wells); Jack Lemmon (Jack Godel); Michael Douglas (Richard Adams); Scott Brady (Herman DeYoung); James Hampton (Bill Gibson); Daniel Valdez (Hector Salas); Peter Donat (Don Jacovich); Wilford Brimley (Ted Spindler).

Chinatown PARAMOUNT, 1974. Screenplay: Robert Towne. Director: Roman Polanski. Cinematography: John Alonso. Cast: Jack Nicholson (Jake Gittes); Faye Dunaway (Evelyn Mulray); John Huston (Noah Cross); Daryll Zwerlind (Hollis Mulwray); Belinda Palmer (Katherine); Burt Young (Curly).

Claudine THIRD WORLD CINEMA / TWENTIETH CENTURY − FOX, 1974. Screenplay: Lester Pine, Tina Pine. Director: John Berry. Cinematography: Gayne Rescher. Cast: Diahann Carroll (Claudine); James Earl Jones (Roop); Lawrence Hilton-Jacobs (Charles); Tamu (Charlene); Eric Jones (Francis).

Coming Home UNITED ARTISTS, 1978. Screenplay: Waldo Salt, Robert C. Jones, based on a story by Nancy Dowd. Director: Hal Ashby. Cinematography: Haskell Wexler. Cast: Jane Fonda (Sally Hyde); Jon Voight (Luke Martin); Bruce Dern (Captain Bob Hyde); Penelope Milford (Vi Munson); Robert Carradine (Billy Munson).

Cooley High AMERICAN INTERNATIONAL, 1975. Screenplay: Eric Monte. Director: Michael Schultz. Cinematography: Paul Vombrack. Cast: Glynn Turman (Preacher); Lawrence Hilton-Jacobs (Cochise); Garrett Morris (Mr. Mason); Cynthia Davis (Brenda).

Death Wish PARAMOUNT, 1974. Screenplay: Wendell Mayes, based on the novel by Brian Garfield. Director: Michael Winner. Cinematography: Arthur J. Ornitz. Cast: Charles Bronson (Paul Kersey); Hope Lange (Joanna Kersey); Vincent Gardenia (Frank Ochoa); Steven Keats (Jack Toby); William Redfield (Sam Kreutzer).

Diner MGM, 1982. Screenplay: Barry Levinson. Director: Barry Levinson. Cinematography: Peter Sova. Cast: Steve Guttenberg (Eddie); Daniel Stern (Shrevie); Mickey Rourke (Boogie); Kevin Bacon (Fenwick); Timothy Daly (Billy); Ellen Barkin (Beth); Paul Reiser (Modell); Kathryn Dowling (Barbara).

Dirty Harry WARNER BROTHERS, 1971. Screenplay: Harry Julian Fink, Rita M. Fink, Dean Riesner, based on a story by Harry Julian Fink and Rita M.

Fink. Director: Don Siegel. Cinematography: Bruce Surtees. Cast: Clint Eastwood (Harry Callahan); Harry Guardino (Bressler); Rene Santoni (Chico);
John Vernon (the Mayor); Andy Robinson (Scorpio).

Easy Rider COLUMBIA, 1969. Screenplay: Peter Fonda, Dennis Hopper,
Terry Southern. Director: Dennis Hopper. Cinematography: Laszlo Kovacs.
Cast: Peter Fonda (Wyatt/Captain America); Dennis Hopper (Billy); Jack
Nicholson (George Hanson).

Fast Times at Ridgemont High UNIVERSAL, 1982. Screenplay: Cameron
Crowe, based on his nonfiction book. Director: Amy Heckerling. Cinematogra-
phy: Bruce Surtees. Cast: Jennifer Jason Leigh (Stacey Hamilton); Sean Penn
(Jeff Spicoli); Judge Reinhold (Brad Hamilton); Brian Backer (Mark "Rat"
Ratner); Robert Romanus (Mike Damone); Phoebe Cates (Linda Barrett); Ray
Walston (Mr. Hand).

Five Easy Pieces COLUMBIA, 1970. Screenplay: Adrien Joyce (penname for
Carol Eastman), Bob Rafelson. Director: Bob Rafelson. Cinematography: Laszlo
Kovacs. Cast: Jack Nicholson (Robert "Bobbie" Dupea); Karen Black (Rayette
Dipesto); Billy Green Bush (Elton); Susan Anspach (Catherine Van Oost); Lois
Smith (Partita Dupea); Ralph Waite (Carl Dupea).

The French Connection TWENTIETH CENTURY – FOX, 1971. Screenplay:
Ernest Tidyman, based on the novel by Robin Moore. Director: William Fried-
kin. Cinematography: Owen Roizman. Cast: Gene Hackman (Popeye Doyle);
Roy Scheider (Buddy Russo); Fernando Rey (Alain Charnier, "Frog 1"); Tony
Lo Bianco (Sal Boca); Marcel Bozzuffi (Pierre Nicoli, the assassin).

Girlfriends CYCLOPS FILMS/WARNER BROTHERS, 1978. Screenplay:
Vicki Polon, based on a story by Claudia Weill and Vicki Polon. Director:
Claudia Weill. Cinematography: Fred Murphy. Cast: Melanie Mayron (Susan
Weinblatt); Anita Skinner (Anne Munroe); Bob Balaban (Martin); Christo-
pher Guest (Eric); Eli Wallach (Rabbi Gold); Viveca Lindfors (Beatrice); Amy
Wright (Ceil); Gina Rojak (Julie).

Hester Street MIDWEST FILMS, 1975. Screenplay: Joan Micklin Silver, based
on the story "Yekl" by Abraham Cahan. Director: Joan Micklin Silver. Cinematography: Kenneth Van Sickle. Cast: Stephen Keats (Jake); Carol Kane (Gitl);
Paul Freedman (Joey); Dorrie Kavanaugh (Mamie); Mel Howard (Bernstein).

Jaws UNIVERSAL, 1975. Screenplay: Peter Benchley, Carl Gottlieb, based
on the novel by Benchley. Director: Steven Spielberg. Cinematography: Bill
Butler. Cast: Roy Scheider (Martin Brody); Robert Shaw (Quint); Richard
Dreyfuss (Hooper); Lorraine Gary (Ellen Brody).

Joe CANNON FILMS, 1970. Screenplay: Norman Wexler. Director: John G. Avildsen. Cinematography: John G. Avildsen. Cast: Peter Boyle (Joe Curran); Susan Sarandon (Melissa Compton); Dennis Patrick (Bill Compton); Patrick McDermott (Frank Russo); Audrey Caire (Joan Compton); K. Callan (Mary Lou Curran).

Killer of Sheep INDEPENDENTLY PRODUCED BY CHARLES BURNETT, 1977. Screenplay: Charles Burnett. Director: Charles Burnett. Cinematography: Charles Burnett. Cast: Henry G. Sanders, Kaycee Moore, Charles Bracy, Angela Burnett, Eugene Cherry, Jack Drummond.

Last Tango in Paris UNITED ARTISTS, 1973. Screenplay: Bernardo Bertolucci, Franco Arcalli. Director: Bernardo Bertolucci. Cinematography: Vittorio Storaro. Cast: Marlon Brando (Paul); Maria Schneider (Jeanne); Jean-Pierre Léaud (Tom); Maria Michi (Rosa's mother); Gitt Magrini (Jeanne's mother); Massimo Girotti (Marcel); Catherine Allegret (Catherine).

Leadbelly PARAMOUNT, 1976. Screenplay: Ernest Kinoy. Director: Gordon Parks. Cinematography: Bruce Surtees. Cast: Roger E. Mosley (Huddie Ledbetter); Art Evans (Blind Lemon Jefferson); Madge Sinclair (Miss Eula); Dana Manno (Margaret Judd); James Brodhead (John Lomax); John Henry Faulk (Governor Neff).

Nashville PARAMOUNT, 1975. Screenplay: Joan Tewkesbury. Director: Robert Altman. Cinematography: Paul Lohmann. Cast: Ronee Blakley (Barbara Jean); Ned Beatty (Delbert Reese); Lily Tomlin (Linnea Reese); Keith Carradine (Tom); Geraldine Chaplin (Opal); Henry Gibson (Haven Hamilton); Michael Murphy (John Triplette); Allen Garfield (Barnett); Timothy Brown (Tommy Brown); Barbara Harris (Albuquerque); Gwen Welles (Sueleen Gay).

The Parallax View PARAMOUNT, 1974. Screenplay: David Giler, Lorenzo Semple Jr., based on the novel by Loren Singer. Director: Alan J. Pakula. Cinematography: Gordon Willis. Cast: Warren Beatty (Joseph Frady); Hume Cronyn (Rintels); Paula Prentiss (Lee Carter); William Daniels (Austin Tucker); Walter McGinn (Parallax Corporation rep.); Kelly Thordsen (Sheriff).

Patton TWENTIETH CENTURY – FOX, 1970. Screenplay: Francis Ford Coppola, Edmund H. North, based on the books *Patton: Ordeal and Triumph,* by Ladislas Farago, and *A Soldier's Story,* by Omar N. Bradley. Director: Franklin J. Schaffner. Cinematography: Fred N. Koenekamp. Cast: George C. Scott (General George S. Patton); Karl Malden (General Omar N. Bradley); Michael Bates (Field Marshal Sir Bernard Montgomery); Stephen Young (Captain Chester B. Hansen); Ed Binns (Major General Walter Bedell Smith); John Doucette (Major General Lucian K. Truscott); James Edwards (Sergeant William G. Meeks).

The Poseidon Adventure 1972. Screenplay: Stirling Silliphant, Wendell Mayes, based on the novel by Paul Gallico. Cinematography: Harold E. Stine. Cast: Gene Hackman (Rev. Frank Scott); Ernest Borgnine (Mike Rogo); Stella Stevens (Linda Rogo); Shelley Winters (Belle Rosen); Jack Albertson (Manny Rosen); Red Buttons (James Martin); Carol Lynley (Nonnie Parry); Roddy McDowell (Acres); Pamela Sue Martin (Susan Shelby); Eric Shea (Robin Shelby).

The Return of the Secaucus Seven SALSIPUEDES PRODUCTIONS, 1979. Screenplay: John Sayles. Director: John Sayles. Cinematography: Austin DeBesche. Cast: Bruce MacDonald (Mike Donnelly); Maggie Renzi (Kate); Adam Lefevre (JT); Gordon Clapp (Chip Hollister); Karen Trott (Maura Tolliver); David Strathairn (Ron); Jean Passanante (Irene).

Shaft MGM, 1971. Screenplay: Ernest Tidyman and John D. F. Black, based on the novel by Ernest Tidyman. Director: Gordon Parks. Cinematography: Urs Furrer. Cast: Richard Roundtree (John Shaft); Moses Gunn (Bumpy Jonas); Charles Cioffi (Lieutenant Vic Anderozzi); Christopher St. John (Ben Buford); Gwenn Mitchell (Ellie Moore); Sherri Brewer (Marcy Jonas).

Shampoo COLUMBIA, 1975. Screenplay: Warren Beatty, Robert Towne. Director: Hal Ashby. Cinematography: Laszlo Kovacs. Cast: Warren Beatty (George); Julie Christie (Jackie); Goldie Hawn (Jill); Lee Grant (Felicia); Jack Warden (Lester); Carrie Fisher (Lorna).

Star Wars TWENTIETH CENTURY–FOX, 1977. Screenplay: George Lucas. Director: George Lucas. Cinematography: Gilbert Taylor. Cast: Mark Hamill (Luke Skywalker); Harrison Ford (Han Solo); Carrie Fisher (Princess Leia); Alec Guinness (Obi-Wan Kenobi); Anthony Daniels (C-3PO); Kenny Baker (R2-D2); David Prowse/James Earl Jones (Darth Vader).

Starting Over PARAMOUNT, 1979. Screenplay: James L. Brooks, based on the novel by Dan Wakefield. Director: Alan J. Pakula. Cinematography: Sven Nykvist. Cast: Burt Reynolds (Phil Potter); Jill Clayburgh (Marilyn Holmberg); Candice Bergen (Jessica Potter); Charles Durning (Michael Potter); Frances Sternhagen (Marva Potter).

Superfly WARNER BROTHERS, 1972. Screenplay: Phillip Fenty. Director: Gordon Parks Jr. Cinematography: James Signorelli. Cast: Ron O'Neal (Priest); Carl Lee (Eddie); Sheila Frazier (Georgia); Julius Harris (Scatter); Charles McGregor (Fat Freddie).

An Unmarried Woman TWENTIETH CENTURY–FOX, 1978. Screenplay: Paul Mazursky. Director: Paul Mazursky. Cinematography: Arthur Ornitz. Cast: Jill Clayburgh (Erica Benton); Alan Bates (Saul Kaplan); Michael Murphy (Martin Benton); Cliff Gorman (Charlie); Lisa Lucas (Patti Benton).

Notes

PREFACE

1. Mikhail Bakhtin, "Discourse in the Novel," in *The Dialogic Imagination*, ed. Michael Holquist, trans. Caryl Emerson and Michael Holquist (Austin: University of Texas Press, 1981), pp. 262–263, 298–300; Robert Stam, *Subversive Pleasures: Bakhtin, Cultural Criticism and Film* (Baltimore: Johns Hopkins University Press, 1989), pp. 187–191.

2. See the essays "From the Prehistory of Novelistic Discourse" and "Forms of Time and Chronotope in the Novel," in Bakhtin's *The Dialogic Imagination*, pp. 41–146.

INTRODUCTION: "NOBODY KNOWS ANYTHING"

1. William Goldman, *Adventures in the Screen Trade* (New York: Warner Books, 1983), p. 39.

2. A "cleaned up" version of this anecdote may be found in Bob Thomas,

King Cohn: The Life and Times of Harry Cohn (New York: G. P. Putnam's Sons, 1967), p. 142.

3. David Bordwell and Kristin Thompson, *Film History: An Introduction* (New York: McGraw-Hill, 1994), p. 697.

4. Robert Sklar, *Movie-Made America*, 2nd (rev.) ed. (New York: Vintage, 1994), p. 302.

5. In film history terms, the split is suggested by two subheadings in Bordwell and Thompson's chapter on recent Hollywood film: "The New Hollywood" and "Hollywood Continues." I like the implication here that these two things are going on simultaneously. Bordwell and Thompson, pp. 711–716.

6. Vincent Canby, commenting on the traditionalism of *Rooster Cogburn*, notes that the producer was Hal Wallis, "who has been making movies since 1922." Canby adds that the stars, Hepburn and Wayne, could have played these same roles thirty-five years earlier. Vincent Canby, "New Movies with That Old Appeal," *New York Times*, 26 October 1975.

7. Paul Monaco, *Ribbons in Time: Movies and Society Since 1945* (Bloomington: Indiana University Press, 1987), p. 100. Monaco takes his definition of nostalgia from Fred Davis, *Yearning for Yesterday: A Sociology of Nostalgia* (New York: Free Press, 1979), p. 22.

CHAPTER 1: HIPPIE GENERATION

1. Ethan Mordden, *Medium Cool: The Movies of the 1960s* (New York: Knopf, 1990), p. 213.

2. Recent scholarship has stressed the contributions of Terry Southern to the screenplay. See Lee Hill, *Easy Rider* (London: British Film Institute, 1996), pp. 15–20, 29; Mark Singer, "Whose Movie Is This?" *New Yorker*, 22 June 1998, pp. 110–116, 118–119.

3. Jamie Diamond, "Peter Fonda Finds a Bit of Henry Within," *New York Times*, 8 June 1997.

4. "50 Top-Grossing Films," *Variety*, 23 July 1969, p. 9.

5. Stephen Farber, "End of the Road?" *Film Quarterly* 23, no. 2 (Winter 1969–1970): 3–4.

6. Dennis Hopper, commentary to the laserdisc of *Easy Rider*, Special Collector's Edition, Columbia Pictures.

7. Hill, pp. 24, 40–42.

8. Jeff Greenfield, "*Easy Rider:* A Turning Point in Film? A Profound Social Message? An Endless Bummer?" *Esquire*, July 1981, p. 90.

9. Diana Trilling, "*Easy Rider* and Its Critics," *Atlantic Monthly*, September 1970, pp. 93–95. Trilling thinks that the drug being bought and sold in *Easy Rider* is heroin. The authors of the film identify it as cocaine, but this should not affect her argument.

10. Margie Burns, "*Easy Rider* and *Deliverance*, or, the Death of the Sixties," *University of Hartford Studies in Literature* 22, no. 2/3 (1990): 44–58.

11. Farber, "End of the Road?" pp. 7–9.

12. Henry D. Herring, "Out of the Dream and into the Nightmare: Dennis Hopper's Apocalyptic Vision of America," *Journal of Popular Film and Television* 10, no. 4 (1983): 145.

13. Ibid., p. 148.

14. Ibid., p. 151.

15. David E. James, *Allegories of Cinema: American Film in the Sixties* (Princeton, N.J.: Princeton University Press, 1989), pp. 17–18.

16. Jonathan Aitken, *Nixon: A Life* (Washington, D.C.: Regnery Publishing, 1993), p. 360.

17. Patrick McGilligan, *Jack's Life: A Biography of Jack Nicholson* (New York: Norton, 1994), p. 196.

18. Herring, p. 149.

19. Anthony Macklin, "*Easy Rider:* The Initiation of Dennis Hopper," *Film Heritage* 5, no. 1 (1969): 9.

20. Robin Wood, *Arthur Penn* (New York: Praeger, 1969), p. 103.

21. Farber, "End of the Road?" pp. 10–11.

22. Wood, *Arthur Penn*, p. 118. Bernard Weinraub, "Director Arthur Penn Takes on General Custer," *New York Times*, 21 December 1969.

23. Vincent Canby, "*Alice's Restaurant*" (review), *New York Times*, 25 August 1969.

24. Thomas Schatz, *Old Hollywood/New Hollywood: Ritual, Art and Industry* (Ann Arbor: UMI Press, 1983), p. 199. For an analysis of *Joe*, see my Chapter 2.

25. The oil field scenes were shot near Bakersfield, California.

26. Gregg M. Campbell, "Beethoven, Chopin and Tammy Wynette: Heroines and Archetypes in *Five Easy Pieces*," *Literature/Film Quarterly* 2, no. 3 (1974): 277.

27. Ibid., p. 279.

28. Stephen Farber, "Easy Pieces," *Sight and Sound* 40, no. 3 (1971): 130.

CHAPTER 2: VIGILANTES AND COPS

1. David Denby, "New York Blues," *Atlantic Monthly*, November 1970, p. 126.

2. Judy Klemesrud, "His Happiness Is a Thing Called 'Joe,'" *New York Times*, 2 August 1970.

3. Denby, p. 125.

4. Kristin Ross, *Fast Cars, Clean Bodies: Decolonization and the Reordering of French Culture* (Cambridge, Mass.: MIT Press, 1995), pp. 71–122.

5. Michael Shedlin, "Police Oscar: *The French Connection*," *Film Quarterly* 25, no. 4 (1972): 8.

6. Shedlin, p. 7.

7. John Baxter, "*Dirty Harry*," in *International Dictionary of Films and Filmmakers*, 2nd ed., vol. 1, "Films," edited by Nicholas Thomas (Chicago: St. James, 1990), p. 246.

8. The doubling theme between Eastwood-as-cop and a criminal antagonist (in this case an ex-cop) is further explored in *Tightrope* (1984), a very interesting film that is not part of the Dirty Harry series.

9. Jack Shadoian, "*Dirty Harry*: A Defense," *Western Humanities Review* 28, no. 2 (1974): 172.

10. Pauline Kael, "Saint Cop," *Deeper into Movies* (Boston: Little-Brown, 1973) pp. 385, 387. This review originally appeared in the *New Yorker*, 15 January 1972.

11. Quoted by Shadoian, p. 166.

12. Quoted by ibid., p. 166.

13. Richard Schickel, *Clint Eastwood* (New York: Knopf, 1996), pp. 269–270.

14. David Edelstein, "Getting Defensive" (interview with John Milius), *Village Voice*, 21 August 1984.

15. Eastwood was de facto producer on *Dirty Harry* because the film was made by his production company, Malpaso.

16. Stuart M. Kaminsky, *Don Siegel, Director* (New York: Curtis Books, 1974), p. 282.

17. Schickel, pp. 279–280.

18. For a more positive view of *Dirty Harry* as a film of legal issues, see Terry Kay Diggs, "Dirty Harry, the Mt. Davidson Cross and Symbols in Conflict," *San Francisco Examiner*, 24 September 1996.

19. Kaminsky, p. 275.

20. The plot of *Death Wish* has similarities to the real-life story of Bernhard Goetz, the "subway vigilante." However, in this case the film (1975) predates the real-life occurrence (1984).

CHAPTER 3: DISASTER AND CONSPIRACY

1. Vincent Canby, "Can 'Bombs' Still Make Money?" *New York Times,* 8 March 1970.

2. Nick Roddick, *"The Poseidon Adventure," Magill's Survey of Cinema, English Language Films,* First Series, vol. 3, edited by Frank Magill (Englewood Cliffs, N.J.: Salem Press, 1980), pp. 1363-1364.

3. Stephen Heath, *"Jaws,* Ideology, and Film Theory," in *Movies and Methods,* vol. 2, edited by Bill Nichols (Berkeley: University of California Press, 1985), pp. 510-511; Robert Phillip Kolker, *A Cinema of Loneliness,* 2nd ed. (New York: Oxford University Press, 1988), p. 272.

4. Stephen E. Bowles, *"The Exorcist* and *Jaws," Literature/Film Quarterly* 4, no. 3 (1976): 200.

5. Kolker, pp. 283-287.

6. Philip M. Taylor, *Steven Spielberg* (New York: Continuum, 1992), p. 87.

7. Heath, p. 510.

8. *Dirty Harry* is a right-wing critique of government, but it does not allege a conspiracy.

9. Loren Singer, *The Parallax View* (Garden City, N.Y.: Doubleday, 1970).

10. Richard Combs, "World without Shadows," *Sight and Sound* 45, no. 3 (1976): 153.

11. Singer, pp. 23-28.

12. Wayne Warga, "Writer Towne: Under the Smog, a Feel for the City," *Los Angeles Times,* 18 August 1974.

13. Virginia Wright Wexman, *Roman Polanski* (Boston: Twayne, 1985), pp. 94-96.

14. Edward W. Said, *Orientalism* (New York: Random House, 1978).

15. Herbert J. Gans, *"Chinatown:* An Anticapitalist Murder Mystery," *Social Policy* 5, no. 4 (1974): 48-49.

16. Kirk Honeycutt, *"Chinatown:* Don't Forget It," *Hollywood Reporter,* 24 April 1995.

17. In the finished film, Curley agrees to take Evelyn and Katherine to Ensenada. He thus figures at least peripherally in the final action.

CHAPTER 4: THE END OF THE SIXTIES

1. Though *M.A.S.H.* (1970) is explicitly about the Korean War, it can be read as an indirect commentary on America's involvement in Vietnam.

2. Filmmakers and spectators know that "Let Me Be the One" is inept, but the character who sings it does not.

3. Helene Keyssar, *Robert Altman's America* (New York: Oxford University Press, 1991), pp. 158–159. This false narrative cue plays with popular memories of My Lai and other atrocities and also with media stereotypes of the crazed Vietnam vet.

4. Ibid., pp. 158–159, 170–171.

5. For discussion of the 1960s New Left and "participatory democracy," see David Caute, *The Year of the Barricades: A Journey Through 1968* (New York: Harper & Row, 1988), pp. 33–36. For political aspects of rock and roll, see Caute, pp. 51–55.

6. Kolker, p. 351.

7. The film was shown at film festivals in 1979 and put into general release in 1980. John Sayles and Gavin Smith, *Sayles on Sayles* (Boston: Faber and Faber, 1998), p. 63.

8. Quoted in Richard K. Ferncase, *Outsider Features: American Independent Films of the 1980s* (Westport, Conn.: Greenwood Press, 1996), p. 28.

9. David Chute, "John Sayles: Designated Writer," *Film Comment* 17 (May–June 1981): 54.

10. Ibid., pp. 54–55. Tom Schlesinger, "Putting People Together: An Interview with John Sayles," *Film Quarterly* 34, no. 4 (1981): 6. Sayles and Smith, pp. 51–52.

11. Joe Klein, "You Can't Get There from Here," *American Film* 9 (October 1983): 61.

12. Lawrence Kasdan and Barbara Benedek, "The Big Chill," first draft screenplay dated 16 July 1982. Available at University of Southern California, Doheny Library, Special Collections.

13. See James Jasinski, "(Re)Constituting Community through Narrative Argument: *Eros* and *Philia* in *The Big Chill*," *Quarterly Journal of Speech* 79, no. 4 (1993): 475–478.

14. Michael Ryan and Douglas Kellner, *Camera Politica: The Politics and Ideology of Contemporary Hollywood Film* (Bloomington: Indiana University Press, 1988), p. 146.

15. Ibid.

CHAPTER 5: *LAST TANGO IN PARIS:* OR ART, SEX, AND HOLLYWOOD

1. Peter Lev, *The Euro-American Cinema* (Austin: University of Texas Press, 1993).

2. Pauline Kael, "Tango," *New Yorker*, 28 October 1972, p. 130.

3. Andre Boucourechliev, *Stravinsky*, trans. Martin Cooper (New York: Holmes & Meier, 1987), p. 64.

4. Michel Leiris, *Francis Bacon* (Barcelona: Ediciones Polígrafa, 1987), pp. 17–20, 24–34.

5. Gideon Bachmann, "Every Sexual Relationship is Condemned" (interview with Bertolucci), *Film Quarterly* 26, no. 3 (1973): 4–5.

6. Yosefa Loshitsky analyzes in some detail the congruence between *Last Tango in Paris* and Marcuse's *Eros and Civilization*. Loshitsky, *The Radical Faces of Godard and Bertolucci* (Detroit: Wayne State University Press, 1995), pp. 68–80.

7. "His boots still give me a shiver," says Jeanne's mother at one point. The film also makes the point that the Colonel's virile power is based on the racist domination of colonialism.

8. Bachmann, p. 7.

9. Quoted in Claretta Micheletti Tonetti, *Bernardo Bertolucci: The Cinema of Ambiguity* (New York: Twayne, 1995), p. 131.

10. Robert B. Ray, *A Certain Tendency of the Hollywood Cinema, 1930–1980* (Princeton: Princeton University Press, 1985). The title is adapted from François Truffaut's seminal article "A Certain Tendency of the French Cinema," which was published in *Cahiers du Cinéma*, January 1954.

11. Ray, p. 57.

12. See Ray on *Angels with Dirty Faces*, pp. 75–77.

13. Note that "the viewers of Hollywood films" refers to a vast international audience, and not just to North American viewers.

14. Bachmann, p. 4.

15. E. Ann Kaplan, "The Importance and Ultimate Failure of *Last Tango in Paris*," *Jump Cut* 4 (1974), p. 9.

16. The back-and-forth "double jeu" of bourgeois and hippie might have required a more experienced actress. Dominique Sanda, who was at one time proposed for the role of Jeanne, probably could have played a bourgeois/bohemian character of some depth. But then *Last Tango* would be a different film.

17. Kaplan, p. 9.

18. Ibid., p. 10.

19. Joan Mellen, "Sexual Politics and *Last Tango in Paris*," *Film Quarterly* 26, no. 3 (1973): 13.

20. Tonetti, p. 131.

21. The "film makes sense" quote comes from Bergman, as cited by Frank

Segers, "'Make It Boy, Film Makes Sense,'" *Variety,* 6 February 1974. The "Jeanne" as "Jean" idea comes from John Simon, "In France We Do It Horizontally," in *Something to Declare: Twelve Years of Films from Abroad* (New York: Clarkson N. Potter, 1983), p. 132.

CHAPTER 6: TEEN FILMS

1. Jon Lewis, *The Road to Romance and Ruin: Teen Films and Youth Culture* (New York: Routledge, 1992), p. 151.

2. I would posit that films about the post–high school years, such as *Animal House,* are still concerned with the dynamics of adolescence.

3. The film was shot mainly in Petaluma, near San Francisco, but the town represented is clearly Modesto, where Lucas grew up.

4. Dale Pollock, *Skywalking: The Life and Films of George Lucas* (Hollywood: Samuel French, 1990), pp. 101, 108.

5. Jon Lewis, p. 137.

6. Pollock, p. 108.

7. Ibid., p. 106.

8. James Woolcott notes that both "Good Times" and *Cooley High* feature "strong, wise, girth-wide women with the world's weight on their wide shoulders." Woolcott, "Film Takes," *Village Voice,* 21 July 1975.

9. This subplot of *Cooley High* anticipates a similar situation, the death of Ricky, in the much later film *Boyz 'n the Hood* (1991).

10. The film makes an interesting observation about the isolation of the college experience from other sectors of American society in a later scene. Four Delta boys bring their dates to a black night club where Otis Day and the Knights are playing. In this context, Otis wants nothing to do with the white boys.

11. The name "Bluto" comes from a villain in "Popeye" cartoons.

12. Levinson attributes the original comparison between *I Vitelloni* and the anecdotes which became *Diner* to Mel Brooks. David Thompson, ed., *Levinson on Levinson* (London: Faber and Faber, 1992), p. 38.

13. Vincent Canby, "Feast of Interesting, Original New Work," *New York Times,* 11 April 1982.

14. *Levinson on Levinson,* p. 38.

15. Cameron Crowe, *Fast Times at Ridgemont High: A True Story* (New York: Simon & Schuster, 1981).

16. Thomas Doherty, *Teenagers and Teenpics: The Juvenilization of American Movies in the 1950s* (Boston: Unwin Hyman, 1988), p. 236.

17. Robin Wood, *Hollywood from Vietnam to Reagan* (New York: Columbia University Press, 1986), pp. 215-221.

CHAPTER 7: GENERAL PATTON AND COLONEL KURTZ

1. The author wishes to thank Jeffrey Chown of Northern Illinois University for generously sharing research suggestions on *Apocalypse Now*.

2. Albert Auster and Leonard Quart, *How the War was Remembered: Hollywood and Vietnam* (New York: Praeger, 1988), pp. 23-73.

3. Ladislas Farago, *Patton: Ordeal and Triumph* (New York: Astor-Honor, 1964).

4. Vincent Canby, *"Patton"* (review), *New York Times*, 8 February 1970.

5. Mel Gussow, "'Patton' Campaign: It Took 19 Years," *New York Times*, 21 April 1971.

6. "Patton" Tells Story of Controversial General in Popular Price Engagement" (Twentieth Century-Fox press release).

7. Stephen Farber, "Coppola and *The Godfather*," *Sight and Sound* 41, no. 4 (Autumn 1972): 220.

8. Ibid. A reading of Coppola's screenplay for *Patton* confirms that the script's criticism of Patton has been toned down by the finished film. For example, in the script, there is a long speech by General Bradley commenting that Patton, with his "dreams of glory," does not understand the struggles of the common soldier. Patton, "stunned" by this speech, leaves without responding. Francis Coppola, first draft screenplay for *Patton*, 27 December 1965, pp. 102-103. Available in the Franklin Schaffner Collection, Archives and Special Collections Department, Shadek-Fackenthal Library, Franklin and Marshall College, Lancaster, Pennsylvania.

9. George C. Scott, "Sorry about That," *Esquire*, December 1965, pp. 208-211, 316-318, 320-322; Rex Reed, "George Is on His Best Behavior Now," *New York Times*, 30 March 1970.

10. Reed, 30 March 1970.

11. Ibid.

12. Jack Hirschberg, interview with Franklin J. Schaffner, transcript of audiotape, p. 4. Franklin J. Schaffner Collection, Archives and Special Collections Department, Shadek-Fackenthal Library, Franklin and Marshall College, Lancaster, Pennsylvania. This interview was probably done by Twentieth Century-Fox for publicity purposes.

13. "Patton became all aflutter, plotting weird schemes to get back to the front." Farago, p. 91.

14. Paul Fussell, "*Patton*," in *Past Imperfect: History According to the Movies*, edited by Mark C. Carnes (New York: Henry Holt, 1995), p. 242.

15. Canby, 8 February 1970.

16. Stanley Kauffmann, *Figures of Light: Film Criticism and Comment* (New York: Harper & Row, 1971), p. 236.

17. Fussell, pp. 244–245.

18. Robert Rosenstone has written on film and postmodern history in relation to the movie *Walker*. Robert Rosenstone, *Visions of the Past: The Challenge of Film to Our Idea of History* (Cambridge, Mass.: Harvard University Press, 1995), pp. 132–151.

19. The Green Beret murder case as a source of *Apocalypse Now* is briefly discussed in Frances FitzGerald, "*Apocalypse Now*," in *Past Imperfect*, edited by Mark C. Carnes (New York: Henry Holt, 1995), p. 285.

20. All charges were eventually dropped.

21. Shelby L. Stanton, *Green Berets at War* (Novato, Calif.: Presidio, 1985), p. 39.

22. Ibid., pp. 39–40.

23. George C. Scott visited the Montagnards during his 1965 trip to Vietnam. He writes, "They have a ritual of beating a water buffalo to death with bamboo sticks and roasting it—hide, head, hooves and all—for a feast." Scott, p. 210.

Eleanor Coppola, in *Notes*, describes witnessing the ritual killing of a "carabao" (a Spanish word meaning "buffalo," in Philippine usage), and convincing her husband to have a look. This serendipitous explanation of the sacrifice scene in *Apocalypse Now* leaves out the link between the Ifugao ritual and similar practices of the Montagnards. Eleanor Coppola, *Notes* (New York: Limelight, 1991), pp. 132–135.

24. John Milius, draft of *Apocalypse Now*, no date, 158 pages. Copy available at the Arts Library-Special Collections, UCLA. This draft includes a reference to the McGovern campaign for President, so it would have been completed at some point after 1972. However, some portions of the draft could certainly have been written earlier. Page numbers within the text refer to this draft.

25. See, for example, "The Case of The Green Berets," *Newsweek*, 25 August 1969, p. 26; "The CIA Talks," *Newsweek*, 8 September 1969, p. 18. Jeff Stein gives an explanation for the origin of the phrase in *A Murder in Wartime* (New York: St. Martin's, 1992), p. 311.

26. My assumption is that John Milius is primarily responsible for the concept and story of *Apocalypse Now*. However, there are other possibilities. Carroll Ballard, a friend of Coppola's from UCLA graduate school days, claims that he was working on an adaptation of *Heart of Darkness* as early as 1967. See Peter

Cowie, *Coppola* (London: Faber & Faber, 1989), p. 117. Jeffrey Chown says that Coppola was the producer of *Apocalypse Now* from 1969, since he negotiated a deal with Warner Brothers to pay Milius for writing the screenplay. Chown adds that Coppola made the "crucial suggestion" that *Heart of Darkness* could provide a structure for Milius's Vietnam script. Jeffrey Chown, *Hollywood Auteur: Francis Coppola* (New York: Praeger, 1988), p. 123. Milius himself has maintained in various forums that adapting *Heart of Darkness* was one of his long-term projects from USC film school. See, for example, the Milius interview in the documentary *Hearts of Darkness.*

27. Frank McCullogh, "The Fall of a Lost Soldier," *Life*, 14 November 1969, pp. 34–39.

28. To my knowledge, no Hollywood fiction films were made in Vietnam during the late 1960s and the early 1970s. The logistics and safety considerations of filming in a war zone would have been daunting.

29. Some variant of this phrase occurs in all four of the *Apocalypse Now* script drafts available at UCLA.

30. John Gallagher, "John Milius" (interview), *Films in Review* 33, no. 6 (1982): 360.

31. The main difference between the Milius script version of this scene and the final filmed version is that Milius stays almost entirely with the attacking American troops. Director-producer Coppola adds shots of the villagers' preparations for imminent attack, of wounded Vietnamese prisoners, and of a Vietnamese woman throwing a grenade into a landed helicopter.

32. The exact text of Willard's voice-over narration is: "If that's how Kilgore fought the war, I began to wonder what they really had on Kurtz."

33. The motto "Apocalypse Now," which appears on a wall in Kurtz's compound, could be seen as calling for no restraints on American conduct of the Vietnam War. It could also suggest the likely result of such a policy—nuclear apocalypse.

34. This version of the script is labeled "*Apocalypse Now*, Original Screenplay by John Milius, Inspired by Joseph Conrad's *Heart of Darkness*, This Draft by Francis Ford Coppola, December 3, 1975." Copies are available at UCLA, USC, and the Academy of Motion Picture Arts and Sciences Library.

35. Fiedler adds both Michael Herr (who wrote Willard's voice-overs) and Marlon Brando to the side of the Doves. Leslie Fiedler, "Mythicizing the Unspeakable," *Journal of American Folklore* 103, no. 410 (1990): 395–396.

36. Ibid., p. 393.

37. A film clip of the press conference is included in the documentary *Hearts of Darkness.*

CHAPTER 8: FROM BLAXPLOITATION TO AFRICAN AMERICAN FILM

1. Ed Guerrero, *Framing Blackness: The African-American Image in Film* (Philadelphia: Temple University Press, 1993), pp. 72–74.

2. Thomas Doherty, "The Black Exploitation Picture," *Ball State University Forum* 24, no. 2 (1983): 31.

3. Guerrero, p. 69.

4. Darius James, *That's Blaxploitation* (New York: St. Martin's Griffin, 1995).

5. James Monaco, *American Film Now* (New York: New American Library, 1979), p. 192.

6. *Sweet Sweetback*, on the other hand, derives much of its power from excess—for example, the excessive display of sexuality and the excessive/forbidden subject of black revolt.

7. Quoted by Daniel J. Leab, *From Sambo to Superspade* (Boston: Houghton Mifflin, 1975), p. 252.

8. Gordon Parks Sr. suggests that before the wave of blaxploitation films it was an "unwritten law" in Hollywood that black actors would be clean-shaven. "A moustache on a black leading man was just *too* macho." Gordon Parks, *Voices in the Mirror: An Autobiography* (New York: Doubleday, 1990), p. 307.

9. David Oestriecher, "Bootstrap Project in the Heart of Harlem," *Los Angeles Times*, 15 September 1973.

10. James Monaco, p. 194.

11. Michael Paris, "Country Blues on the Screen: The Leadbelly Films," *Journal of American Studies* 30, no. 1 (1996): 123–124.

12. Gordon Parks, *Half Past Autumn: A Retrospective* (Boston: Little Brown, 1997), p. 320.

13. James Monaco, p. 197.

14. Ntongela Masilela, "The Los Angeles School of Black Filmmakers," in *Black American Cinema*, edited by Manthia Diawara (New York: Routledge, 1993), pp. 107–117.

15. Berenice Reynaud, "An Interview with Charles Burnett," *Black American Literature Forum* 25, no. 2 (1991), p. 328.

16. I wrote this comparison to the myth of Sisyphus before discovering that Charles Burnett had made the same linkage in a 1988 interview. See Phyllis Rauch Klotman, ed., *Screenplays of the African American Experience* (Bloomington: Indiana University Press, 1991), p. 95.

17. For laudatory comments, see Guerrero, p. 170, and Armond White, "Charles Burnett: Sticking to the Soul," *Film Comment* 33.1 (1997), p. 38. *Killer*

of Sheep was named to the National Film Registry of the Library of Congress, a major honor, in 1990.

CHAPTER 9: FEMINISMS

1. Sonya Michel, "*Yekl* and *Hester Street:* Was Assimilation Good for the Jews?" *Literature/Film Quarterly* 5, no. 2 (1977): 143.

2. Compare the nastier but more plausibly drawn painter played by Nick Nolte in Scorsese's *Life Lessons.*

3. Bernard Drew, "The Basic Training of Jill Clayburgh," *American Film,* April 1979, pp. 22–23.

4. Judy Klemesrud, "Too Intelligent to Be a Movie Star?" *New York Times,* 15 December 1976.

5. Barbara Koenig Quart, *Women Directors: The Emergence of a New Cinema* (New York: Praeger, 1988), p. 55.

6. Karen Hollinger, *In the Company of Women: Contemporary Female Friendship Films* (Minneapolis: University of Minnesota Press, 1998), pp. 55–56.

7. Quart, p. 55.

8. Molly Haskell, *From Reverence to Rape,* 2nd ed. (Chicago: University of Chicago Press, 1987), pp. 377–378, 394–395.

9. The 1982 version is ninety-six minutes long; the 1979 release would be slightly longer.

10. Wood, *Hollywood from Vietnam to Reagan,* p. 214.

11. The 1979 version of this film is available to researchers at the Library of Congress.

12. See James Atlas, "How 'Chilly Scenes' Was Rescued," *New York Times,* 10 October 1982, for an account of the re-release of the film.

13. Cecile Starr, "Claudia Weill Discusses *Girlfriends,*" *Filmmakers* 11, no. 12 (1978): 28.

14. For detailed career studies of Jane Fonda, see Barbara Seidman, "'The Lady Doth Protest Too Much, Methinks': Jane Fonda, Feminism and Hollywood," in *Women and Film,* edited by Janet Todd (New York: Holmes and Meier, 1988), pp. 186–230; Tessa Perkins, "The politics of 'Jane Fonda'," Christine Gledhill, ed., *Stardom: Industry of Desire* (London: Routledge, 1991), pp. 237–250; Fred Lawrence Guiles, *Jane Fonda: The Actress in Her Time* (Garden City, N.Y.: Doubleday, 1982); and Richard Dyer, *Stars* (London: British Film Institute, 1986), pp. 72–98.

15. The company's name eventually became International Pictures Corpo-

ration, and then Fonda Films. Bill Davidson, *Jane Fonda: An Intimate Biography* (New York: Dutton, 1990), p. 208.

16. Kirk Honeycutt, "The Five-Year Struggle to Make 'Coming Home,'" *New York Times*, 19 February 1978; Thomas Kiernan, *Jane Fonda: Heroine for Our Time* (New York: Delilah Books, 1982), pp. 305–306.

17. *Coming Home* is a landmark film about people with disabilities. See Martin Norden, *The Cinema of Isolation* (New Jersey: Rutgers University Press, 1994), pp. 265–270.

18. Tania Modleski argues that this love scene is not "a symbol or a metaphor" saying something about the men. It is, rather, a scene about the woman's pleasure, "made at a time when feminists were vociferously proclaiming the myth of the vaginal orgasm and agitating for the requisite attention to be paid to the clitoris." Modleski, "A Rose Is a Rose? Real Women and a Lost War," in *The New American Cinema*, edited by Jon Lewis (Durham: Duke University Press, 1998), p. 127.

19. The song title is "Out of Time," by Mick Jagger and Keith Richards.

20. Kiernan, p. 309.

21. Kai Erickson, *A New Species of Trouble* (New York: Norton, 1994), p. 139.

22. Jill Clayburgh is a good example of a star working within the collaborative, but also hierarchical, Hollywood system, with much less autonomy and control than a Jane Fonda or a Woody Allen. A career study of Clayburgh would be a good test of the "star-image" methodology proposed by Richard Dyer in his book *Stars*.

23. Quoted in Seidman, p. 209.

24. Tessa Perkins discusses a possible link between guidance by men within the films and guidance by men in Fonda's personal life—e.g., the influence of Tom Hayden on her politics in the 1970s. Perkins, pp. 247–248.

CHAPTER 10: WHOSE FUTURE?

1. Unless otherwise noted in the text, my analysis refers to the film *Star Wars*, not to the *Star Wars* trilogy. Similarly, I will be discussing the film *Alien*, and not its sequels, with any exceptions specifically noted in the text.

2. On the literary roots of *Star Wars*, see David Wyatt, "*Star Wars* and the Productions of Time," *Virginia Quarterly Review* 58 (1982): 600–615; Robert G. Collins, "*Star Wars*: The Pastiche of Myth and the Yearning for a Past Future," *Journal of Popular Culture* 11, no. 1 (1977): 1–10.

3. David Wyatt, pp. 609–610.

4. John J. Pierce, "Creative Synergy and the Art of World Creation," in *Retrofitting Blade Runner,* edited by Judith B. Kerman (Bowling Green, Ohio: Bowling Green Popular Press, 1991), pp. 201, 209.

5. Dale Pollock, p. 178.

6. John Seabrook, "Why Is the Force Still with Us?," *New Yorker* 6 January 1997, pp. 45, 50.

7. Pollock, pp. 139–140.

8. Ibid., pp. 139–140.

9. David S. Meyer, "Star Wars, *Star Wars,* and American Political Culture," *Journal of Popular Culture* 26, no. 2 (Fall 1992), p. 99.

10. See Paul M. Sammon's *Future Noir: The Making of Blade Runner* (New York: HarperCollins, 1996), pp. 71-75, for a description of how Ridley Scott's art direction skills transformed the script for *Blade Runner.*

11. Robbie Robertson, "Some Narrative Sources of Ridley Scott's *Alien,*" in *Cinema and Fiction: New Modes of Adapting, 1950-1990,* edited by John Orr and Colin Nicholson (Edinburgh: Edinburgh University Press, 1992), pp. 175–176.

12. Scott Bukatman, *Terminal Identity: The Virtual Subject in Postmodern Film* (Durham: Duke University Press, 1993), pp. 262–267.

13. Every army presents medals with pomp and ceremony, but the music used here recalls *Triumph of the Will.*

14. Wood, *Hollywood from Vietnam to Reagan,* pp. 162–165.

15. The connection between Raymond Chandler's literary detective and the chivalrous knight is outlined in Philip Durham's *Down These Mean Streets a Man Must Go* (Chapel Hill: University of North Carolina Press, 1963).

16. The lines from Blake begin, "Fiery the angels rose" (*America: A Prophecy,* lines 115–116). For interpretation of this near-quote, see Wood, pp. 183–187; Rachela Morrison, "*Casablanca* Meets *Star Wars:* The Blakean Dialectics of *Blade Runner,*" *Literature/Film Quarterly* 18, no. 1 (1990): 3.

17. Morrison, p. 3.

18. After writing these words, I learned that George Lucas collects Norman Rockwell's work! Rockwell's paintings hang prominently on the walls of the Skywalker Ranch, Lucas's business headquarters. See Seabrook, p. 43.

19. Vivian Sobchack, "On the Virginity of Astronauts," in *Alien Zone,* edited by Annette Kuhn (London: Verso, 1990), pp. 103–115.

20. See, for example, C. J. Cherryh, *Merchanter's Luck* (New York: Daw, 1982).

21. Sobchack, p. 106.

22. Pollock, p. 142.

23. Sobchack, p. 106.

24. Ibid., p. 107.

25. Thanks to Rebecca Pauly for suggesting the importance of Jonesy the cat.

26. Wood, p. 187.

CONCLUSION

1. Fredric Jameson, *Postmodernism, or, the Cultural Logic of Late Capitalism* (Durham: Duke University Press, 1991), p. 296.

2. I am leaving to the side the "underground film" of Maya Deren, Kenneth Anger, Stan Brakhage, and others, as well as the work of European modernists such as Godard.

3. Peter N. Carroll, *It Seemed Like Nothing Happened: The Tragedy and Promise of America in the 1970s* (New York: Holt, Rinehart and Winston, 1982), pp. 326–327.

4. Ibid., pp. ix, 348–350.

5. It would be interesting to chart antifeminist or nonfeminist films in this same period, from *Love Story* and *Airport* to James Bond and the male "buddy movies."

6. "The Directors: Woody Allen and Martin Scorsese," *New York Times Magazine*, 16 November 1997, p. 92.

7. Peter Biskind, *Easy Riders, Raging Bulls* (New York: Simon & Schuster, 1998), pp. 401–402.

8. See Biskind, pp. 133–136.

9. Pauline Kael, "Why Are Movies So Bad? or, The Numbers," *New Yorker*, 23 June 1980, pp. 84, 92.

10. Fiona Lewis, "Daring All," *New Yorker*, 23 February 1998, pp. 70–76. The quote is from p. 71.

11. I would extend Scorsese's comment to fit the entire decade.

Bibliography

Aitken, Jonathan. *Nixon: A Life*. Washington, D.C.: Regnery Publishing, 1993.

Auster, Albert, and Leonard Quart. *How the War Was Remembered: Hollywood and Vietnam*. New York: Praeger, 1988.

Bachmann, Gideon. "Every Sexual Relationship Is Condemned" (interview with Bertolucci). *Film Quarterly* 26, no. 3 (1973): 2–9.

Bakhtin, M. M. *The Dialogic Imagination*. Edited by Michael Holquist. Translated by Caryl Emerson and Michael Holquist. Austin: University of Texas Press, 1981.

Biskind, Peter. *Easy Riders, Raging Bulls*. New York: Simon & Schuster, 1998.

Bordwell, David, and Kristin Thompson. *Film History: An Introduction*. New York: McGraw-Hill, 1994.

Boucourechliev, André. *Stravinsky*. Trans. Martin Cooper. New York: Holmes & Meier, 1987.

Bowles, Stephen E. "*The Exorcist* and *Jaws*." *Literature/Film Quarterly* 4, no. 3 (1976): 196–214.

Brinkley, Alan. *The Unfinished Nation* (New York: Knopf, 1993).

Bukatman, Scott. *Terminal Identity: The Virtual Subject in Postmodern Film.* Durham: Duke University Press, 1993.

Burns, Margie. "*Easy Rider* and *Deliverance,* or, the Death of the Sixties." *University of Hartford Studies in Literature* 22, no. 2/3 (1990): 44–58.

Cagin, Seth, and Philip Dray. *Born to be Wild.* Boca Raton: Coyote, 1994.

Campbell, Gregg M. "Beethoven, Chopin and Tammy Wynette: Heroines and Archetypes in *Five Easy Pieces.*" *Literature/Film Quarterly* 2, no. 3 (1974): 275–283.

Carroll, Kent E., ed. *Closeup: Last Tango in Paris.* New York: Grove Press, 1973.

Carroll, Peter N. *It Seemed Like Nothing Happened: The Tragedy and Promise of America in the 1970s.* New York: Holt, Rinehart and Winston, 1982.

Carruth, Gorton. *The Encyclopedia of American Facts and Dates,* 9th ed. New York: HarperCollins, 1993.

Caute, David. *The Year of the Barricades: A Journey Through 1968.* New York: Harper & Row, 1988.

Cherryh, C. J. *Merchanter's Luck.* New York: Daw, 1982.

Chown, Jeffrey. *Hollywood Auteur: Francis Coppola.* New York: Praeger, 1988.

Chute, David. "John Sayles: Designated Writer." *Film Comment* 17, no. 4 (May–June 1981): 54–59.

Collins, Robert G. "*Star Wars:* the Pastiche of Myth and the Yearning for a Past Future." *Journal of Popular Culture* 11, no. 1 (1977): 1–10.

Combs, Richard. "World without Shadows." *Sight and Sound* 45, no. 3 (1976): 153.

Coppola, Eleanor. *Notes.* New York: Limelight, 1991. Originally published by Simon & Schuster, 1979.

Coppola, Francis. "Apocalypse Now." Draft of screenplay, 3 December 1975. Available at UCLA, USC, and Academy of Motion Pictures Arts and Sciences Libraries.

———. "Patton." First draft screenplay, 27 December 1965. Available in the Franklin Schaffner Collection, Archives and Special Collections Department, Shadek-Fackenthal Library, Franklin and Marshall College, Lancaster, Pa.

Cowie, Peter. *Coppola.* London: Faber and Faber, 1989.

Crowe, Cameron. *Fast Times at Ridgemont High: A True Story.* New York: Simon & Schuster, 1981.

Daniel, Clifton, ed. in chief. *Chronicle of the 20th Century.* Mount Kisco, N.Y.: Chronicle Publications, 1987.

Davidson, Bill. *Jane Fonda: An Intimate Biography.* New York: Dutton, 1990.

Davis, Fred. *Yearning for Yesterday: A Sociology of Nostalgia.* New York: Free Press, 1979.

Denby, David. "New York Blues." *Atlantic Monthly*, November 1970, pp. 124–129.

Doherty, Thomas. "The Black Exploitation Picture." *Ball State University Forum* 24, no. 2 (1983): 30–39.

———. *Teenagers and Teenpics: The Juvenilization of American Movies in the 1950s*. Boston: Unwin Hyman, 1988.

Drew, Bernard. "The Basic Training of Jill Clayburgh." *American Film*, April 1979, pp. 19–24.

Durham, Philip. *Down These Mean Streets a Man Must Go*. Chapel Hill: University of North Carolina Press, 1963.

Dyer, Richard. *Stars*. London: British Film Institute, 1986.

Erickson, Kai. *A New Species of Trouble*. New York: Norton, 1994.

Farago, Ladislas. *Patton: Ordeal and Triumph*. New York: Astor-Honor, 1964.

Farber, Stephen. "Coppola and *The Godfather*." *Sight and Sound* 41, no. 4 (1972): 217–223.

———. "Easy Pieces." *Sight and Sound* 40, no. 3 (1971): 128–131.

———. "End of the Road?" *Film Quarterly* 23, no. 2 (1969–1970): 3–15.

Ferncase, Richard K. *Outsider Features: American Independent Films of the 1980s*. Westport, Conn.: Greenwood Press, 1996.

Fiedler, Leslie. "Mythicizing the Unspeakable." *Journal of American Folklore* 103, no. 410 (1990): 390–399.

FitzGerald, Frances. "*Apocalypse Now*." In *Past Imperfect: History According to the Movies*, edited by Mark C. Carnes, pp. 284–287. New York: Henry Holt, 1995.

Fussell, Paul. "*Patton*." In *Past Imperfect: History According to the Movies*, edited by Mark C. Carnes, pp. 242–245. New York: Henry Holt, 1995.

Gallagher, John. "John Milius" (interview). *Films in Review* 33, no. 6 (1982): 357–361.

Gans, Herbert J. "*Chinatown*: An Anticapitalist Murder Mystery." *Social Policy* 5, no. 4 (1974): 48–49.

Goldman, William. *Adventures in the Screen Trade*. New York: Warner Books, 1983.

Greenfield, Jeff. "*Easy Rider*: A Turning Point in Film? A Profound Social Message? An Endless Bummer?" *Esquire*, July 1981, pp. 90–91.

Guerrero, Ed. *Framing Blackness: The African-American Image in Film*. Philadelphia: Temple University Press, 1993.

Guiles, Fred Lawrence. *Jane Fonda: The Actress in Her Time*. Garden City, N.Y.: Doubleday, 1982.

Haskell, Molly. *From Reverence to Rape*, 2nd ed. Chicago: University of Chicago Press, 1987.

Heath, Stephen. "*Jaws*, Ideology and Film Theory." In *Movies and Methods*, vol. 2, edited by Bill Nichols, pp. 509–514. Berkeley: University of California Press, 1985.

Herring, Henry D. "Out of the Dream and into the Nightmare: Dennis Hopper's Apocalyptic Vision of America." *Journal of Popular Film & TV* 10, no. 4 (1983): 144–154.

Hill, Lee. *Easy Rider*. London: British Film Institute, 1996.

Hirschberg, Jack. Interview with Franklin J. Schaffner, transcript of audiotape. Franklin J. Schaffner Collection, Archives and Special Collections Department, Shadek-Fackenthal Library, Franklin and Marshall College, Lancaster, Pennsylvania.

Hollinger, Karen. *In the Company of Women: Contemporary Female Friendship Films*. Minneapolis: University of Minnesota Press, 1998.

Jacobs, Diane. *Hollywood Renaissance*. South Brunswick, N.J.: A. S. Barnes, 1977.

James, Darius. *That's Blaxploitation*. New York: St. Martin's Griffin, 1995.

James, David E. *Allegories of Cinema: American Film in the Sixties*. Princeton, N.J.: Princeton University Press, 1989.

Jameson, Fredric. *Postmodernism, or, the Cultural Logic of Late Capitalism*. Durham: Duke University Press, 1991.

Jasinski, James. "(Re)Constituting Community through Narrative Argument: *Eros* and *Philia* in *The Big Chill*." *Quarterly Journal of Speech* 79, no. 4 (1993): 467–486.

Kael, Pauline. "Saint Cop." In her *Deeper into Movies*, pp. 385–388. Boston: Little-Brown, 1973.

——. "Tango." *New Yorker*, 28 October 1972, pp. 130–134, 137–138.

——. "Why Are Movies So Bad? or, The Numbers." *New Yorker*, 23 June 1980, pp. 82, 85–93.

Kaminsky, Stuart. *Don Siegel, Director*. New York: Curtis Books, 1974.

Kaplan, E. Ann. "The Importance and Ultimate Failure of *Last Tango in Paris*." *Jump Cut* 4 (1974): 1, 9–11.

Kasdan, Lawrence, and Barbara Benedek. "The Big Chill." First draft screenplay, 16 July 1982. Available at Special Collections, Doheny Library, University of Southern California.

Kauffmann, Stanley. *Figures of Light: Film Criticism and Comment*. New York: Harper & Row, 1971.

Kerman, Judith B., ed. *Retrofitting Blade Runner: Issues in Ridley Scott's Blade*

Runner and Philip K. Dick's *Do Androids Dream of Electric Sheep?* Bowling Green, Ohio: Bowling Green Popular Press: 1991.

Keyssar, Helene. *Robert Altman's America.* New York: Oxford University Press, 1991.

Kiernan, Thomas. *Jane Fonda: Heroine for Our Time.* New York: Delilah Books, 1982.

Klein, Joe. "You Can't Get There from Here." *American Film,* October 1983, pp. 40–44, 61.

Klotman, Phyllis Rauch, ed. *Screenplays of the African-American Experience.* Bloomington: Indiana University Press, 1991.

Kolker, Robert Phillip. *A Cinema of Loneliness,* 2nd ed. New York: Oxford University Press, 1988.

Laffey, Sheila A. The Bildungsfilm or the "Coming of Age" Film as Seen in "The Graduate," "You're a Big Boy Now," and "Girl Friends." Ph.D. dissertation, New York University, 1983.

Leab, Daniel J. *From Sambo to Superspade.* Boston: Houghton Mifflin, 1975.

Leiris, Michel. *Francis Bacon.* Barcelona: Ediciones Polígrafa, 1987.

Lev, Peter. *The Euro-American Cinema.* Austin: University of Texas Press, 1993.

Lewis, Fiona. "Daring All." *New Yorker,* 23 February 1998, pp. 70–76.

Lewis, Jon. *The Road to Romance and Ruin: Teen Films and Youth Culture.* New York: Routledge, 1992.

Loshitsky, Yosefa. *The Radical Faces of Godard and Bertolucci.* Detroit: Wayne State University Press, 1995.

Macklin, Anthony. "*Easy Rider:* The Initiation of Dennis Hopper." *Film Heritage* 5, no. 1 (1969): 1–12.

Man, Glenn. *Radical Visions: American Film Renaissance 1967–76.* Westport, Conn.: Greenwood, 1994.

Masilela, Ntongela. "The Los Angeles School of Black Filmmakers." In *Black American Cinema,* edited by Manthia Diawara, pp. 107–117. New York: Routledge, 1993.

McCullogh, Frank. "The Fall of a Lost Soldier." *Life,* 14 November 1969, pp. 34–39.

McGilligan, Patrick. *Jack's Life: A Biography of Jack Nicholson.* New York: Norton, 1994.

Mellen, Joan. "Sexual Politics and *Last Tango in Paris.*" *Film Quarterly* 26, no. 3 (1973): 9–19.

Meyer, David S. "Star Wars, *Star Wars* and American Political Culture." *Journal of Popular Culture* 26, no. 2 (1992): 99–115.

Michel, Sonya. "*Yekl* and *Hester Street:* Was Assimilation Good for the Jews?" *Literature/Film Quarterly* 5, no. 2 (1977): 142–146.

Milius, John. "Apocalypse Now." Three draft screenplays. Available at Arts Library–Special Collections, UCLA.

Modleski, Tania. "A Rose Is a Rose? Real Women and a Lost War." In *The New American Cinema,* edited by Jon Lewis, pp. 125–145. Durham: Duke University Press, 1998.

Monaco, James. *American Film Now.* New York: New American Library, 1979.

Monaco, Paul. *Ribbons in Time: Movies and Society since 1945.* Bloomington: Indiana University Press, 1987.

Mordden, Ethan. *Medium Cool: The Movies of the 1960s.* New York: Knopf, 1990.

Morrison, Rachela. "*Casablanca* Meets *Star Wars:* The Blakean Dialectics of *Blade Runner.*" *Literature/Film Quarterly* 18, no. 1 (1990): 2–10.

Norden, Martin. *The Cinema of Isolation.* New Jersey: Rutgers University Press, 1994.

Palmer, William J. *The Films of the Seventies.* Metuchen, N.J.: Scarecrow, 1987.

Paris, Michael. "Country Blues on the Screen: The Leadbelly Films." *Journal of American Studies* 30, no. 1 (1996): 119–125.

Parks, Gordon. *Half Past Autumn: A Retrospective.* Boston: Little Brown, 1997.

———. *Voices in the Mirror: An Autobiography.* New York: Doubleday, 1990.

Perkins, Tessa. "The Politics of 'Jane Fonda.'" In *Stardom: Industry of Desire,* edited by Christine Gledhill, pp. 237–250. London: Routledge, 1991.

Pierce, John J. "Creative Synergy and the Art of World Creation." In *Retrofitting Blade Runner,* edited by Judith B. Kerman, pp. 201–211. Bowling Green, Ohio: Bowling Green Popular Press, 1991.

Pollock, Dale. *Skywalking: The Life and Films of George Lucas.* Hollywood: Samuel French, 1990.

Pye, Michael, and Linda Myles. *The Movie Brats: How the Film Generation Took Over Hollywood.* New York: Holt, Rinehart and Winston, 1979.

Quart, Barbara Koenig. *Women Directors: The Emergence of a New Cinema.* New York: Praeger, 1988.

Ray, Robert B. *A Certain Tendency of the Hollywood Cinema, 1930–1980.* Princeton: Princeton University Press, 1985.

Reynaud, Berenice. "An Interview with Charles Burnett." *Black American Literature Forum* 25, no. 2 (1991): 323–334.

Robertson, Robbie. "Some Narrative Sources of Ridley Scott's *Alien.*" In *Cinema and Fiction: New Modes of Adapting, 1950– 1990,* edited by John Orr and Colin Nicholson, pp. 171–179. Edinburgh: Edinburgh University Press, 1992.

Rosenstone, Robert A. *Visions of the Past: The Challenge of Film to Our Idea of History.* Cambridge, Mass.: Harvard University Press, 1995.

Ross, Kristin. *Fast Cars, Clean Bodies: Decolonization and the Reordering of French Culture.* Cambridge, Mass.: MIT Press, 1995.

Ryan, Michael, and Douglas Kellner. *Camera Politica: The Politics and Ideology of Contemporary Hollywood Film.* Bloomington: Indiana University Press, 1988.

Said, Edward W. *Orientalism.* New York: Random House, 1978.

Sammon, Paul M. *Future Noir: The Making of Blade Runner.* New York: HarperCollins, 1996.

Sayles, John, and Gavin Smith. *Sayles on Sayles.* London: Faber and Faber, 1998.

Schatz, Thomas. *Old Hollywood/New Hollywood: Ritual, Art and Industry.* Ann Arbor: UMI Research Press, 1983.

Schickel, Richard. *Clint Eastwood.* New York: Knopf, 1996.

Schlesinger, Tom. "Putting People Together: An Interview with John Sayles." *Film Quarterly* 34, no. 4 (1981): 1–8.

Scott, George C. "Sorry about That." *Esquire,* December 1965, pp. 208–211, 316–318, 320–322.

Seabrook, John. "Why Is the Force Still with Us?" *New Yorker,* 6 January 1997, pp. 40–53.

Seidman, Barbara. "'The Lady Doth Protest Too Much, Methinks': Jane Fonda, Feminism and Hollywood." In *Women and Film,* edited by Janet Todd, pp. 186–230. New York: Holmes and Meier, 1988.

Shadoian, Jack. "*Dirty Harry:* A Defense." *Western Humanities Review* 28, no. 2 (1974): 166–179.

Shedlin, Michael. "Police Oscar: *The French Connection.*" *Film Quarterly* 25, no. 4 (1972): 2–9.

Simon, John. "In France We Do It Horizontally." In *Something to Declare: Twelve Years of Films Abroad,* pp. 128–134. New York: Clarkson N. Potter, 1983.

Singer, Loren. *The Parallax View.* Garden City, N.Y.: Doubleday, 1970.

Singer, Mark. "Whose Movie Is This?" *New Yorker,* 22 June 1998, pp. 110–119.

Sklar, Robert. *Movie-Made America,* 2nd ed. New York: Vintage, 1994.

Sobchack, Vivian. "On the Virginity of Astronauts." In *Alien Zone,* edited by Annette Kuhn, pp. 103–115. London: Verso, 1990.

Stam, Robert. *Subversive Pleasures: Bakhtin, Cultural Criticism, and Film.* Baltimore: Johns Hopkins University Press, 1989.

Stanton, Shelby L. *Green Berets at War*. Novato, Calif.: Presidio, 1985.

Starr, Cecile. "Claudia Weill Discusses *Girlfriends*." *Filmmakers* 11, no. 12 (1978): 26–28.

Stein, Jeff. *A Murder in Wartime*. New York: St. Martin's, 1992.

Taylor, Philip M. *Steven Spielberg*. New York: Continuum, 1992.

Thomas, Bob. *King Cohn: The Life and Times of Harry Cohn*. New York: G. P. Putnam's Sons, 1967.

Thompson, David, ed. *Levinson on Levinson*. London: Faber and Faber, 1992.

Tonetti, Claretta Michelletti. *Bernardo Bertolucci: The Cinema of Ambiguity*. New York: Twayne, 1995.

Trilling, Diana. "*Easy Rider* and its Critics." *Atlantic Monthly*, September 1970, pp. 90–95.

Wexman, Virginia Wright. *Roman Polanski*. Boston: Twayne, 1985.

White, Armand. "Charles Burnett: Sticking to the Soul." *Film Comment* 33, no. 1 (1997): 38–41.

Wood, Robin. *Arthur Penn*. New York: Praeger, 1969.

——. *Hollywood from Vietnam to Reagan*. New York: Columbia University Press, 1986.

Wyatt, David. "*Star Wars* and the Productions of Time." *Virginia Quarterly Review* 58 (1982): 600–615.

Index

Academy Awards, xiii, xix, 16, 108, 130
Adventures of the Wilderness Family, xix
Agnew, Spiro, xxi, 66
Airport, 41–43, 183; class and age of characters, 41–42, 47; popularity, 17; and technology, 44, 161–162, 182
Airport 75, 41
Aitken, Jonathan, 11
Albertson, Jack, 44
Alexander, Field Marshall Harold, 113
Alice Doesn't Live Here Any More, xix
Alice's Restaurant, 6, 12–17, 20, 182, 183; religious theme, 15–16, 44–45; song, 12, 13; and youth culture, 21, 22, 25, 41
Alien, 165–166, 168–172, 183; illustrations, 170, 171; and sexuality, 176–177; as social criticism, 165, 174, 179
Allen, Karen, 100

All the President's Men, 50
Alonso, John, 55
Altman, Robert, 62–63
American Graffiti, xv, xx, 90–95; illustrations, 92, 93; as model for teen comedies, xx–xxi, 96–98, 99, 100–101, 103–106; nostalgia, xx, 90–92, 103–104, 181–183
American International Pictures, 3, 95
American patriotism, 24, 113–114
American Zoetrope, 124
Anders, Allison, 184
Anderson Platoon, The, 118
Anger, Kenneth, 78
Animal House, 91, 98–100, 102, 105
Anspach, Susan, 19
Apocalypse Now, 77, 107, 108, 116–126, 182; illustrations, 121, 123
April Fools, 5
Arnott, Mark, 70

Ashby, Hal, 157, 159, 160, 164
Auster, Albert, 107
Author!, Author!, 152
Avalon, Frankie, 90
Avildsen, John, 23

Backer, Brian, 104
Bacon, Francis, 78–79, 80, 88
Bacon, Kevin, 101
Bakhtin, Mikhail, xii, 75
Balaban, Bob, 149
Band, The, 8
Barbieri, Gato, 78
Barkin, Ellen, 101
Barron, Fred, 68
Basil, Toni, 7
Bates, Alan, 147
Baxter, John, 34
BBS Productions, 4, 17
Beattie, Ann, 154–156
Beatty, Warren, 50, 53, 65
Belafonte, Harry, 127
Belushi, John, 99
Berenger, Tom, 71
Bergen, Candice, 152
Bergman, Ingmar, 78, 88, 152
Berry, John, 136
Bertolucci, Bernardo, 77, 80, 83, 85, 86, 87
Between the Lines, 61–62, 68–69, 70, 72, 73, 154
Bicycle Thief, The, 140
Big Chill, The, 61–62, 70, 71–73, 183
Big Sleep, The, 55, 129
Biskind, Peter, 184
Bisset, Jacqueline, 41, 42
Black, John D. F., 131
Black, Karen, 18, 63
Blackboard Jungle, The, 90
Blade Runner, 165–166, 168, 169, 185;
    illustrations, 173, 178; and sexuality,
    177–179; as social criticism, 166,
    173–174, 177–179
Blakley, Ronee, 62, 63
Blake, William, 172, 178
Blauner, Steve, 4

blaxploitation, 128–133, 136, 138. *See
    also* B movies, exploitation films
B movies, 3, 4, 98. *See also* blaxploita-
    tion, exploitation films
Bob & Carol & Ted & Alice, 16
Boeing, William, 43
Boeing Aircraft, 43
Bonnie and Clyde, xvi, 60, 68, 115,
    182
Bordwell, David, xviii
Borgnine, Ernest, 44
Boucourechliev, André, 78
Boyle, Peter, 23, 24
Bozzuffi, Marcel, 27
Bradley, General Omar, 109, 111, 113,
    115
Brakhage, Stan, 78
Brando, Marlon, 79, 85–86, 117
Bridges, James, 160, 164
Brimley, Wilfred, 161
British documentary school, 140
Bronson, Charles, xix, 37–39
Bryant, Anita, 142
"Buffalo Ghosts" (script), 157
Bukatman, Scott, 169
Burnett, Charles, 139, 140, 141, 184
Burns, Margie, 7
Burtt, Ben, 166
Buttons, Red, 44
Byrds, The, 8, 9

Cahan, Abraham, 143
Caldwell, Ben, 140
Cambridge, Godfrey, 135
Campbell, Gregg M., 19
Campbell, Joseph, 166
Canby, Vincent, 17, 43, 101, 109, 113–
    114
Cannes Film Festival, 16, 125
Cannon Group, 22
Carradine, Keith, 62, 63
Carroll, Diahann, 133, 136
Carroll, Peter N., 182–183
Carter, Jimmy, 40, 162
Cassidy, Joanna, 177
Chandler, Raymond, 55, 129

Chaplin, Geraldine, 63
Che, 5
Cherryh, C. J., 175
Chilly Scenes of Winter, 154–156
China Syndrome, The, 151, 156, 160–164, 185; illustration, 163
Chinatown, xx–xxii, 54–59, 185; as conspiracy film, 49–50, 56–58, 61; illustrations, 57, 58; as nostalgia, xxi, 59, 182; as social criticism, xxi–xx, 54–59, 174, 183
Chitty Chitty Bang Bang, 5
Christie, Julie, 65
Cioffi, Charles, 129
Cisco Pike, xvii, 17
Clapp, Gordon, 70
Clark, Candy, 91
Clark, Larry, 140
Claudine, 133–137, 140, 183; illustration, 134
Clayburgh, Jill, 143, 146–149, 152, 153, 164
Cleopatra Jones and the Temple of Gold, xix
Clockwork Orange, A, xviii
Close, Glenn, 71
Cohn, Harry, xvi
Cold War, 168
Collier, James, xix
Collins, Steven, 69
Coming Home, 156, 157–160, 163, 182, 183; and *Last Tango in Paris*, 82, 158; and Vietnam War, 116, 157–159, 163
Conan the Barbarian, 122
Conformist, The, 77
Conrad, Joseph, 108, 116
conspiracy movies, 49–57
Conversation, The, 49
Cooley High, xix, 91, 95–98, 101, 105; illustration, 97
Coppola, Eleanor, 116
Coppola, Francis, 77; *Apocalypse Now*, 107, 108, 124–125; *Patton*, 108, 109–110, 115
Corman, Roger, xix, 3, 109
Costner, Kevin, 71

counterculture, xviii, xxi, 17, 18, 183; *Dirty Harry*, 31; *Easy Rider*, 5, 6, 8; *Joe*, 23–25, 27; *Nashville*, 65; *Shampoo*, 67
Cousineau, Maggie, 70
Crazy Mama, xix
Cronyn, Hume, 53
Crouse, Lindsay, 69
Crowe, Cameron, 104, 105

Daly, Timothy, 101
Davis, Ossie, 135
Day of the Locust, 157
Death Wish, 37–39; illustration, 39
Deer Hunter, The, 116
Denby, David, 24
De Niro, Robert, xvi
De Pasquale, Frederic, 28
Dern, Bruce, 157, 159, 160
de Sica, Vittorio, 136, 140
Dick, Philip K., 168, 173
Diller, Barry, 139, 184
Diner, 100–103, 105
Dirty Harry, 30–37, 39, 41, 142, 183, 185; and *Death Wish*, 38; and legal issues, 33–36; illustrations, 32, 33; and religion, 35, 44; vigilantism, 35–37
disaster movies, 40–49
Disney Co. *See* Walt Disney Co.
Dispatches, 108
Do Androids Dream of Electric Sheep?, 173
Doherty, Thomas, 104, 128
Donat, Peter, 160
Douglas, Michael, 160, 164
Dowd, Nancy, 157, 164
Downhill Racer, 16
Dreyfuss, Richard, 45, 91
Dr. Strangelove, 176
drugs and drug culture, 17; *Easy Rider*, 4, 7, 11, 133; *The French Connection*, 27, 29–30; *Joe*, 24; *Superfly*, 132–133
Drum, 185
Dunaway, Faye, xxi, 55

Durning, Charles, 152
Duvall, Robert, 117
Duvall, Shelley, 63
Dylan, Bob, 8, 12

Earthquake, 41
Eastman, Carol, 20
Eastwood, Clint, xix, 30, 36–37, 38
Easy Rider, xv, 3–12, 21, 22, 43, 142,
    183, 185; and drug culture, 4, 7, 11,
    133; and films of "The Sixties," xii–
    xiii, 5–6, 182; illustration, 8; re-
    ligious theme, 11–12, 44, 92; and
    social class, 11, 18, 25; and youth cul-
    ture, xvi, xvii, 5, 16, 17, 41, 60–61
Ebert, Roger, 35
Eiger Sanction, The, xix
Eikenberry, Jill, 68
Eisenhower, General Dwight D., 109,
    111, 113
Erickson, Kai, 162
E.T., 49
Euro-American cinema, 77
Exorcist, The, 167
exploitation film, 3, 4, 10, 22, 27. *See
    also* blaxpoitation, B movies

Fanaka, Jamaa, 140
Farago, Ladislas, 108, 111, 113
Farber, Stephen, 5, 7, 14, 20
Fast Times at Ridgemont High, 103–106
Fauvism, 88
Fellini, Federico, 78, 101
Female Trouble, xix
feminism and film, 72–73, 87–88, 142–
    164
Fiedler, Leslie, 124–125
Fielding, Henry, 51
film noir, 173
Fisher, Carrie, 65, 166
Five Easy Pieces, 17–21, 22, 25, 183;
    illustration, 21
Fonda, Jane, 82, 143, 156–164
Fonda, Peter, 3–9, 11, 61
Ford, Harrison, 91, 166, 172
Ford, John, 6

Forrest, Frederick, 117
Four Tops, The, 95
Freedman, Paul, 144
French Connection, The, 27–30, 39, 131,
    142, 183; illustration, 29; kinetic
    style, 27–28, 167; police subculture,
    29–30, 37
French New Wave, xvii, 86
Friedan, Betty, 142
Friedkin, William, 28, 29, 167
Funicello, Annette, 90
Funny Girl, 5
Funny Lady, xix
Fun with Dick and Jane, 156
Furst, Stephen, 99
Fussell, Paul, 113, 115–116
Fury, The, 185

Gabriel, Teshome, 140
Gai Savoir, Le, 80
Gans, Herbert J., 58
George VI, King of England, 116
Gerima, Haile, 140, 141, 184
German silent film, xvii
Getting Straight, xvi, xvii, 17
Gibson, Henry, 63
Gilbert, Bruce, 157, 160
Girlfriends, 149–152, 156, 157, 164
Godard, Jean-Luc, 11, 78, 80
Godfather, The, xii, xv, 52, 142
Godzilla, 168
Goldblum, Jeff, 65, 68, 71
Goldman, William, xv–xvi
Gone With the Wind, 127
Goodbye Columbus, 16
"Good Times" (TV show), 96
Gould, Elliott, 61
Graduate, The, xvi, 60
Graham, Reverend Billy, xix
Grand Hotel, 43
Grant, Cary, 136
Grant, Lee, 65
Grease, 91, 100
"Green Beret murder case," 118–121,
    125
Green Berets, The, 107, 122

Greenfield, Jeff, 7, 10
Guerrero, Ed, 128
Guest, Christopher, 149
Gulf War, 168
Gunn, Moses, 129
Gussow, Mel, 109
Guthrie, Arlo, 12–15, 17, 19
Guthrie, Woody, 13, 14, 19
Guttenberg, Steve, 101

Hackman, Gene, 27, 44
Hamill, Mark, 166
Hammett, Dashiell, 55, 129
Hannah, Daryl, 174
"Happy Days" (TV show), 95
Harris, Barbara, 64
Harris, Julius, 133
Hauer, Rutger, 172, 178
Hawn, Goldie, 65
Hayes, Isaac, 130
Head, 17
Head Over Heels. See Chilly Scenes of Winter
Heard, John, 69, 154
Heart of Darkness (novel), 108, 116–120, 125
Hearts of Darkness (documentary film), 116
Heath, Stephen, 46, 49
Heckerling, Amy, 105
Hellman, Lillian, 156
Hendrix, Jimi, 8
Hepburn, Katherine, xix
Herndon, Venable, 12
Hero with a Thousand Faces, The, 166
Herr, Michael, 108, 122
Herring, Henry D., 9, 10, 11
Hester Street, xix, 143–146, 149, 156, 183; illustration, 145
Hiding Place, The, xix
"high concept," 184
High Noon, 156
Hill, Lee, 6
Hilton-Jacobs, Lawrence, 96, 135
Hindenberg, The, xix
Hirschberg, Jack, 110

Hitchcock, Alfred, 50
Hitler, Adolf, 54
Hoffman, Dustin, xvi
Hollinger, Karen, 150
Holm, Ian, 172
Hopper, Dennis, 3–9, 11, 185
Howard, Mel, 144
Howard, Ron, 91, 95
Hulce, Tom, 99
Hurricane, 41
Hurt, William, 71
Huston, John, xxi, 56
Huyck, Willard, 95

I Am Curious, Yellow, 5
If, 5, 16
If This is Tuesday, It Must Be Belgium, 5
Independence Day, 41, 184
IPC Films, 157, 160
Italian neorealism, xvii, 140
Ivory, James, xix

Jagger, Mick, 159
James, Darius, 128
James, David, 10
Jameson, Fredric, 181–182
Jarmusch, Jim, 141, 184
Jaws, 45–49, 142, 161–162, 184, 185; illustrations, 46, 48; and patriarchal authority, 48–49, 183; as prototype for blockbusters, xvii, xix
Jefferson, Blind Lemon, 137
Joe, 17, 22–27, 37, 39, 41, 183
Johns, Jasper, 114
Jones, Eric, 135
Jones, James Earl, 134–136
Jones, Robert, 157
Joyce, Adrien. *See* Eastman, Carol
Julia, 156–157, 163, 183
"Julia" (TV show), 136

Kael, Pauline, 35, 78, 80, 185
Kafka, Franz, 50
Kallionotes, Helena, 18
Kaminsky, Stuart, 36
Kane, Carol, 143–144

Kaplan, E. Ann, 87–88
Kasdan, Lawrence, 71, 73
Katz, Gloria, 95
Kauffmann, Stanley, 114
Kavanaugh, Dorrie, 143
Keats, Stephen, 143
Kellner, Douglas, 72
Kennedy, George, 42
Kennedy, John F., 52, 182
Kennedy, Robert, xviii
Kerouac, Jack, 1
Keyssar, Helene, 1, 63–64
Killens, John O., 135
Killer of Sheep, 139–141, 183
King Jr., Martin Luther, xviii
Kirby, Bruno, 68
Klein, Joe, 71
Kline, Kevin, 71
Klute, 143
Kolker, Robert, 46, 47, 65
Kovacs, Laszlo, 3, 7, 9
Kramer vs. Kramer, 49, 152, 156
Kubrick, Stanley, 25

Ladd, Diane, 55
Lancaster, Burt, 42
Last Detail, The, 157
Last Movie, The, xvi, 185
Last Picture Show, The, xvi
Last Summer, 16
Last Tango in Paris, xviii, 77–89, 158; illustration, 81
"Laverne and Shirley" (TV show), 95
Leadbelly, 137–139, 183, 185
Lean on Me, 23
Léaud, Jean-Pierre, 80, 86
Ledbetter, Huddie, 137–139
Lee, Carl, 133
Lefevre, Adam, 70
Leiris, Michel, 78
Le Mat, Paul, 91
Lemmon, Jack, 160
Leone, Sergio, 35, 39

Levinson, Barry, 100–101
Lewis, Fiona, 185
Lewis, Jon, 90
Lisztomania, 185
Little Fauss and Big Halsey, 17
Lomax, Alex, 137
Lomax, John, 137, 139
Lord of the Rings, 166
Love Bug, The, 5
Love Story, 17
Lucas, Marcia, 175
Lucas, George, 122; American Graffiti, xxi, 92, 94, 98, 100; Star Wars, xvii, 166–168, 170–171, 175, 179
Lynley, Carol, 44

MacKenna's Gold, 5
Magnificent Ambersons, The, 155
Magnum Force, The, 37
Maltese Falcon, The, 55, 129
Man for all Seasons, A, 156
Man Who Would be King, The, 122
Marcuse, Herbert, 81
Marshall, General George C., 111, 113
Martin, Dean, 41
Martin, Pamela Sue, 44
M.A.S.H., xvi, 60–61
Masilela, Ntongela, 139
Matheson, Tim, 99
Matisse, Henri, 88
Mayberry, Billy, 140
Mayfield, Curtis, 132, 133
Mayron, Melanie, 149, 151
Mazursky, Paul, 146–149
McCarthy, Frank, 109–110, 111
McDaniel, Hattie, 127
McDonald, Bruce, 69
McGilligan, Patrick, 11
McWilliams, Cary, 54
Medium Cool, 16, 60–61
Mellen, Joan, 88
Method Acting, 85
Metro-Goldwyn-Mayer, 101
Metropolis, 41

Meyer, Russ, xix
Micheaux, Oscar, 127
Michel, Sonya, 145
Midnight Cowboy, xviii, 142, 157, 182; Academy Award, 16; and youth culture, xvi, xvii, 5, 6, 60–61
Milius, John, 36, 119–120, 121–125
Millar, Stuart, xix
Millett, Kate, 142
Minnelli, Vincente, xviii
Mississippi Freedom Riders, 7
Mitchell, Joni, 14
Mitford, Penelope, 157
Moby Dick, 49
Monaco, James, 75, 128, 139
Monaco, Paul, xx
Monkees, The, 5, 17
Montagnards, 118–119, 120
Monte, Eric, 96
Montgomery, Field Marshal Bernard, 109, 113, 115
Mordden, Ethan, 3
Moreno, Rita, 135
Motion Picture Production Code, xviii, 42–43, 85, 94
Motown Records, 95–96
Move!, 17
Mr. Mom, 152
Mulholland, William, 54
Murder My Sweet, 129
Murphy, Michael, 62, 147

Nashville, 61, 62–65, 68, 70, 174,; illustration, 64; and political exhaustion, xix, 63, 72–73, 182, 183; and sexuality, 63, 72
National General, 5
Neff, Roy, 137, 138
New York Film Festival, 78
Nicholson, Jack, xvi, xx; *Chinatown*, xxi, 55; *Easy Rider*, 3, 4, 11; *Five Easy Pieces*, 17–18
Night Moves, xix, 50, 54, 61
Nixon, Richard, 66, 114
North, Edward, 108

nostalgia in films, xx–xxi, 90–92, 95, 182
Notes (nonfiction book), 116
Nunez, Victor, 184
Nykvist, Sven, 152

Obanheim, William, 13
Oliver, 5
Olmos, Edward James, 177
Once Upon a Time in the West, 39
O'Neal, Ron, 132
One Flew Over the Cuckoo's Nest, xix–xx, 50, 61–62, 174
One From the Heart, 77
OPEC oil cartel, xviii, xxi, 40, 61
Otis Day and the Knights, 99

Pacino, Al, xvi, 149
Pakula, Alan J., 53, 152
Paradise Lost, 166
Parallax View, The, 49, 50–54, 55, 61, 183; illustration, 51
Paramount, xv, 5, 139, 184
Paris, Michael, 137
Parks, Gordon, 128, 129–131, 138–139, 184
Parks Jr., Gordon, 128, 132–133
Passanante, Jean, 70
Patton, 107, 108–116, 125–126; illustrations, 112, 114
Patton, General George S., 108–116, 125–126
Patrick, Dennis, 24
Penn, Arthur, 12, 14
Penn, Sean, 105
Pentimento, 156
Peters, Brock, 135
Phillips, Mackenzie, 91
Pierce, John J., 166
Pierrot le fou, 11
Place, Mary Kay, 71
Poitier, Sidney, 127
Polanski, Roman, xxi, 55, 56, 57, 59
Pollard, Michael J., 68
Pollock, Dale, 93, 167, 175

Porky's, xv, 100
Poseidon Adventure, The, 41, 43–45, 54, 161,; and corporate responsibility, 43, 47, 172
Prentiss, Paula, 51
Presley, Elvis, 90
Prisoner of Second Avenue, The, xix
Putney Swope, 5, 16

Quart, Barbara Koenig, 150
Quart, Leonard, 107

Rabe, David, 149
Rafelson, Bob, 4, 17
Raiders of the Lost Ark, xv
Rain People, The, 16
Rauschenberg, Robert, 114
Ray, Nicholas, 90
Ray, Robert B., 84
Reagan, Ronald, 168
Rebel Without a Cause, 90
Red Dawn, 122
Redgrave, Vanessa, 157
Reinhold, Judge, 105
religion in films, 7, 11–12, 15, 35, 44–45
Renzi, Maggie, 69
Return of the Secaucus Seven, 61–62, 69–70, 72, 73, 183
The Revolutionary, 17
Rey, Fernando, 27
Reynolds, Burt, xix, 152
Riefenstahl, Leni, 171
Riegert, Peter, 100
Reiser, Paul, 101
Rheault, Colonel Robert B., 108, 118, 120
Risky Business, 104
Robertson, Robbie, 168
Robinson, Andy, 30
Rock around the Clock, 90
rock music in films, xx; *American Graffiti*, xx, 91–92; *Apocalypse Now*, 117, 124; *Cooley High*, 95–96; *Easy Rider*, 8–9
Rockwell, Norman, 174
Rocky, xv, 23

Rocky Horror Picture Show, The, 100
Roddick, Nick, 44
Rolling Stones, The, 159
Romanus, Robert, 105
Romeo and Juliet, 5
Roosevelt, Franklin D., 111, 113
Rooster Cogburn, xix
Ross, Kristin, 26
Roundtree, Richard, 129–130
Rourke, Mickey, 101
RPM, 17
Ryan, Michael, 72

"Sacre du Printemps, Le" (ballet), 78
Sagan, Françoise, xvii
Said, Edward, 57
Salt, Waldo, 157, 160, 164
Sanderson, William, 174
Sands, Diana, 135
Sankofa, 141
Sarandon, Susan, 23
Sarris, Andrew, 35
Saturday Night Fever, 22, 100
"Saturday Night Live" (TV show), 98
Save the Tiger, 23
Savoca, Nancy, 184
Sayles, John, 69, 70, 184
Schaffner, Franklin, 110–111
Schatz, Thomas, 17
Scheider, Roy, 27, 45
Schickel, Richard, 35
Schlafly, Phyllis, 142
Schneemann, Carolee, 78
Schneider, Abe, 4
Schneider, Bert, 4
Schneider, Maria, 79, 85–86, 87, 158
Schoendorffer, Pierre, 118
Scorsese, Martin, 183
Scott, George C., 109–110
Scott, Ridley, 168, 169, 177, 179
Seabrook, John, 167
Seberg, Jean, 42
Seeger, Pete, 14
Serpico, 157
sexuality in films, 72, 104–105; *American Graffiti*, 94; *The Big Chill*, 71;

Coming Home, 158; *Cooley High*, 96–97; *Dirty Harry*, 31; *Fast Times at Ridgemont High*, 104–105; *Last Tango in Paris*, 78–83; *Nashville*, 63; *Shampoo*, 67; science fiction films, 169, 174–179
Shadoian, Jack, 34
Shaft, 128–132, 136, 183; illustrations, 129, 130
Shampoo, xix, 61–62, 65–68, 70, 73, 183; illustration, 66
Shaw, Robert, 45
Shea, Eric, 44
Sheen, Martin, 117
Siegel, Don, 36
Signoret, Simone, 88
"Silent Majority," 25, 114
Silver, Joan Micklin, 143, 164; *Between the Lines*, 68, 73; *Chilly Scenes of Winter*, 154–156; *Hester Street*, xix, 143, 144
Silver, Raphael, 68, 146
Simon, John, 88
Simon, Neil, xix
Sinclair, Max, 139
Singer, Loren, 50, 54
Skinner, Anita, 149
Sklar, Robert, xviii
Smile, xix
Smith, Charles Martin, 91
Smith, General Bedell, 113
Smith, Kevin, 184
Sobchack, Vivian, 174–177
Somers, Suzanne, 93
Sound of Music, The, xvi
Southern, Terry, 4
Southern California Country, 54
Spielberg, Steven, xix, 45, 47, 49
Stanton, Shelby L., 118
Star!, xvi
Star Wars, xvii, 49, 165–168, 169, 179, 183, 185; conservative values in, 165–166, 170–171, 174, 179; and nostalgia, 167, 174, 182; and sexuality, 175–176
"Star Wars" missile defense system, 168

Starting Over, 152–154, 156
Staying Alive, 23
Steinem, Gloria, 142
Stepford Wives, The, xix
Steppenwolf (musical group), 8, 9
Stern, Daniel, 101
Sternhagen, Frances, 152
Stevens, Stella, 44
St. John, Christopher, 129
Stranger than Paradise, 141
Strawberry Statement, The, xvi, 17
Streep, Meryl, xvi
Streisand, Barbra, xvi, xix
Storaro, Vittorio, 77, 85
Stravinski, Igor, 78
Sunshine Boys, The, xix
Superfly, 128, 132–133
Supervixens, xix
Sutherland, Donald, 61, 100
Sweet Charity, 5
Sweet Sweetback's Badasssss Song, 128

Tamu, 135
Taxi Driver, xii
teen films, xx, 90–106
Temptations, The, 95
Tewkesbury, Joan, 63
That Cold Day in the Park, 16
They Shoot Horses, Don't They?, 16
Third World Cinema Corporation, 135–136
Thomas, Piri, 135
Thompson, Kristin, xviii
Three Mile Island nuclear plant, 162
Tidyman, Ernest, 131
Titanic, 184
Tomlin, Lily, 162
Tonetti, Claretta Micheletti, 88
Tootsie, 152
To Sleep with Anger, 141
Towering Inferno, The, 41
Towne, Robert, xxi, 54, 55, 57, 59
Trial, The, 50
Trilling, Diana, 7
Trip, The, 3
Trott, Karen, 70

True Grit, 5
Turman, Glynn, 96
Turning Point, The, 157
Twentieth Century-Fox, 107, 109
2001: A Space Odyssey, 5

United Artists, 107, 155
Unmarried Woman, An, 146–149, 150,
　151, 156, 183

Valdez, Daniel, 160
Van Peebles, Melvin, 128
Van Sant, Gus, 184
Van Vogt, A. E., 168
Vernon, John, 99
Vietnam War, xvii, xx, 40; *Alice's Res-
taurant*, 13, 15; *American Graffiti*, 91,
94; *Apocalypse Now*, 107–108, 116–
126; *Coming Home*, 157, 159; *Dirty
Harry*, 36–37; *Joe*, 24–25; *Patton*,
107–108, 110, 115; *Return of the Se-
caucus Seven*, 69
Vitelloni, I, 101
Voight, Jon, 157, 160, 164

Wagner, Richard, 125
Wallace, George, 11
Wallach, Eli, 150
Wakefield, Dan, 152
Walt Disney Co., 5
Warden, Jack, 65
Warhol, Andy, 78
Warner Brothers, 124, 149
Watergate scandal, xviii, 40, 49–50, 54,
61, 183; and *Chinatown*, xxi, 55, 59;
and *Jaws*, 46–47
Waters, John, xix
Wayne, John, xix, 5, 122
Weaver, Sigourney, 172

Weill, Claudia, 143, 149, 156
Weinstein, Hannah, 135
Welles, Gwen, 63, 69
Welles, Orson, 155
Western genre, 6, 10, 166
Wexler, Haskell, 159
Wexler, Norman, 22–23
Wexman, Virginia Wright, 55–56
Where Eagles Dare, 5
Wild Angels, The, 3
Wild Bunch, The, xviii, 5, 60
Wild in the Streets, 3
Wild One, The, 90
Wild Party, The, xix
Wilder, Billy, xviii
Williams, Cindy, 91, 95
Williams, Jo-Beth, 71
Willis, Gordon, 52
Winters, Shelley, 44
Wise, Robert, xix
Wolfman Jack, 92
Wonder, Stevie, 96
Wood, Robin, 14, 155, 171
Woodstock, 60–61, 67, 182
Wright, Basil, 140
Wynette, Tammy, 18, 19
Wynter, Dana, 42

Yablans, Frank, 184
Yekl, 143
Young, Burt, 55
Young, Sean, 172

Zabriskie Point, xvi, 17
Zanuck, Darryl, 109, 110
Zeffirelli, Franco, 5
Zinman, Sharon, 101
Zinnemann, Fred, 156